SAGE PAYROLL in easy steps

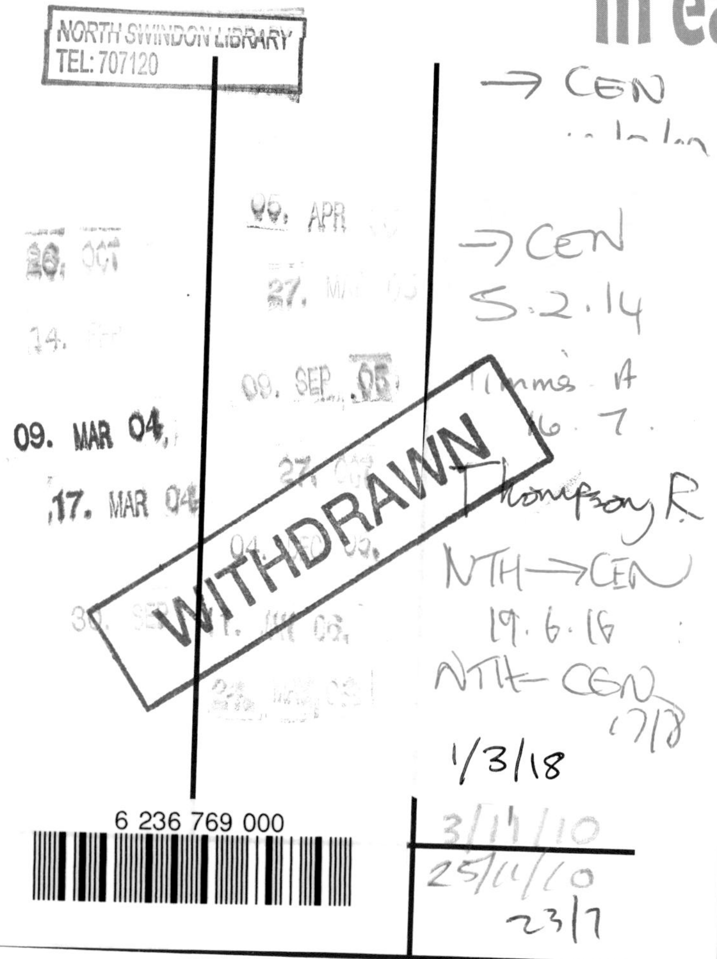

In easy steps is an imprint of Computer Step
Southfield Road . Southam
Warwickshire CV47 OFB . England

http://www.ineasysteps.com

Notice of Liability
Every effort has been made to ensure that this book contains accurate and current information. However, Computer Step and the author shall not be liable for any loss or damage suffered by readers as a result of any information contained herein.

Trademarks
Sage® is a registered trademark of The Sage Group Plc. All other trademarks are acknowledged as belonging to their respective companies.

Printed and bound in the United Kingdom

ISBN 1-84078-081-9

Table of Contents

Getting Started

This chapter takes you through the stages of preparing Sage Payroll for use once it has been installed on your computer. It explains initial procedures for setting up defaults required by the program before you start entering data.

Covers

Chapter One

Introduction

Whilst Sage Payroll is a flexible, user friendly program, it is still very important to ensure you enter payroll information carefully and accurately.

For many businesses manual payroll is often a very time consuming, laborious task. Computerised payroll programs can save businesses valuable time and money by processing payroll routines quickly and easily. However, like any computerised system, the accuracy of the results depends entirely on information being entered correctly and without error in the first place.

This book explains and describes in easy to follow stages how to computerise your payroll requirements using the Sage Payroll package. It is full of handy hints and advice about how to enter, maintain and process your information quickly and easily and thus avoid making costly mistakes.

To avoid making mistakes on your company payroll, you can always practice on the demonstration data first. Select the Open Company option from the File menu. Choose Demonstration Data from the list and click OK. Enter your User Name and Password and click OK to continue. To return to your company data when you have finished practising, select Open Company from the File menu and choose your company. See page 22.

It takes you through, in a step by step guide, the various stages involved in running a company payroll system and covers all important payroll legislation.

Preparing to use Sage Payroll

Before you can do any payroll processing a certain anount of preparation is required. Employee, Company and Government Legislation information needs entering so that from this, complex tasks such as Tax Calculations, NI, SSP/SMP and holiday entitlements can be processed quickly and easily. This book guides you through all of this preparation in easy to follow steps.

Employee and Company records store very detailed information. Because of the confidential nature of payroll, this book shows you how to set up passwords and different levels of security to protect this information from unauthorised access.

Many statutory forms are produced during payroll processing. You will be advised of the various forms and reports required at different stages and of the importance of regularly backing up your data.

Overview

Use the Quick New Employee Entry option from the File menu to speed up entering new employee details.

The concepts used by Sage Payroll are very easy to grasp and understand and are similar to a manual system. It basically records information using three sets of 'cards'.

For every employee there is an Employee Record card to store information such as Name, National Insurance Number, Tax Code and Payment Details etc. This information is grouped into a number of sections, accessed by clicking on the corresponding tab.

The following is an example of an Employee Record and shows Employment details:

For detailed help, pressing the F1 key at any time in Sage Payroll brings up the Help facility.

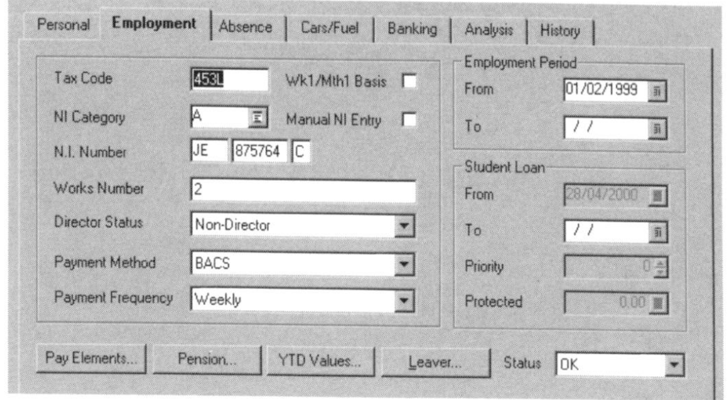

Accuracy reduces errors and prevents costly mistakes.

For every employee, there is also an Employee Payment card, such as the one below, for recording Basic Pay, Overtime Rates and Bonuses, together with any regular Deductions, Attachments and Statutory Sick Pay (SSP), etc.

Always make sure you are up to date with the latest Government legislation relating to payroll.

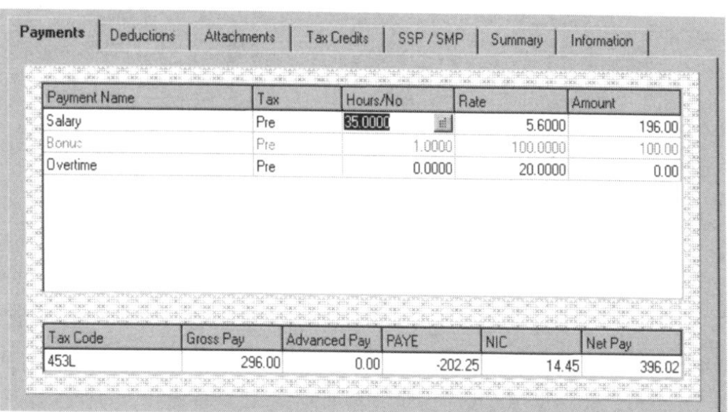

To run the latest version of Sage Payroll, the minimum computer hardware requirements are now a Pentium processor running at 133 MHz or higher and at least 50Mbyte of free hard disc space and 32MByte of RAM memory, plus an SVGA monitor.

Location of Payroll Data

The installation procedure copies all the necessary files onto your PC for you, though it is sometimes handy to know how Sage Payroll is stored on your computer.

Typically, the Payroll program will be stored on drive C:, in the C:\PAYROLL or \PROGRAM FILES\SAGE PAYROLL folder. This folder is then further sub-divided as follows:

PAYROLL\COMPANY.001	contains the PAYDATA and PICTURES folders.
PAYROLL\COMPANY.001\PAYDATA	holds the employee records and payments cards as well as the parameters cards.
PAYROLL\COMPANY.001\PICTURES	contains the bitmap files of employee photos, where used.
PAYROLL\DEFAULTS	used to hold the default page header information for a report designer file.
PAYROLL\REPORTS	holds the report writer files.
PAYROLL\TEMPLATE	holds the Stationery layout templates (Payslips, Giros, Cheques).

To quickly install Sage Payroll without making changes, simply select the 'Typical' option.

You can link Sage Payroll to Sage Line 50 or Sage Line 100 accounting software and make automated postings to update your Profit and Loss and Balance Sheet with payroll journals.

Press Function key F1 to open the Sage Payroll online help system.

Working through Sage Payroll in easy steps

This book explains how to perform the main tasks required for keeping a computerised payroll system. The following chapters show you how to:

- Check and amend Government Legislation settings.
- Record comprehensive Employee and Company details.
- Provide Payroll Security.
- Create a nominal link to Sage Line 50 Accounts.
- Pay your Employees weekly, fortnightly or monthly.
- Deal with Statutory Sick Pay and Statutory Maternity Pay.
- Record and maintain your Company Pension Schemes.
- Set up and process Deductions and Attachments.
- Process Payroll runs and print Statutory Forms.
- Run your Year End Routine.
- Carry out File Maintenance.

Familiarise yourself with Sage Payroll's features and practice with the demonstration company provided with the program until you are ready to start entering your own data for real.

Preparing to start checklist

Make sure you do the following before using Payroll for the first time:

- Collate all your employee record information.
- Check your government parameters are recorded correctly.
- Have company details and pay elements to hand.
- Plan, then check your nominal link settings.
- Decide about payroll security.
- Set up a backup facility.

Let the Tax Year End Wizard guide you through the year end procedure.

If you want to make use of the Internet facilities your computer must be equipped with a modem.

Key Functions

Setting up the F11 and F12 keys to perform frequently used actions can save you considerable time.

The following shortcut features are available to help you whilst working with your Sage Payroll program. Make full use of them to save time.

Function keys

F1	Opens the online help system.
F2	Displays the system calculator.
F4	Displays the calendar, calculator or Finder search if the selected text box has any of these special buttons attached.
F11	User defined - you can set up this function key using the Environment tab, from the View, Options menu, to open a frequently used action of your choice.
F12	This key can also be user defined or used to minimise your program if 'Configure F12 as Hide Key' is ticked on the Environment tab.

Function keys and Keystrokes are provided for frequently used actions. Practice using them regularly and you will find Sage Payroll easier to use.

Keystrokes

ESC	Exits the current screen without saving.
TAB	Accepts an entry and moves to the next field or entry box.
SHIFT+TAB	Moves back to the previous field or box.
END	Moves the cursor to the last character of the last word in the field.
HOME	Moves the cursor to the start of the field.
CTRL+RIGHT ARROW	Moves to the first character of the next word in the field.
CTRL+LEFT ARROW	Moves the cursor to the first character of the previous word in the field.

A quick method of accessing an option from the Menu bar is to hold down the Alt key and press the underlined letter of the function required (i.e., Alt+T pulls down the Tasks menu).

The Payroll Desktop

The Desktop features a menu bar, a stacked toolbar, an application toolbar and a split screen, with tree view on the left and list view on the right.

When working from the Payroll stacked toolbar, the New button creates a new employee, whereas the New button from the Company stacked toolbar creates a new company, provided you have purchased a multi-company licence.

The main program options are quickly accessed using the stacked toolbars by clicking on the Payroll, Company or Desktop buttons. Many of these options are also available from, or similar to those on, the application toolbar.

Payroll Desktop

1 Application toolbar for working with your Employee and Company data.

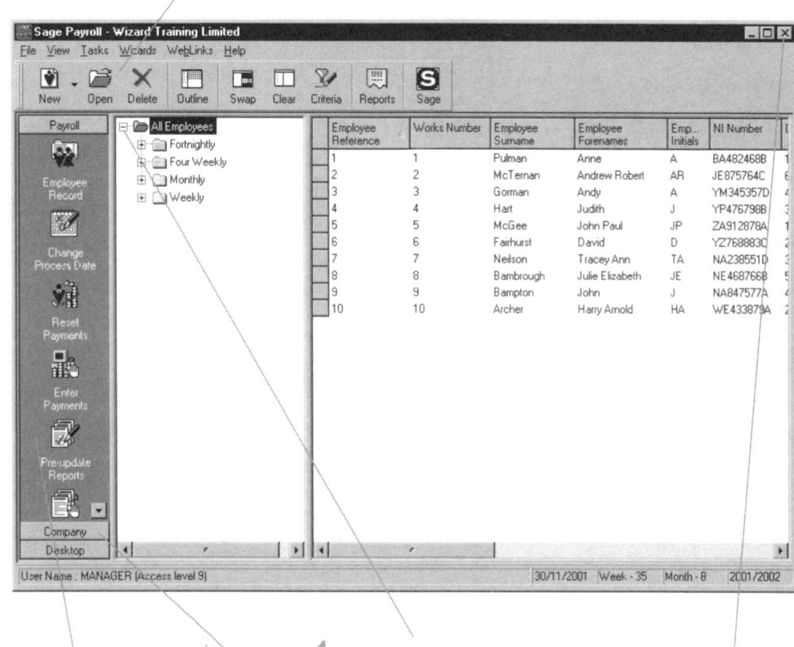

You can use the Tasks menu as an alternative method of quickly accessing the majority of payroll functions, such as changing the process date, entering payments, changing passwords, etc.

4 Click here to view specific information.

2 The main program options are contained on the stacked toolbar.

5 Click here to Close.

3 Click here to move between stacked toolbar options.

Sorting your information to meet your requirements

When required you can easily sort your payroll information into a different order. For example, to sort your employees by surname order do the following:

To sort on a particular field just click on the field name at the top of a column.

1 Click once here to sort into ascending order (A–Z).

2 To revert the sort to its original order, simply click here again.

Use the mouse to drag columns into any new order you prefer to work with.

Clicking on the Outline button in the toolbar removes the tree view and maximises the list view, allowing you to see more record columns.

Reorganising your columns

To reorganise the employee column list, do the following:

1 Point to the required column heading and hold down the left mouse button.

2 Drag the column to the required position, then simply release the mouse button.

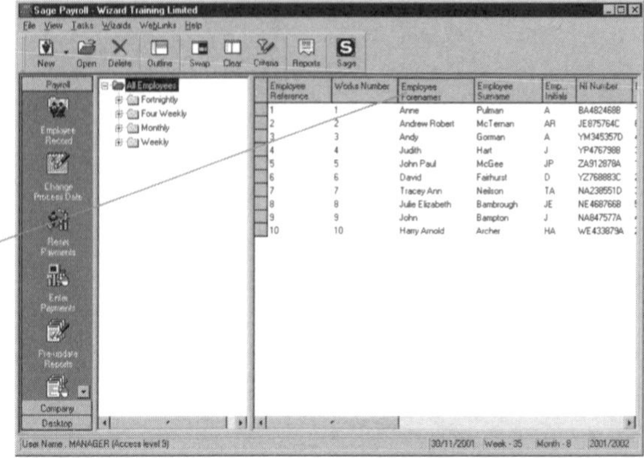

To restore the tree view just click on the Outline button again.

Setting up Desktop Options

Options can also be set up by selecting the Options icon from the Desktop stacked toolbar.

You can change the appearance of the desktop to suit your preferences. The following options are available:

Toolbar

1. From the Menu bar click View, then Options.
2. Tick here for text labels under each toolbar button.

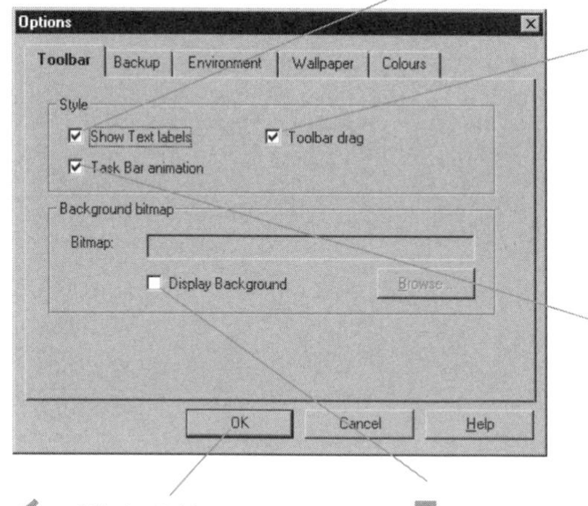

3. A tick here lets you drag your application toolbar to any position on the desktop.
4. Tick here to change the way you move between stacked toolbars.
5. Tick here to use a background.
6. Click OK to save or Cancel to abandon.

To drag your toolbar, place the cursor on the lines on the left of the toolbar, hold down the left mouse button and drag to a new position.

Use the Browse button to help you find a path for the background bitmap.

Backup

To change the backup drive:

1. From the Menu bar click View, then Options.
2. Select the Backup tab.
3. Enter the new backup path here.
4. Click OK to save.

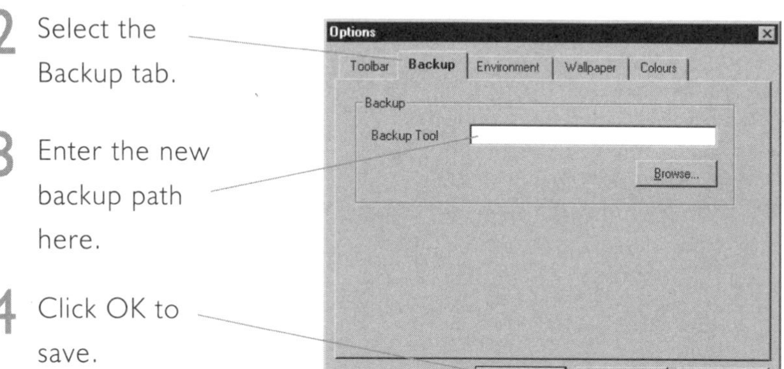

To exit without saving your changes, just click on the Cancel button.

Environment

To set your environment defaults do the following:

1. From the Menu bar click View and Options.
2. Click the Environment tab.

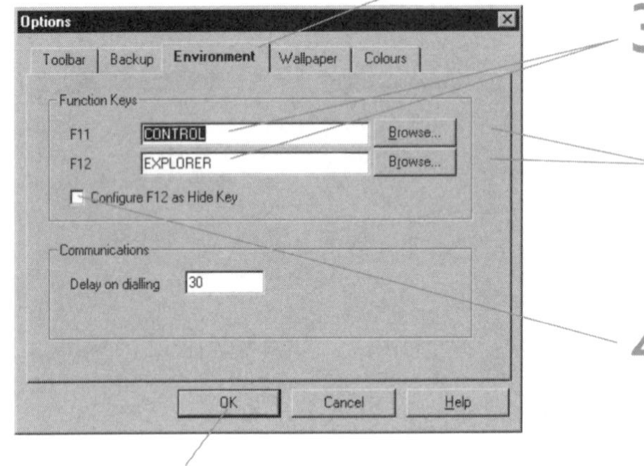

3. Enter a command for F11 and F12. Use Browse buttons as necessary.
4. Click this box to use F12 as a minimise key.
5. Click OK to save changes.

If you select the 'Configure F12 As Hide Key' check box you can then press F12 at any time and minimise your screen, instantly hiding confidential information from view.

The default setting for the modem port is COM3. This may need changing if your modem is connected to a different port.

Wallpaper

1. From the Menu bar click View and Options.
2. Click the Wallpaper tab.
3. Click here to use wallpaper.
4. Enter path of the bitmap file you require.
5. Choose your prefered list style here.
6. Click OK to save.

With the Line 50 style selection you can select more than one employee at a time using the mouse. If you are using the Windows 95 style list, you can only select more than one employee by using the mouse and holding down the SHIFT key.

Colours

To set up your colour defaults do the following:

1. From the Menu bar click View and Options.
2. Click the Colours tab.
3. Ensure this box is not ticked.
4. Click this box to change text colour.

If you do not want to show colours on your windows simply select the Ignore colours check box.

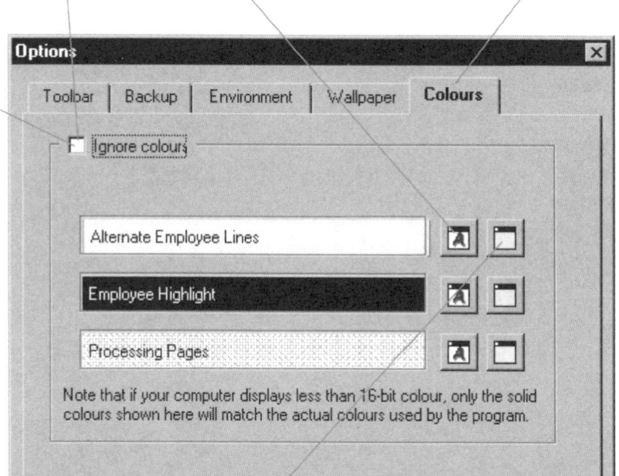

You can also specify alternate colours to display your employee list or highlighted employees. Just click on the appropriate text or background box and do step 5.

7. Click here to change background colour.
8. Repeat steps 5 & 6.

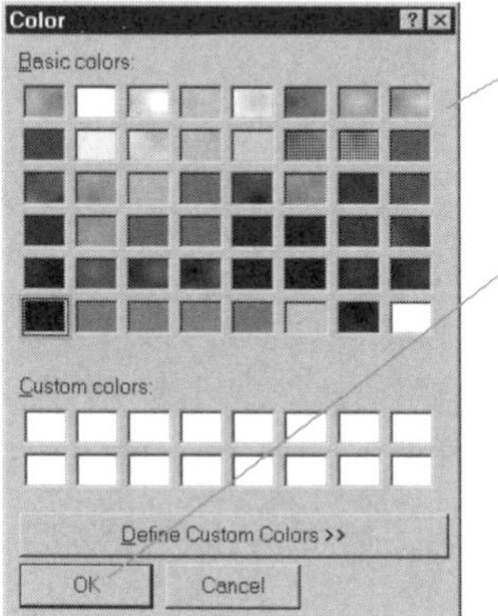

5. Select colour here.
6. Click OK.
9. Click OK to close the Options window.

Using Criteria

You can also invoke the Criteria function from the Desktop stacked toolbar.

This feature is very useful for quickly supplying you with categorised levels of employee information, e.g., list of weekly paid staff together with their department. You can also use the Criteria option for excluding unnecessary records from your processing list, such as Leavers, staff on holiday and those On Hold.

The following example shows you how to list only employees who are paid weekly in cash:

It is always advisable to reset the Criteria filters once you have finished to avoid confusion later. Simply ensure the Payment Periods and Payment Methods boxes are all ticked and set the filters to None.

1 Click the Criteria button on the application toolbar.

2 Select the By Payment Period filter here.

3 Select By Payment Method here.

4 Tick only Include Weekly.

5 Tick only Include Cash.

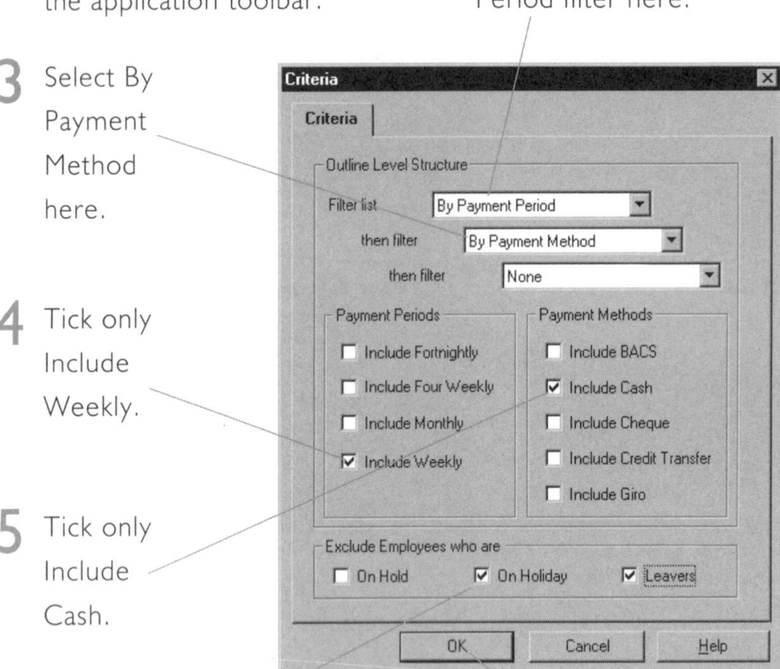

6 Tick here to exclude as required.

7 Click OK to accept.

Remember that you will not see employee lists that match your selected criteria until you step down the appropriate levels in the Tree view.

8 In the Tree view, double-click on All Employees to bring up the Weekly folder only.

9 Double-click on Weekly.

10 Click on Cash. The list shows employees paid weekly in cash.

Government Legislation Settings

These settings should not need changing unless there is a change to Government Legislation.

Government legislation can change from time to time, such as when there is a budget. Sage Payroll comes with settings for legislation relating to the current tax year. If legislation changes for a new tax year then you will be sent an update disk by Sage, with installation instructions.

Before you start entering employee and company details it is advisable to familiarise yourself with your current payroll legislation settings, as follows:

You can also use the Reports option from the application toolbar to check and print out current legislation settings.

1 Click on Company from the stacked toolbar.

2 Click on the Government Legislation button.

3 From the PAYE tab check the Bandwidths and Rates are correct.

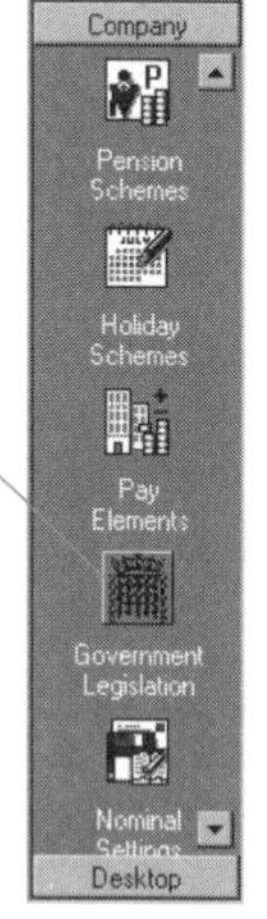

Remember to always refer to the Employer's Annual Pack for the most up to date legislation information. If you do not have this pack, simply order one via the Inland Revenue Employer's Orderline.

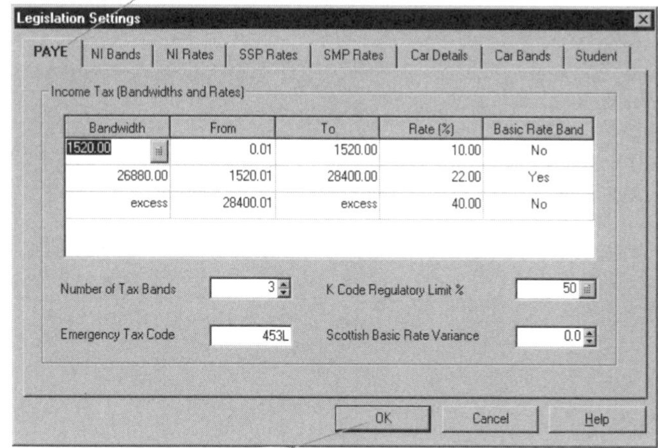

4 Click OK to close.

To check your SSP and SMP legislation settings

It is very important to remember that you should not edit these bandwidths or rates unless government legislation changes, or unless you are advised to do so by Sage.

It is also important to be very familiar with Statutory Sick Pay and Statutory Maternity Pay. Check these settings as follows:

1. From the Company stacked toolbar click on Government Legislation.
2. Click on the SSP Rates tab and note the settings.

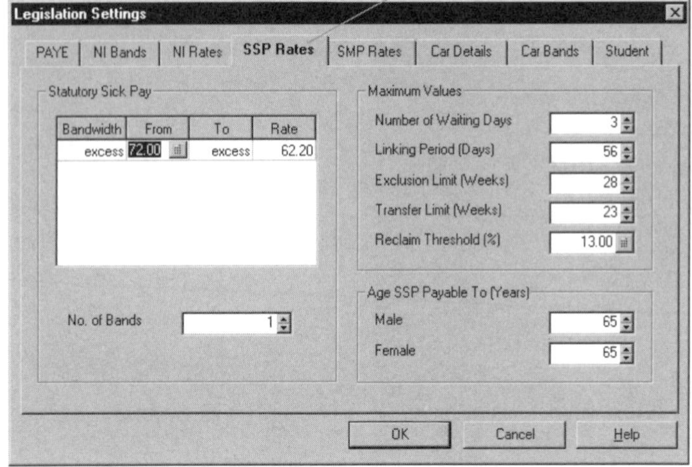

If you make a mistake and accidentally alter a setting, simply click on the Cancel button.

3. Click on the SMP tab.
4. When finished, click OK.

As well as doing it to familiarise yourself with Government Legislation settings, it is advisable that you check your legislation settings are correct before you enter any company or employee details.

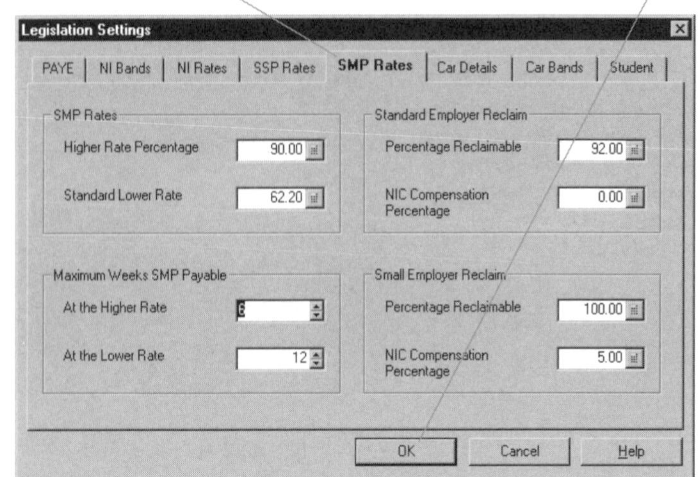

To check Car Details and Car Bands

Another area that can change in annual budgets is the legislation for the use of a company car. Check and familiarise yourself with these rates as follows:

Legislation was introduced in the 1991 budget regarding the liability for national insurance contributions (NIC) on the value of company cars and the fuel they use. Employers are liable for NIC on the value of company cars and fuel provided by them, therefore accurate records need to be kept of business mileage for each company car.

1. From the Company stacked toolbar click on Government Legislation.
2. Select the Car Details and Car Bands tabs and note the settings.

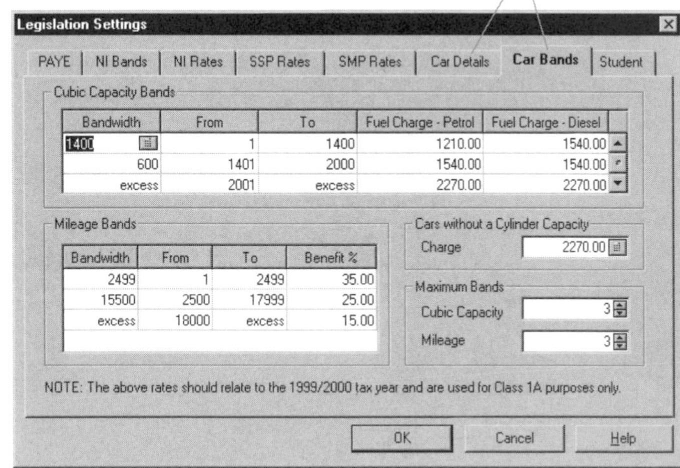

Repayment of student loans

1. Click on the Student tab to view the income threshold.

From 6 April 2000 the collection of student loan repayments is made through the payroll system.

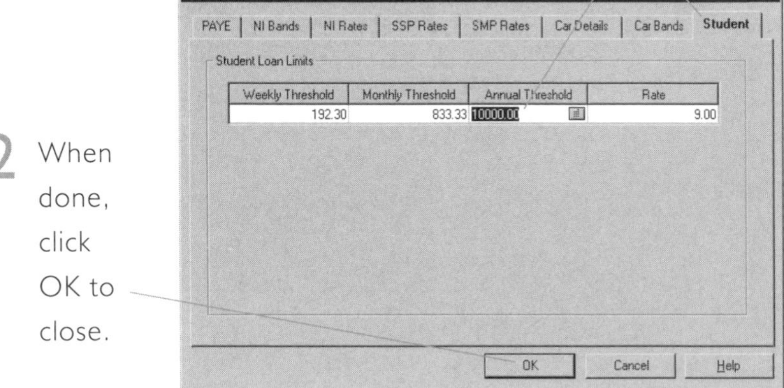

2. When done, click OK to close.

Demonstration Data

Use the Finder button to help you quickly search for previously set up records. You may even only have to enter the first few characters, numbers, etc.

So that you can become familiar with using Sage Payroll without altering your own data, you are provided with demonstration data to practice on. To open the demonstration company, do the following:

1 From the File menu choose the Open Company option.

2 Select the Demonstration Data from the list.

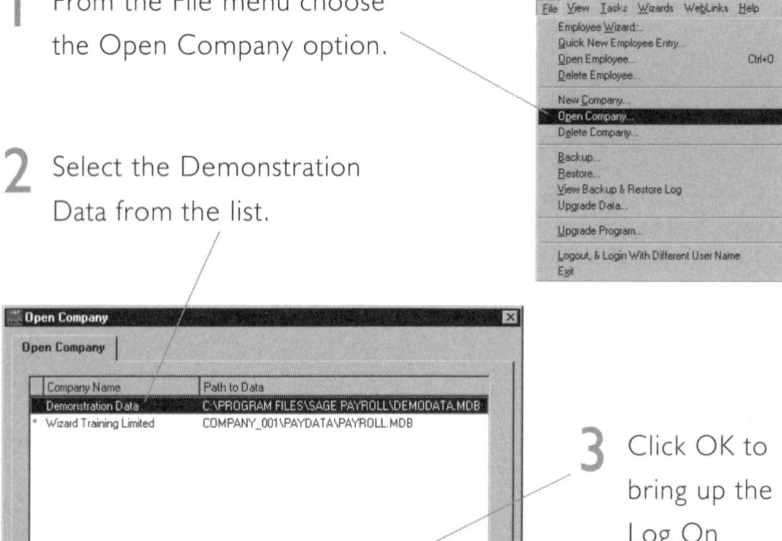

3 Click OK to bring up the Log On screen.

An asterisk marks the currently selected company in the Open Company window.

4 Note processing date and tax period, then click OK.

To delete a Company select the Delete Company option from the File Menu.

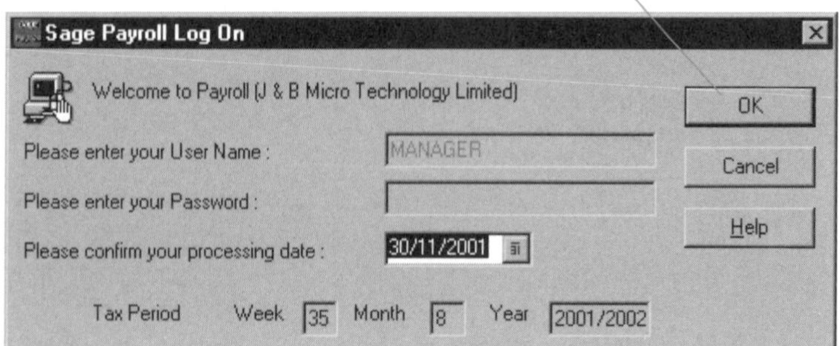

5 To return to your own company, repeat the above steps.

Payroll Security

In this chapter you will learn how to set up any security requirements for your Payroll program to ensure that only authorised users can access the data. This includes setting up user names and access rights as well as editing and deleting existing user names. You will also learn how to customise access levels and create and change passwords for added security.

Covers

Chapter Two

User Names and Access Rights

You must log on as MANAGER the first time you use Sage Payroll, though a password will not be required.

Sage Payroll provides you with the facility to restrict access to the system to authorised users only. After installation, initial access to the program is available via the user name MANAGER. Unless you have given the permission to another user, normally only the MANAGER would set up access rights for other users.

Using the Access Rights option from the Tasks menu, the MANAGER can create a table of users and passwords. Users can then be restricted from various areas of the payroll program.

Setting a MANAGER password

When you first install Sage Payroll, no password is allocated to the user name MANAGER, so the first thing you should do is to set one up otherwise the payroll system is left open to unauthorised access. To do this:

When you use Sage Payroll for the first time remember to secure your data by setting up a password for MANAGER.

1 Click on Tasks on the menu bar.

2 Click on Security, then the Change Personal Password option.

3 Enter your password here, and again here.

If you run more than one company, the MANAGER can set up the security system for each company differently.

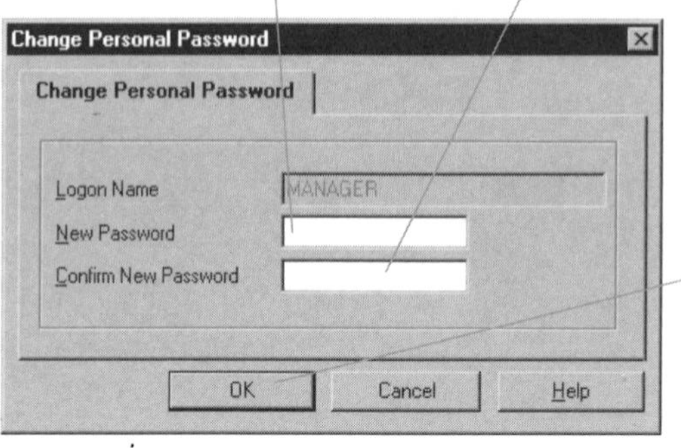

5 Click on OK to save, or Cancel to abandon.

Access Levels

Once you have set up a password for MANAGER, be careful never to lose it.

Having logged onto the Payroll system as MANAGER, you can now set up new users. Each user can then be allocated their own password and different levels of access, as appropriate.

The list below highlights the different payroll areas associated with each Access Level.

For security reasons and to avoid problems later it is always advisable to structure your payroll access rights so that each authorised user can only access their own particular area of interest.

Access Level	**Company Areas**
Company	Company Details (Edit, New & Delete) Pay Elements Nominal Settings
Legislation	Government Legislation
Employee	Employee Record (Edit, New & Delete)
Process	Reset Payments Enter Payments Recalculate
Reports	Pre-update Reports Main Reports
Update	Update Records Nominal Link Tax Year End Rollback Advance Absence Year
Utilities	Global Changes Upgrade Program Upgrade Data
Access Rights	Access Rights Change Program Password
Internet	Internet

Access rights are not required to use the Sage Payroll desktop and utilities, nor to use the data backup or restore facility.

Before processing your first payroll, take some time to work out the security levels you need. You can then set this up as shown in the following pages.

Setting up a User

A Logon Name can be up to 30 characters.

Start the Sage Payroll program and log in as MANAGER. You are now in a position to create a new user, with or without a password. To do this, do the following:

1. Click on Tasks on the menu bar.

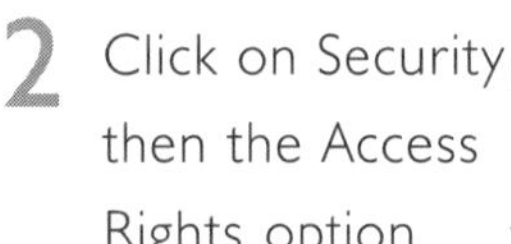

2. Click on Security, then the Access Rights option.

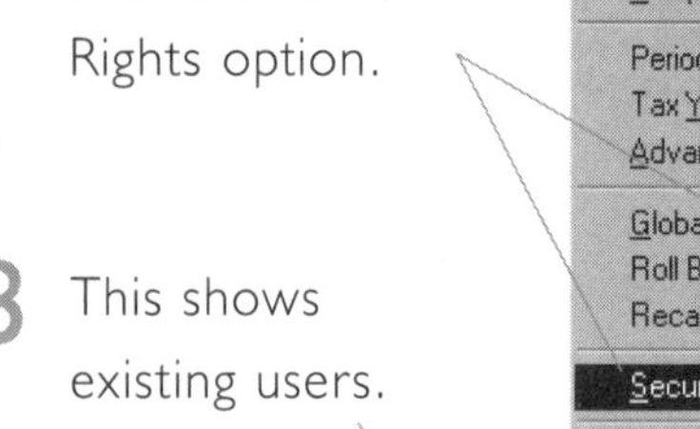

A Password can be up to 10 characters and is not case sensitive.

3. This shows existing users.

Leaving the Password box blank means the user will not need a password to access Sage Payroll. It also means anyone else who knows the user name can also access payroll!

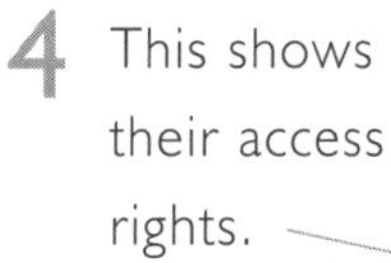

4. This shows their access rights.

5. Click Add.

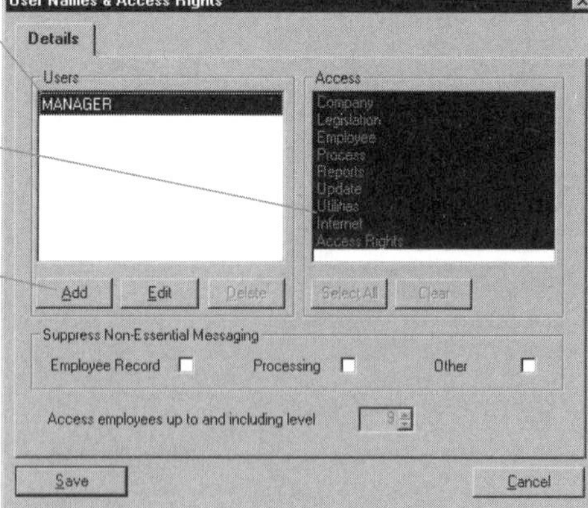

6. Enter new user name here.

To set up access rights immediately after you add a user, after doing Step 8 continue from Step 3 on Page 27.

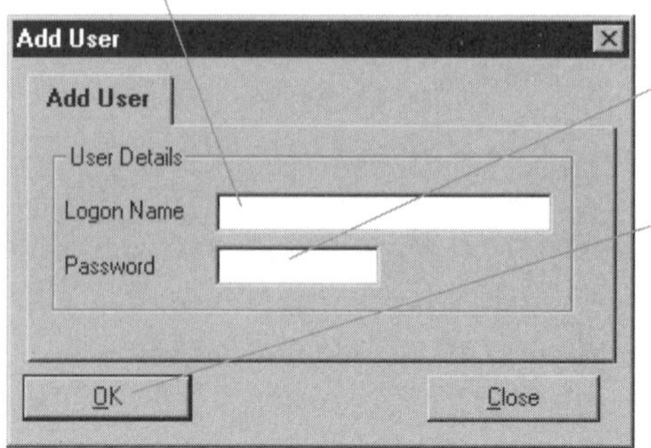

7. Enter Password here.
8. Click OK to accept.
9. Click Save again to close user names window.

Allocating Access Levels

Refer to page 25 for the full list of Access Levels.

Having decided which areas of the program you want each of your users to have access to, you are now ready to allocate the appropriate access levels to each user. The following steps guide you through this process.

1 Click on Tasks on the menu bar.

Once access rights have been set up and the user logs on he or she will only have access to the areas you have specified.

2 Click on Security, then the Access Rights option.

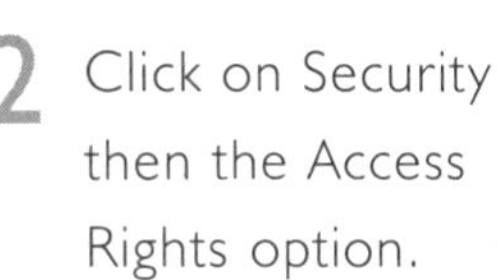

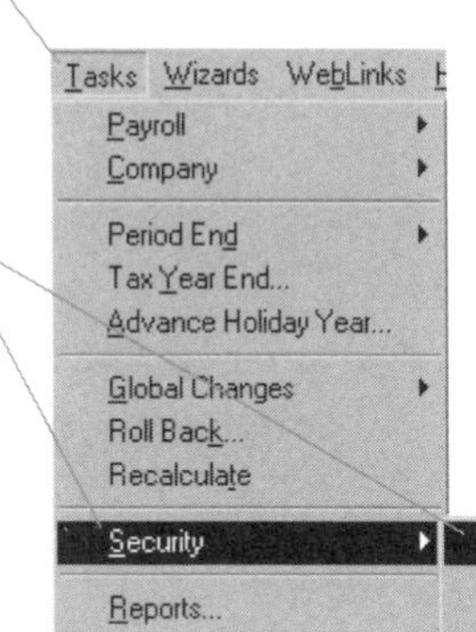

3 Click on the required user here.

Use the Select All button to allocate full access to a user.

4 Click on each Access level you wish to give the user here.

Use the Clear button to deselect any access rights settings.

5 Click Save to record your settings.

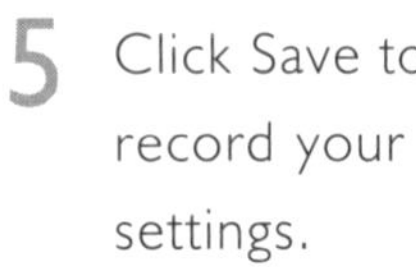

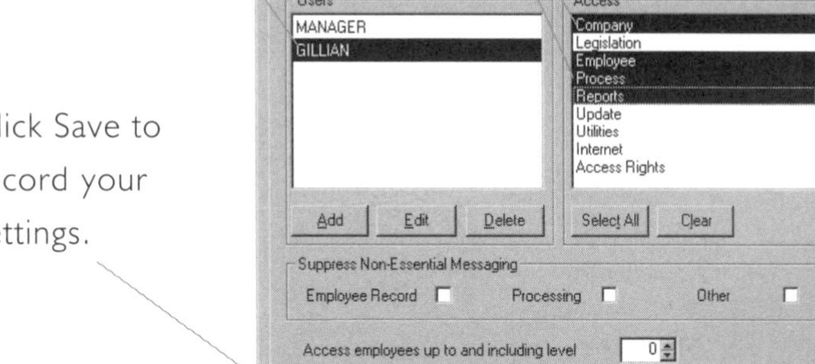

Where access to an area is prohibited the icon will appear in grey.

6 Repeat Steps 1 to 5 as necessary to set up access rights for any other users.

Editing User Names

To quickly deselect all access settings just click the Clear button.

Sage Payroll allows you to edit user names, access rights and passwords. To do this however, the task must be carried out by the manager or another user with access to the Access Rights area.

To edit Access Rights, do the following:

1. From the menu bar click Tasks, then Security and Access Rights to bring up the User Names & Access Rights box.

As part of your security measures, change user passwords on a regular basis.

2. Select the user whose details need amending.

3. Click on the access areas to be added or removed.

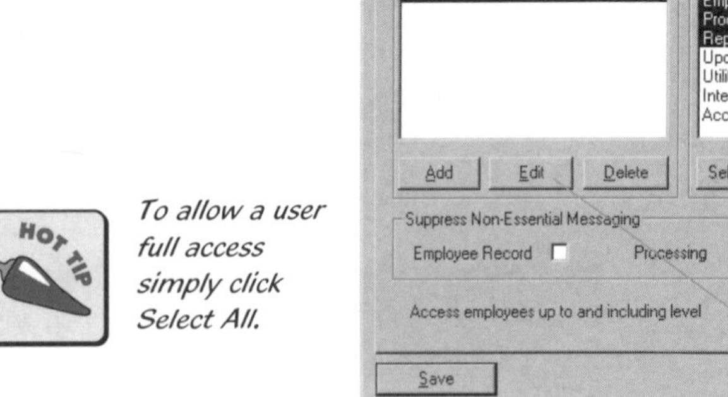

To allow a user full access simply click Select All.

To edit a user's password:

1. Select the required user and click on the Edit button.

For security reasons, change passwords when a user leaves.

2. Delete the existing password and enter a new one.

3. Click OK to save the changes then Save to return to the desktop.

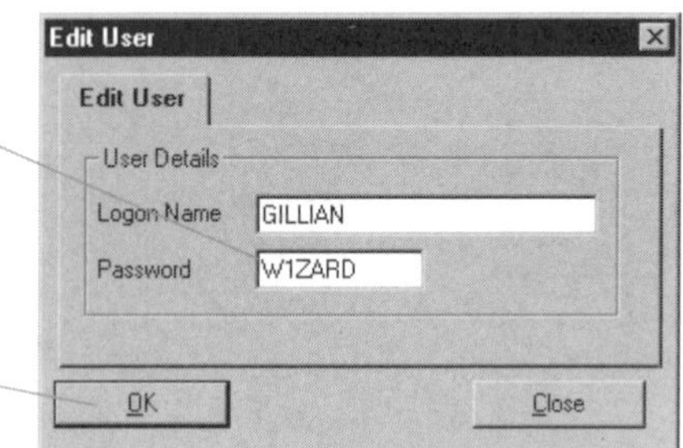

Deleting User Names

You also have the facility to permanently delete a user's details from the Sage Payroll program. You may want to do this, for example, when a payroll user leaves your company.

Once a payroll user leaves your company you should delete their details immediately from the Users list.

To delete a user name, do the following:

1. From the menu bar click Tasks, Security then Access Rights to bring up the User Names & Access Rights box.

2. Select the user whose details you need to delete from the Users list.

3. Click the Delete button.

When a user leaves but a new one is to take over the same tasks, simply edit the previous user name and password to the new details instead of deleting the old user details and then setting up a new user.

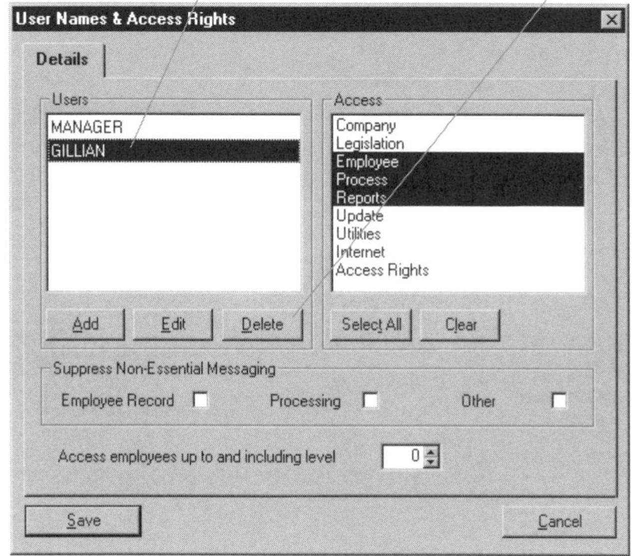

If you accidentally select the incorrect user to delete, simply press No when asked to confirm and repeat from Step 2.

4. Click Yes to confirm you want to delete the user, else No to cancel.

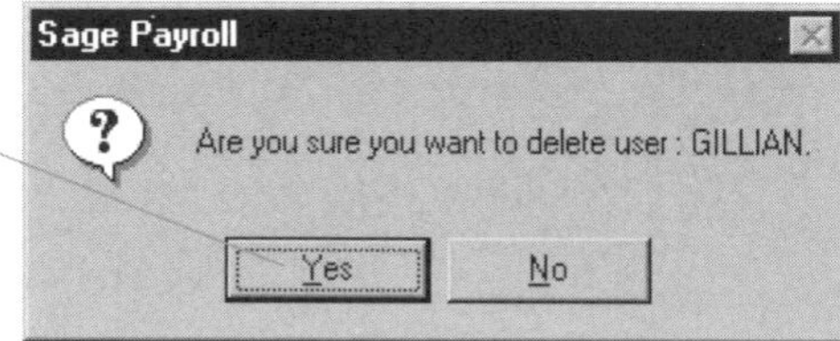

5. Click Save to record changes.

Passwords

Once you have set up a password for MANAGER, you must take great care not to lose it.

Sage provides you with two levels of security password for using the Payroll program. Firstly the system manager can set up a personal password for each user. This is the user's personal password and can be changed as and when required.

The second option involves the setting up of a program password by the manager. All users must enter this password to gain access to the Payroll program irrespective of whether they have their own personal password or not.

Only users with access to the Access Rights area can set up the program password.

To change the program password

1. From the Tasks menu click Security, then Change Program Password.
2. Enter existing password here or leave blank if there is no program password set up.
3. Enter new password here.
4. Re-enter new password here to confirm.
5. Click OK.

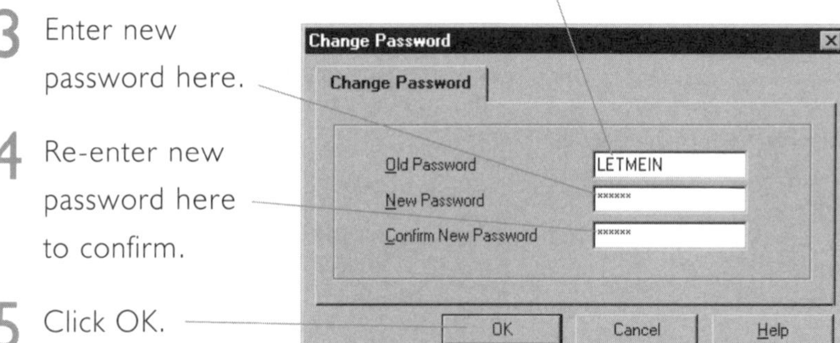

A user can change their personal password at any time.

Passwords can be up to 10 characters and are not case sensitive.

To change your personal password

1. Click Tasks, Security then Change Personal Password.
2. Enter new password.
3. Re-enter new password here to confirm.
4. Click OK.

Change Personal Password
Change Personal Password
Logon Name
GILLIAN
New Password
Confirm New Password
OK
Cancel
Help

If you have purchased a multi company licence, passwords can be set up to limit access to specific companies.

Company Settings

This chapter shows you how to enter and configure your company defaults, which must be set up before you start using the program. This includes company and bank details, holiday and pension schemes, coinage requirements and, if required, departments and cost centres. You will also be shown how to use the Pay Elements option to record payments, deductions and attachment types for your employees.

Covers

Chapter Three

Entering Your Company Details

Simply press the F1 key for help or use the Library for additional information about Company Settings.

Before you can start using Sage Payroll for the first time you must enter your company defaults. These include details such as your name, address, tax office, bank, coinage and department details. Company holiday and absence schemes need recording too, as well as any pension schemes you may have.

To first enter your company details:

Use the TAB key to quickly move to the next row or input box.

Pressing SHIFT+TAB moves you to the previous row or input box.

Whilst setting your company details, check also that your SSP patterns are correctly set up.

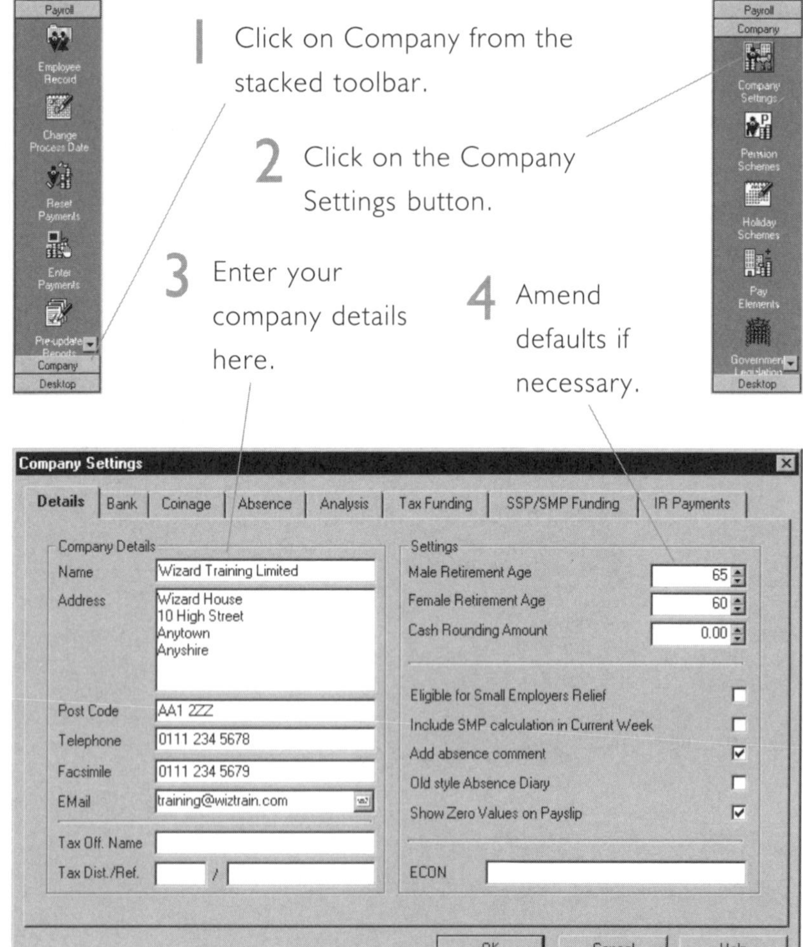

1 Click on Company from the stacked toolbar.

2 Click on the Company Settings button.

3 Enter your company details here.

4 Amend defaults if necessary.

5 Click OK to record your company details.

The Retirement Age defaults are 65 for men and 60 for women.

Normally, the default settings will not need altering, but if necessary, they can be amended. The following explains what the various settings do:

You can enter either a negative or positive value between - 10.00 and +10.00 for the Cash Rounding Amount. A negative value rounds the employee's pay down to the nearest multiple whilst a positive number rounds up to the nearest multiple.

By default, SMP is paid in arrears.

After recording your company details, see page 42 if you want to use departments and cost centres .

Retirement Age	Although set by default, this can be amended to any age between 50 and 70.
Cash Rounding Amount	For employees paid by cash, you can enter here whether to round the payment up or down to the nearest multiple.
Eligible for Small Employers Relief	Tick this box if you qualify as a small employer. If unsure, contact your local DSS office.
Include SMP calculation in Current Week	If ticked, the current week of processing will include any SMP calculations.
Add absence comment	If this box is ticked you can then include comments on the absence diary.
Old style Absence Diary	Should you be familiar with previous versions of Sage Payroll and prefer to view the absence diary in the earlier style, tick here.
Show Zero Values on Payslip	A tick here allows values that are zero to appear and be printed on your employees' payslips.
ECON	This box contains the Employers Contracted Out Number, though you do not need to enter the first alpha character, e.g., E. Note that an employer should only have one ECON.

Company Bank Details

You can use up to 30 characters per line for the Bank Name, Address and Account Name.

The Bank tab from the Company Settings window allows you to set up your company's bank details. This is necessary as Sage Payroll will use this information when printing cheque and giro details. Enter your company bank details as follows:

1. From the Company stacked toolbar, click Company Settings.
2. Click on the Bank tab.
3. Enter your Bank Name here.
4. Enter bank address and other contact details here.
5. Click here and choose the account type.

You must enter an eight digit number for an account number. No spaces, letters or special characters are allowed.

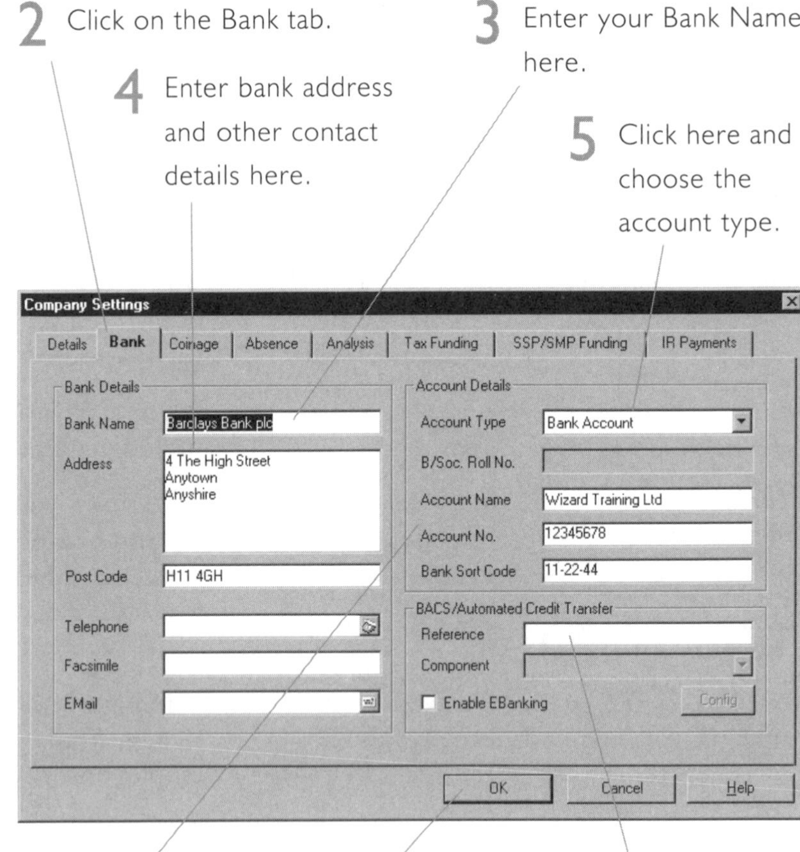

You can only enter a building society roll number if you selected building society from the Account Type drop-down list.

6. Enter the rest of your Account Details here.
7. Enter Reference here if you use BACS/automated credit transfer to pay your employees.
8. Click OK to save changes.

The Bank Sort Code should be entered in the format shown, for example, 12-34-56.

Setting Up Coinage Requirements

If you do not wish to specify a number for the Minimum Quantity of a particular note or coin, simply leave the entry as zero.

This facility enables you to set up a minimum quantity of notes and coins that you would like to use when paying your employees in cash.

To set up minimum coinage quantities:

1. From the Company stacked toolbar, click Company Settings.

2. Click on the Coinage tab.

3. Enter the minimum number of each type of note required here.

4. Enter the minimum number of each type of coin required here.

If needed, you can quickly generate a Company report for Coin Analysis using the Reports option on the application toolbar.

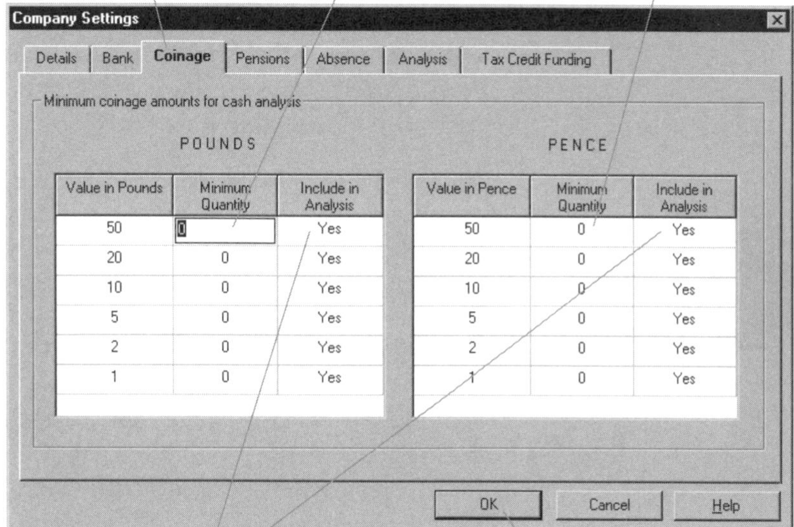

When you need help for a particular setting, whilst in that window, pressing the F1 key brings up the Sage Payroll Help already open on that topic for you.

5. Select No in each entry in this column here if you want to exclude the bank note or coinage from the payment calculation.

6. Click OK here to save, or Cancel to abandon your changes.

Company Pension Schemes

A pension will be made up of the basic State pension plus any additional entitlement provided by SERPS.

Types of Pensions

When all employed earners reach retirement age, they are entitled to receive the basic State pension. Employees who have paid Class 1 NI contributions are entitled to an additional State pension provided by the State Earnings Related Pension Scheme, better known as SERPS.

However, many employers also decide to offer their employees the opportunity to join a company or occupational pension scheme. These schemes provide much better benefits on retirement than the State's basic pension.

You must keep your employees pension contributions up to date and any changes to the scheme always have to be recorded, i.e., joiners and leavers or amendments to employee's and employer's contributions.

These pension schemes can be contracted in or contracted out of SERPS. A contracted in scheme means that the occupational pension is in addition to SERPS, whilst a contracted out scheme means the company pension scheme is in place of SERPS.

For a scheme which is contracted out of SERPS, both the employer and the employee pay a reduced rate of National Insurance Contributions (NIC).

Where the employer does not provide their employees with a company or occupational pension scheme, employees can make contributions into a personal pension scheme of their own to increase pension benefits on retirement.

AVC stands for Additional Voluntary Contribution and AEO stands for Attachment of Earnings Order.

Employees contributing to an occupational scheme

Where an employer provides an occupational pension scheme, rules, conditions and benefits must be clearly defined and made available so that employees can decide for themselves whether or not they wish to become members. An employer is not allowed to make membership a compulsory condition of employment.

For national insurance purposes, pension contributions and AVCs are not deducted from gross pay prior to calculating NI contributions for the employer and employee.

However, for exempt approved occupational schemes, employees receive tax relief for contributions made through the payroll.

For contracting out of SERPS, the employer must have a contracting out certificate issued by the Occupational Pensions Board.

Contributions made from the employee's pay into the pension scheme must be deducted from the employee's gross pay before calculating the tax due on the pay. This is known as a 'net pay arrangement'. Where an employee decides to pay AVCs into the pension scheme, these are treated the same as the pension contributions and are also deducted from gross pay before tax is calculated.

Employees contracting out of SERPS

Some occupational pension schemes are contracted out of SERPS. For these schemes both the employees who are members and the employer pay a reduced rate of NIC. The employer must have a contracting out certificate issued by the Occupational Pensions Board. This certificate includes a final salary scheme which offers a guaranteed minimum pension (GMP) increasing in line with inflation and a money purchase scheme that provides a pension under the protected rights test giving the employee a similar GMP.

Within Sage Payroll V7 you can have an unlimited number of different pension schemes, but only one can be applied to any employee at any one time, i.e., you cannot have a fixed amount and a percentage contribution applied to the same employee.

Getting started pension checklist

Before entering your pension, work through this checklist:

1. Which scheme–fixed amount or percentage?
2. Is the pension paid on all elements amounting to gross or just on certain payments?
3. Is the pension contribution subject to COMPS or to the NIC rebate?
4. Do you wish to add the rebate for COMPS amount to your fixed or percentage contribution or do you just require the rebate figure only?
5. For NIC purposes do you require your pension figure to be calculated between the Lower and Upper Earnings Limit?
6. Do you wish to include in your pension calculation SSP and SMP payments?
7. Does tax relief apply to your pension amount?

If you have queries regarding pension contributions, check with your pension adviser BEFORE setting up your pension details.

You need to enter pension information for both employee and employer contributions.

To set up your company pension scheme details

You need to record the details of any company pension scheme so that Sage Payroll can then automatically calculate the pension contributions. To set up or edit your company pension scheme details do the following:

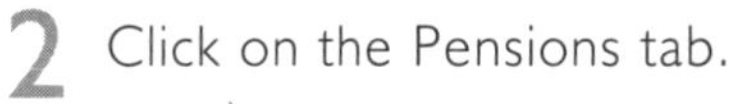

1. From the Company stacked toolbar, click Company Settings.

2. Click on the Pensions tab.

3. Enter a new pension scheme Reference and press TAB or use the Finder button to select a scheme to edit.

You will need to enter a description for data which has been converted from a previous version of Payroll.

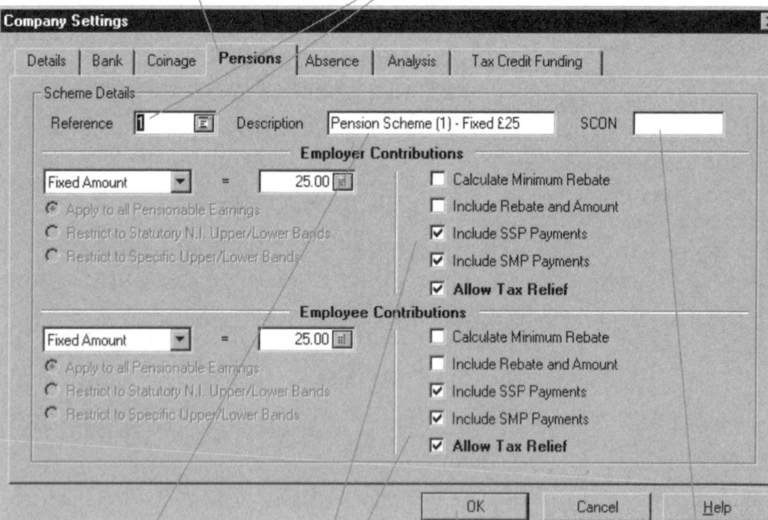

You can enter up to 30 characters for a pension Description.

Refer to page 141 for assigning pension schemes to an employee.

4. Type a Description here.

5. Enter your Scheme Contracted Out Ref. Number here if applicable.

6. Enter pension information for employer and employee in these boxes.

7. Click OK to save.

Additional notes on entering your company pension scheme details

Use the Calculator button to enter an amount or fixed percentage.

In the Scheme Details area you need to select either Percentage or Fixed Amount from the drop down list for both employer and employee, then enter the value of the percentage or amount in the next box.

If a percentage scheme is in use you need to select one of the following options so that Sage Payroll knows how to calculate the percentage contribution:

To apply the pension percentage to the NI earnings band only, select Restrict to Statutory N.I. Upper/Lower Bands.

Apply to all Pensionable Earnings	This applies the percentage to the employee's total earnings.
Restrict to Statutory N.I. Upper/Lower Bands	Check this to apply the pension percentage to the NI earnings bands only.
Restrict to specific Upper/Lower Bands	This will apply the percentage to the limits specified by you in the Upper and Lower limits boxes which appear when you select this option.

Other scheme details you can specify are:

The Restrict to Specific Upper/Lower Bands option allows you to set your own defined earnings limit. Once selected, you can enter your own earning limits into the Lower and Upper limits boxes which appear automatically.

Calculate Minimum Rebate	If checked, calculates the NI contracted out rebate.
Include Rebate and Amount	Select to total the percentage and minimum rebate values.
Include SSP Payments	If selected, Payroll includes any SSP payments in the total pensionable pay.
Include SMP Payments	If selected, Payroll includes any SMP payments in the total pensionable pay.
Allow Tax Relief	If checked, allows tax relief on pension contributions. Tax is deducted from gross before tax.

Company Holiday Schemes

Payroll V7 has 10 holiday schemes ready set up for you to edit as required.

Your company's holiday and absence scheme details also need setting up. The start date of your holiday and absence year needs recording together with the statutory sickness payment qualifying patterns. To enter this information:

1 From the Company stacked toolbar, click Holiday Schemes.

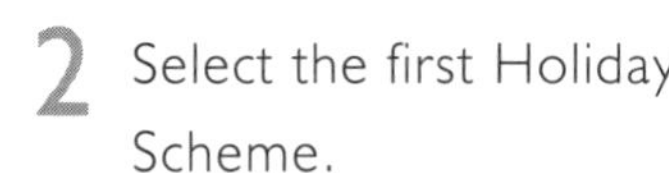

2 Select the first Holiday Scheme.

The Holiday Scheme Name can be up to 30 characters long.

3 Click Edit.

4 Enter a name for the scheme here.

5 Enter Entitlement details here.

If a new starter begins halfway through the pay period and you wish to accrue holiday for the full period, select the Include Starting Pay Month check box.

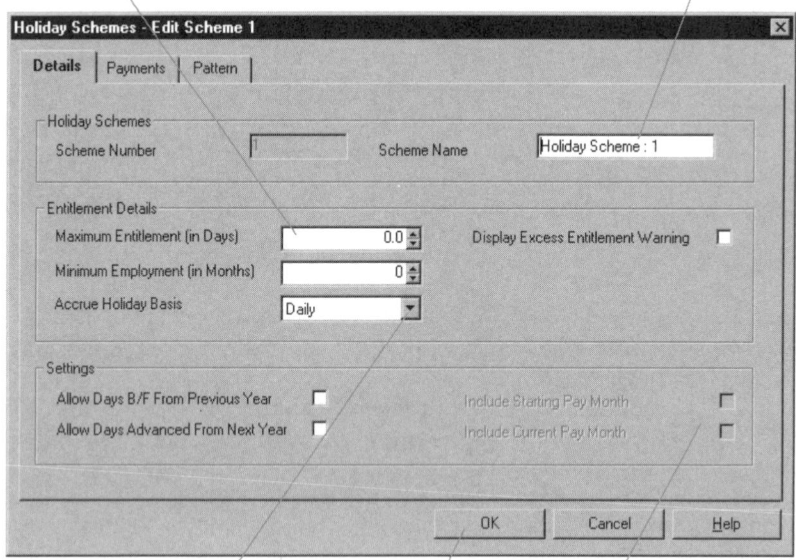

To process an employee's payroll during a pay period and accrue holiday for the full period, select the Include Current Pay Month check box.

6 Select how the holiday entitlement is to accrue here, either Daily or Calendar Monthly.

7 Complete the remaining settings as appropriate. Note that some only appear when Calendar Monthly is selected.

8 Click OK to save.

Qualifying days are days when an employee is contractually required to work.

Additional notes on setting up your company holiday schemes

The Sage Payroll Holiday Schemes screen offers a number of options which allow you to exactly tailor each holiday scheme your company operates.

The remaining options not covered on the previous page are as follows:

When entering SSP Qualifying Patterns:

Q = Qualifying
N = Non-qualifying.

SSP Qualifying Patterns run from Sunday to Saturday, so a normal five day working week (Monday to Friday) would be:

NQQQQQN.

Allow Days B/F From Previous Year	A tick in this box allows any holiday not taken during the year to be carried forward and added to next year's entitlement.
Include Starting Pay Month	Where a new starter joins the company halfway through the current pay period, a tick in this box allows holiday to be accrued for the full period.
Include Current Pay Month	If you process an employee's payroll part way through a period but want to accrue holiday for the full period, place a tick in this box.
Display Excess Entitlement Warning	A tick here makes Sage Payroll display a warning whenever an employee exceeds their holiday entitlement.

You can set up a number of qualifying patterns for an employee, e.g., where someone works shift patterns that change on a weekly basis.

Use the Payments tab to select how the holiday fund is to be accrued.

1. Select the Pattern tab.
2. Click in the pattern box, then the Finder Button.
3. Select pattern and click OK.

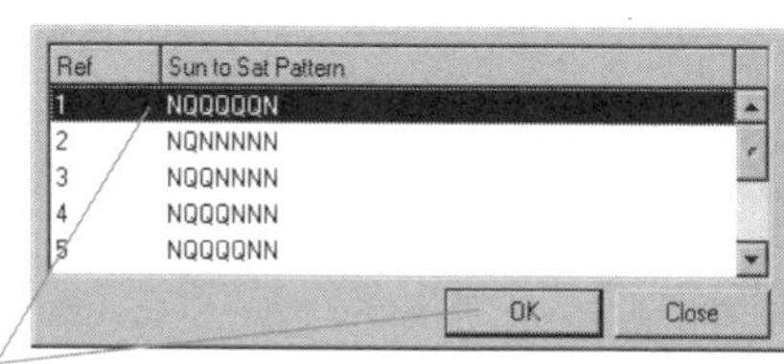

Departments and Cost Centres

The use of Cost Centres is only applicable for users of Sage Line 100.

Should you want to, an unlimited number of Departments and Cost Centres can be easily set up in Sage Payroll and then allocated to each employee. To set up your Departments and Cost Centres do the following:

To accept an entry and move to the next field press the TAB key.

To delete a department from the list, simply select it and press the Delete button on your keyboard, then press TAB to accept the changes.

1. From the Company stacked toolbar, click Company Settings.
2. Click on the Analysis tab.
3. The Analysis tab window displays Departments and Cost Centres already set up.
4. Click here and type a new Department name.

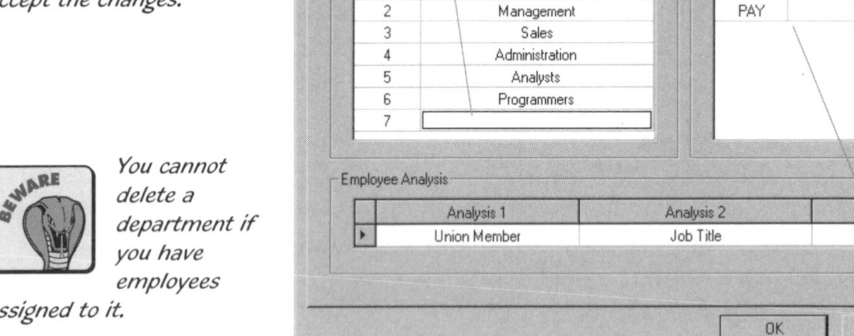

You cannot delete a department if you have employees assigned to it.

5. Press the TAB key to accept the entry.
6. To create a new Cost Centre, click here and type the Cost Centre name.
7. To edit a Department or Cost Centre name, just click on the one required and type a new name.
8. Click OK to save.

Use Employee Analysis to record employee specific information.

Pay Elements

Use the Edit button to amend Payments and Deductions details.

Use the Delete button to remove a Payments or Deductions type.

Use the Employee Wizard from the File menu to help you assign payments and deduction types to an employee from the start of their employment.

Payments and deductions can also be assigned to employees by selecting the Employment tab from the Employee Record and clicking the Pay Elements button.

The Pay Elements option is where payment and deduction types are set up. You will find that Attachments have already been set up for you. Pay Elements need setting up before you enter your employee details, after which the payment and deduction types can be applied to each individual.

Sage Payroll lets you create an unlimited number of payment and deduction types. Payments are divided into three types, namely global, fixed and variable. For global payment types, any changes to the payment elements will affect all employees assigned to them whereas for fixed payment types, the rate/amount is fixed by the value entered in each individual employee record. Variable payment types allow the user more flexibility in recording changes to rates or hours. To set up payment types:

1 From the Company stacked toolbar, click Pay Elements.

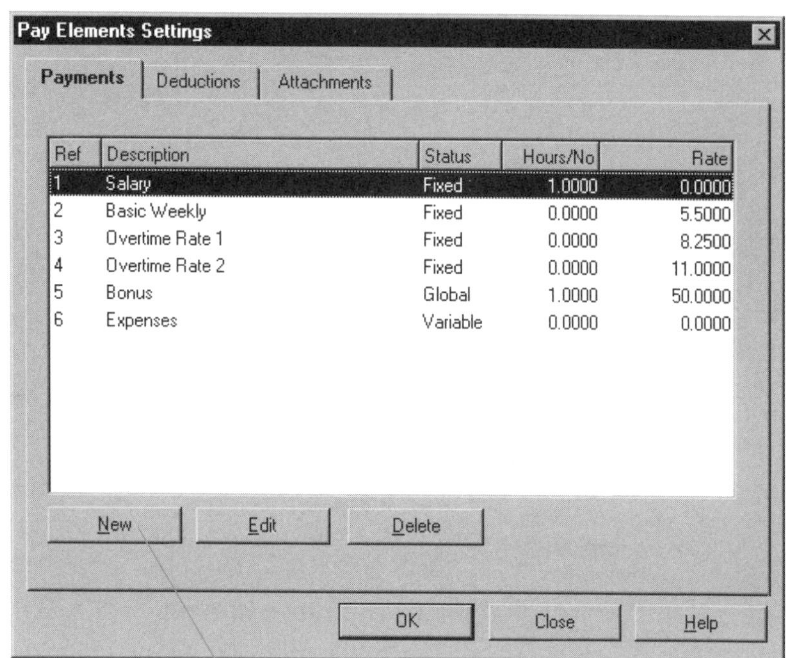

2 Click New to add a new payment type.

Enter a default number of hours for Default Hours/No, to save time later when processing, otherwise each employee's Payments tab will need individually updating.

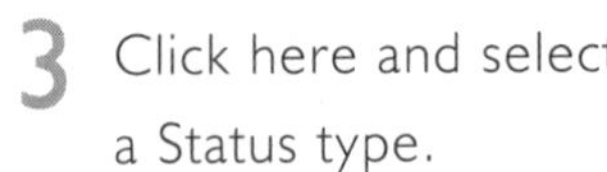

3 Click here and select a Status type.

4 Enter a payment Description.

5 Enter the Default Number of Hours for this payment.

6 Set up a default Rate only if necessary.

Unless all your employees receive the same rate of pay, it is advisable to leave the Default Rate as zero.

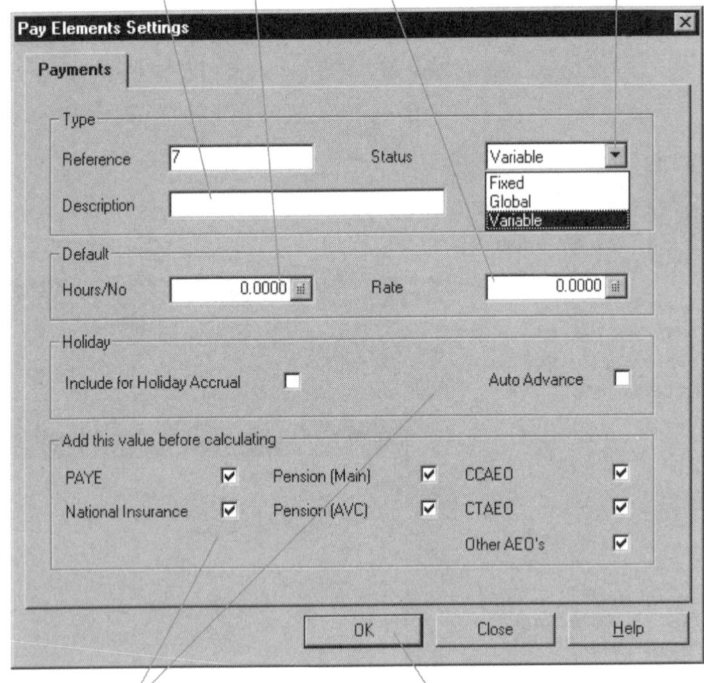

The term CCAEO is used for Community Charge Attachment of Earnings Order.

7 Tick here for options required.

8 Click OK to save or Close to abandon.

Auto Advance uses the last updated pay period values to advance holiday pay.

To edit a payment type

Select the payment type you wish to edit from the payments tab, click on the Edit button, then follow steps 3 to 8 above.

Deduction Types

Use the F1 help key for more information about Deductions.

As with payment types, an unlimited number of deduction types can be set up. Information which needs amending can be updated quickly and easily by using the Edit button. Any unwanted Deductions can be removed by using the Delete button. Deductions can be set up to cater for all your employment requirements, for example, union fees, professional subscriptions to the firm's sports & social club, etc.

Once Deductions have been set up, you can assign them to your employee details.

To set up deduction types do the following:

1 From the Company stacked toolbar, click Pay Elements.

2 Click the Deductions tab.

3 Click New to create a new deduction type.

4 Click here and select a Status type.

CTAEO refers to Council Tax Attachment of Earnings Order.

AVC stands for Additional Voluntary Contribution and AEO stands for Attachment of Earnings Order.

Use the TAX Credit Funding tab to record the amount of Inland Revenue funding received.

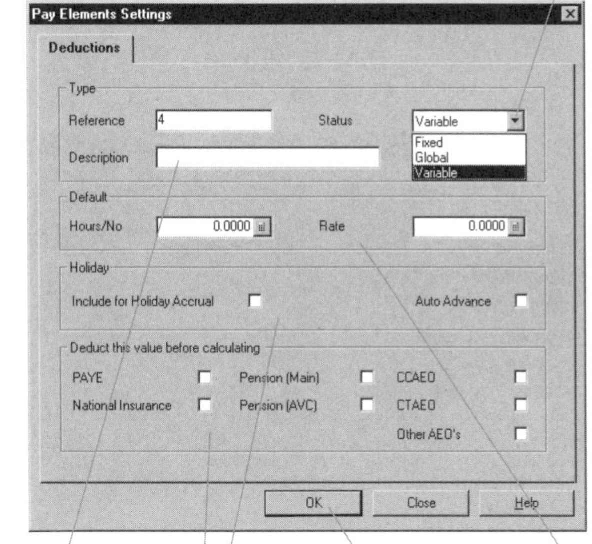

5 Enter a Description here.

6 Enter the Default Hours and Rate (if necessary).

7 Tick as appropriate.

8 Click OK to save.

Attachments

Use the F1 help key for additional information about Attachments.

An attachment of earnings order is an official form issued by a court and legally binding to an employer, instructing them to deduct an outstanding debt from an employee's wages. These Attachments are always taken from the employee's net pay, referred to as Attachable Earnings. The court sets a protected earnings amount to ensure that the employee has sufficient income after deductions have been made. The difference between the protected and attachable earnings is the sum from which the deduction is actually made.

Employers are allowed to deduct an administration fee from employees for administering any attachment of earnings. The rate is £1 per attachment in England, Wales and Northern Ireland and 50 pence per attachment in Scotland.

These payments are usually on a weekly or monthly basis. Examples of these orders include the non payment of council tax, fines and child support payments etc.

Sage Payroll provides some Attachments. A user can add or edit the descriptions where appropriate and later assign them to an employee's details. To view Attachments:

1 From the Company stacked toolbar, click Pay Elements.

2 Click the Attachments tab.

To deduct an administration fee from an employee's net pay, create a Deductions type within Pay Elements and call it Administration Fee. This Deductions type can then be assigned to the employee concerned.

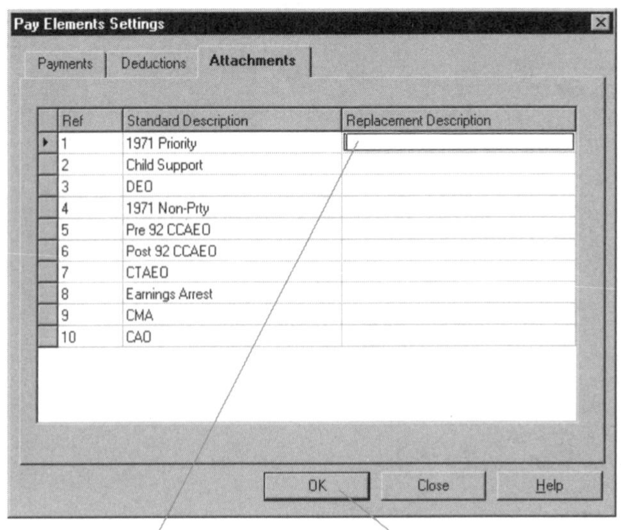

3 Type your own description here if desired.

4 Click OK when finished.

The Nominal Link

This chapter shows you how to set up the Nominal Link. This allows payroll data to be automatically transferred into your Sage accounting package and hence appear in your Nominal Ledger. When you then produce your Balance Sheet and Profit and Loss reports, these will show up-to-date payroll information.

Covers

Chapter Four

Setting up the Nominal Link

The nominal link needs setting up BEFORE processing your payroll.

To transfer your payroll information directly to the nominal ledger of your accounts program, it is important to set up the Nominal Settings before processing your first payroll. To set up the Nominal Settings do the following:

Make a note of the directory path where your accounts package is installed, e.g., c:\programfiles\Line 50.

Your payroll data can be posted directly to Sage Line accounts packages or saved to a file to import into other accounting packages.

1 Click on Company from the stacked toolbar.

2 Click on the Nominal Settings button. Use the down arrow until it appears if necessary

3 Ensure Use Nominal Link is ticked.

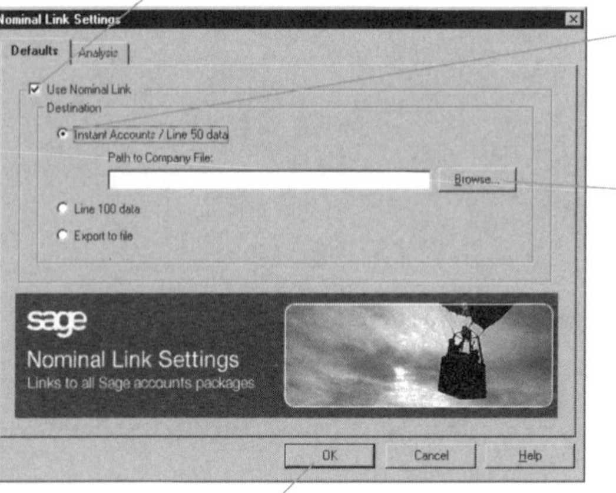

4 Select a Destination, e.g., Line 50.

5 For Instant Accounts or Line 50, use the Browse button to enter your Company file path.

6 Click OK to save.

If you are linking to Line 100 accounts the pathname is automatically displayed after retrieving the SVN4WIN.INI file.

Setting up Nominal Codes

Your deductions can be either a Profit and Loss or Balance Sheet code depending upon the deduction type. The codes will need customising to your business needs.

Default nominal codes are already set up by Sage but if you use different company nominal codes these will want setting up before posting your payroll information. To do this:

1 From the Nominal Link Settings window click the Analysis tab.

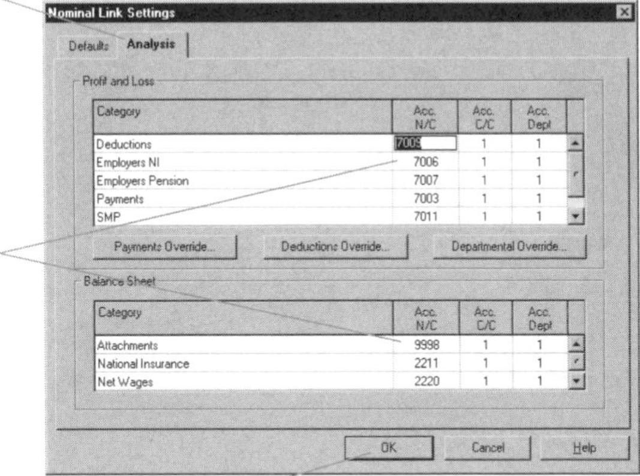

2 Enter any company nominal code changes here or retain Sage's default nominal codes.

Use the vertical scroll bars to view your Profit and Loss and Balance Sheet nominal codes.

3 Click OK to save changes or Cancel to abandon.

Default Nominal Link codes

For your reference, here are the default codes already set up for you in Sage Payroll:

For analysis purposes Sage Line 100 users can record an account cost centre (Acc. C/C) and an accounts department (Acc. Dept) against each nominal code.

Profit and Loss

Employers NI	7006
Employers Pension	7007
Staff Salaries	7003
Adjustments	7009
SSP Reclaimed	7010
SMP Reclaimed	7011

Balance Sheet

Net Wages	2220
PAYE	2210
NI	2211
Pension	2230
Attachments	9998
Tax Credits	9998
Student Loans	9998

Payments Override

Use Payments Override when different payments need posting to different nominal codes and departments.

There are three types of Override options, namely, Payment, Deduction and Departmental Override. The Payments/ Deductions Override facility allows you to post your payments or deductions types to different nominal codes. This allows you to differentiate between the many types of expense payments, for example, payments made for accommodation, travel, etc.

Note: An accounts department can also be set up against each nominal code.

The Payments Override allows you to produce a detailed breakdown of your employee's gross pay, e.g., you may find it helpful to post basic staff wages to a different nominal code from your bonus payments.

1 From the Analysis tab click the Payments Override button.

2 Click here to bring up a list of payment types you can override.

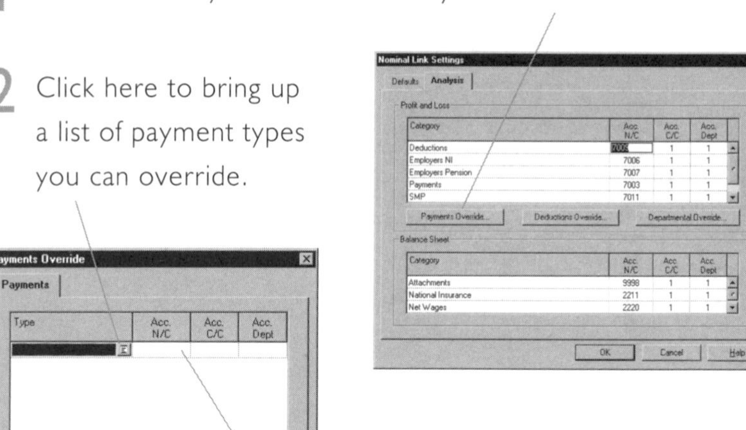

3 Select the payment type.

4 Click OK.

5 Enter your Nominal Code here.

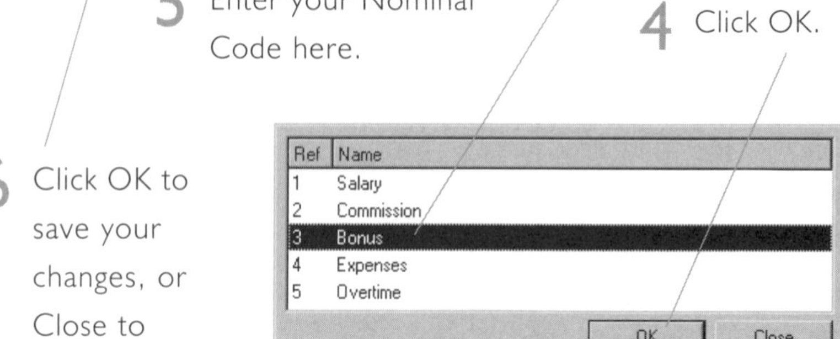

6 Click OK to save your changes, or Close to abandon.

Different nominal codes can also be set up for certain payment/ deduction types within different departments using the Departmental Override facility.

Deductions Override

Use the Deductions Override facility to keep certain deductions separate from the rest of your deduction types. For example, you may want to post car repayments for your employees to a separate deduction nominal code.

Deductions can either be a Profit and Loss or Balance Sheet nominal code (see page 49). To allow more detailed analysis of your deductions payments follow the steps below:

1 From the Analysis tab click the Deductions Override button.

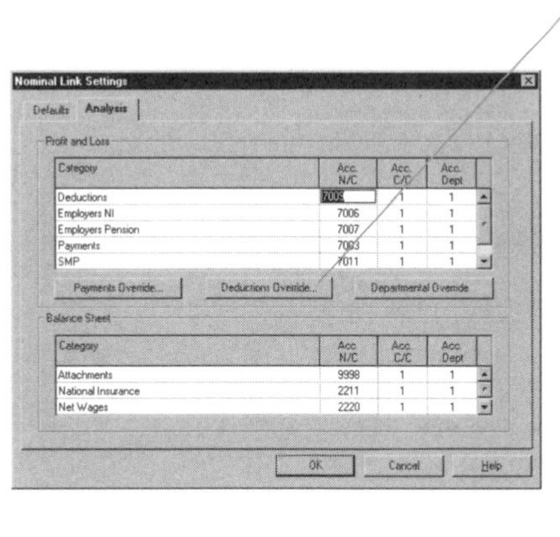

2 Click here to bring up a list of deduction types you can override.

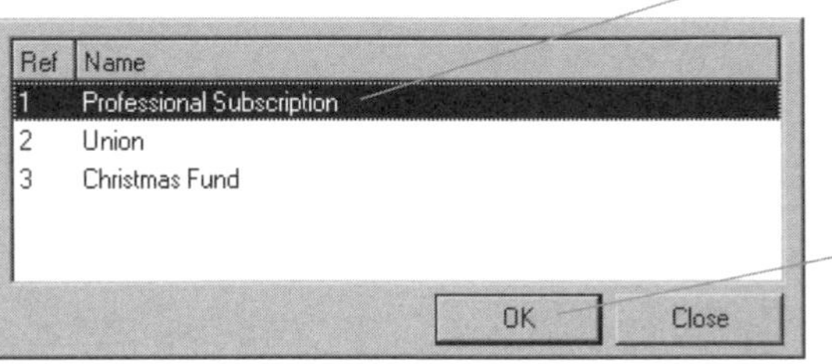

3 Select the deduction type.

4 Click OK.

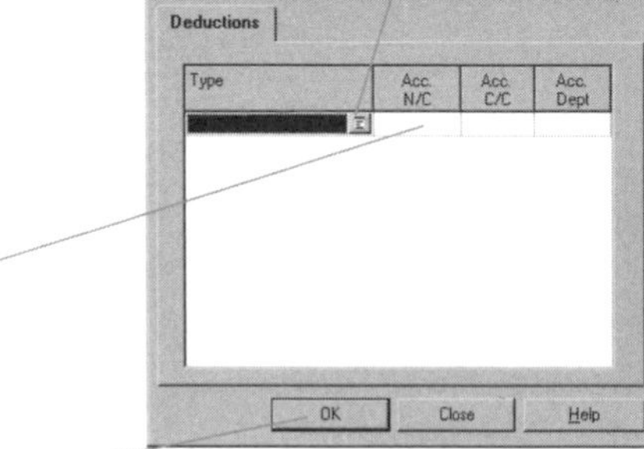

5 Enter your Nominal Code here.

6 Click OK to save your changes, or Close to abandon.

To create a new or edit an existing deduction type, select Pay Elements from the Company stacked toolbar, then Deductions tab.

If you are a Sage Line 100 user an account Cost Centre can be entered against each nominal code for more detailed reporting.

Departmental Override

Where a full departmental breakdown is required the Departmental Override must be set up.

Sage Payroll provides you with the facility to set up and anaylse your payments and deductions by Department. The example below shows you, using customised nominal codes, how to select the Sales department and post employees' wages to a different nominal code from their overtime payments. This information will then be used within the Profit and Loss report.

Use the Override column from the Departmental Override dialog box for checking overrides allocated against departments.

1. From the Analysis tab click Departmental Override button.
2. Select department required.

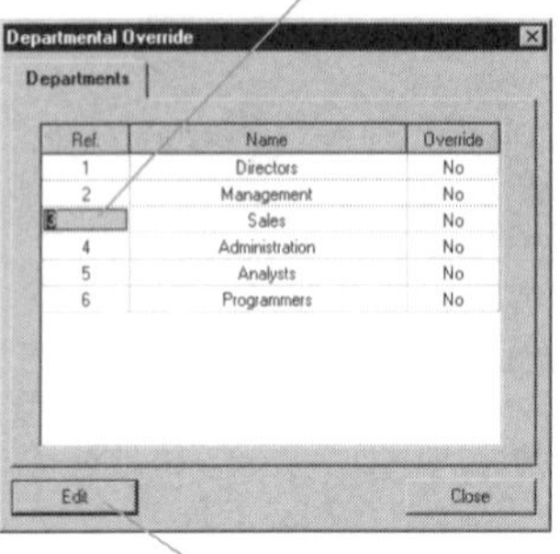

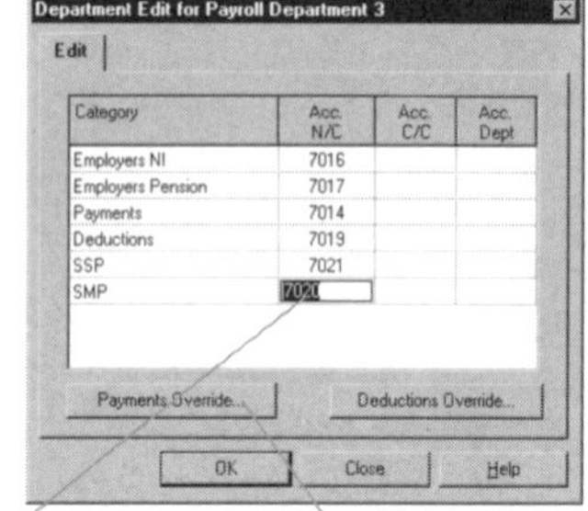

Using the Payments and Deductions Override buttons within the Departmental Override option allows even more detailed analysis.

3. Click Edit.
4. Enter your additional nominal codes here.
5. Click the Payments Override button.
6. Click here and select your payment types from the list. To set up new pay elements see page 43.
7. Enter your nominal codes here.
8. Click OK and OK again to return to the Departments window. Note the Override column says Yes.
9. Click Close to return to the Analysis tab. Note the Departmental Override button is now displayed in bold.

You can specify a different department from Payroll to post to within your accounts.

Nominal Link Postings

Let the Nominal Link Wizard guide you through posting your payroll payments directly to your accounts program.

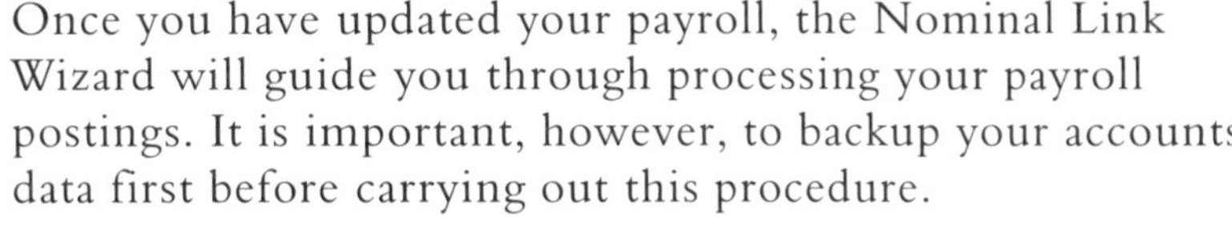

Once you have updated your payroll, the Nominal Link Wizard will guide you through processing your payroll postings. It is important, however, to backup your accounts data first before carrying out this procedure.

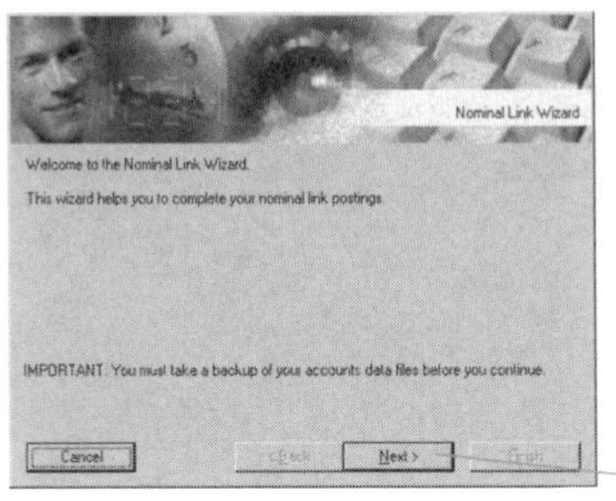

1 Make a backup of your accounts data files.

2 From the Payroll stacked toolbar click Nominal Link to start the Wizard.

3 Click Next to continue.

Your nominal link settings must be configured before you can use the Nominal Link.

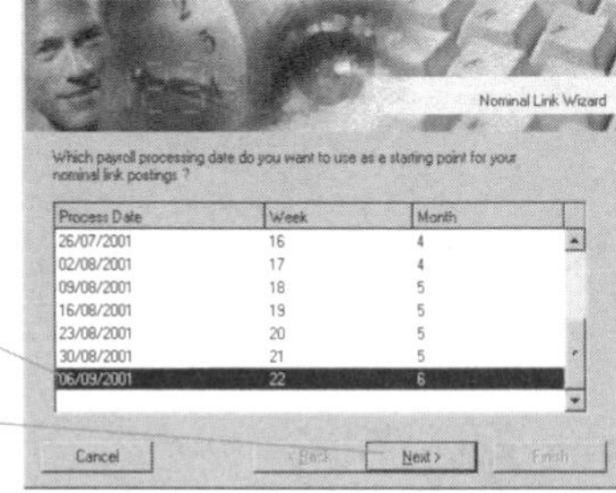

4 Select the Process Date you require.

5 Click Next to continue.

The Nominal Link can only be posted after the payroll has been updated.

6 Check information is correct. Use the Cancel button if you need to make any change, else click Next.

The Nominal Link can only post one payment type at a time, i.e., monthly, weekly.

7 If you have Sage Line 50 multi-company, select the company here, else go to Step 8.

8 Click Next to continue.

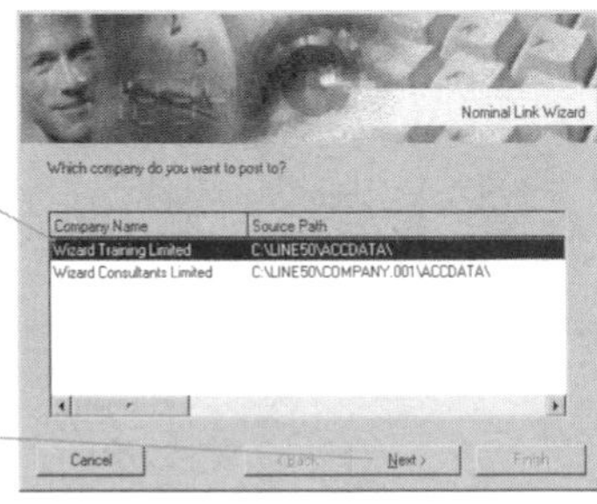

Always print a list of payroll transactions for checking purposes before updating your accounts package.

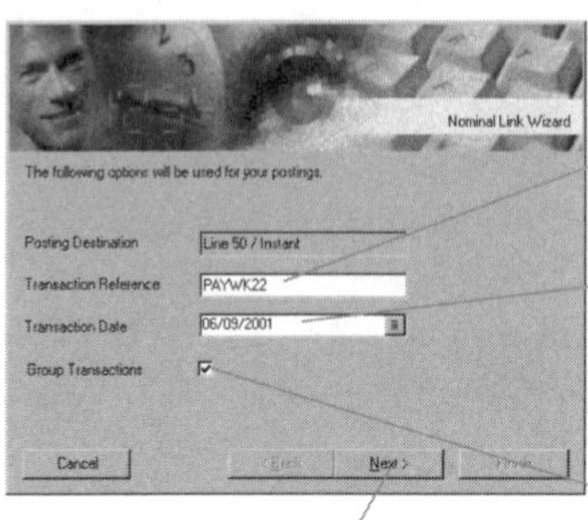

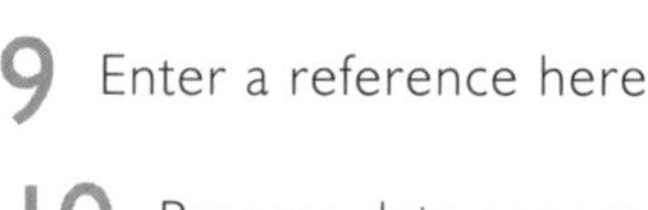

9 Enter a reference here.

10 Process date appears here automatically but another date may be specified.

11 Click here to group nominal codes, or deselect to produce a list of nominal code values for each individual employee.

Make sure there are no errors because once you have clicked Finish, the transactions will be added to the audit trail within your Sage accounts package.

12 Click Next to create a posting file.

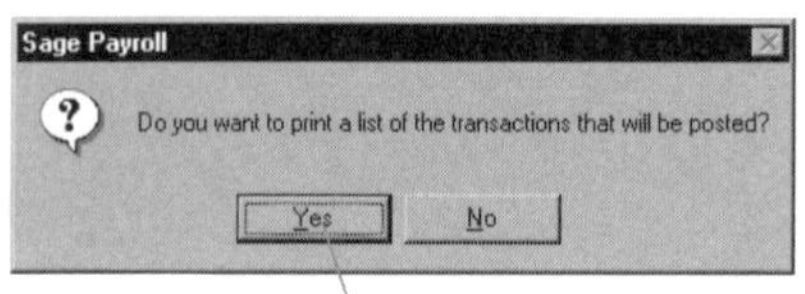

13 Click Yes to print transactions.

14 Then click Print and Close.

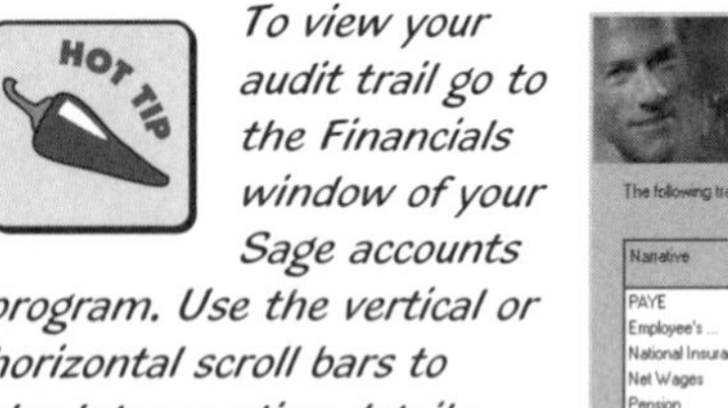

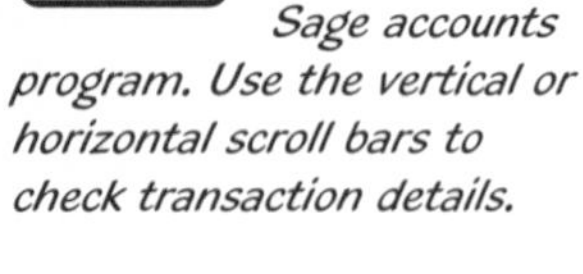

To view your audit trail go to the Financials window of your Sage accounts program. Use the vertical or horizontal scroll bars to check transaction details.

15 Click Finish to post transactions to your accounts program.

16 Enter your accounts Logon Name and Password here.

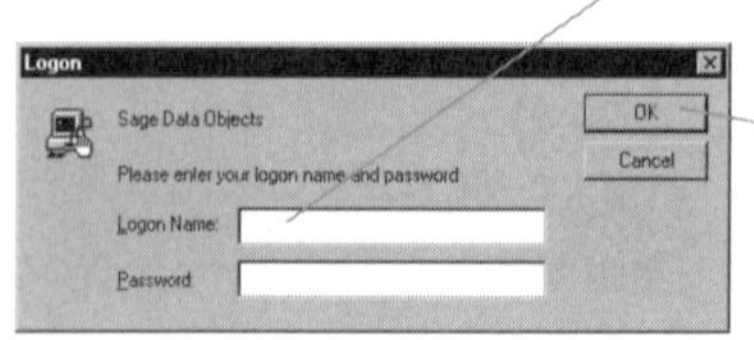

17 Click OK to perform the postings.

If a nominal code does not exist, you will receive an error message.

18 Click OK to complete the operation.

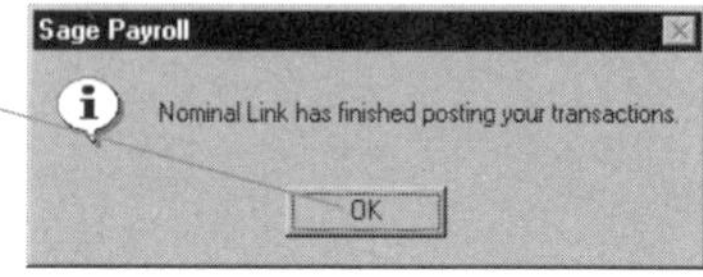

Employee Records

This chapter explains how to set up and maintain your employees' personal records and keep track of their payments. These details include items such as tax codes, rates of pay, bank account and absence information. These details will be then be used automatically during payroll processing.

Covers

Chapter Five

Creating Employee Records

Let the Employee Wizard guide you through creating your new employee records.

When setting up new employee records, use the Employee Wizard to help you enter the majority of your employee payroll details, for example, personal, bank and payment details. Certain information is essential and must be entered, i.e., Surname, Tax Code, NI Number, Date of Birth, Start Date, etc.

To quickly enter basic, essential details for your new employees click Quick New Employee Entry from the File menu. *See page 60.*

Where employees have joined your organisation part way through the tax year, cumulative figures from their previous employment need to be entered. These figures, gathered from the employee's P45 are entered into the Taxable Gross Pay and Total Tax Paid boxes. If an employee does not supply you with a P45, then they must complete a P46. The Wizard will detail necessary instructions to successfully complete your payroll information.

New employee records can be created at any time. Additional information can be entered, or amendments made, using the Employee Record button from the Payroll stacked toolbar.

On the main payroll desktop, click the right mouse button for additional facilities when dealing with your employees' records.

To set up a new Employee Record, do the following:

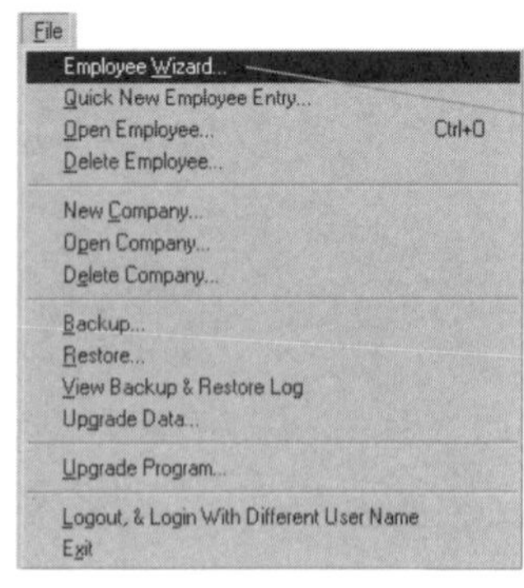

1. From the File menu click Employee Wizard.

Click the Cancel button if you wish to abandon setting up a new employee record.

2. Click Next to enter your new employee.

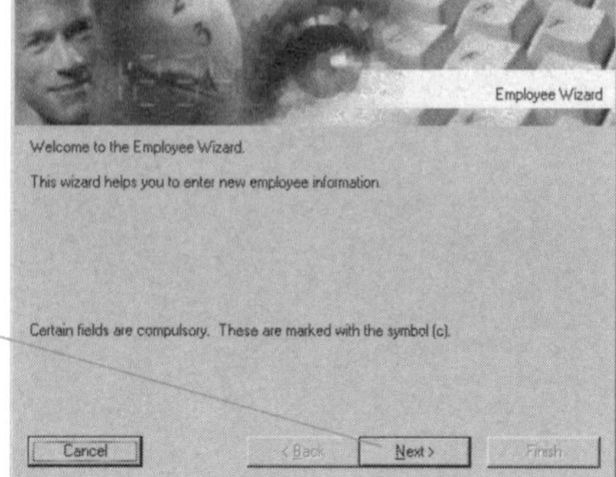

All fields marked with (c) must be completed, e.g., Employee's Tax Code.

3 Enter your new employee's reference number here.

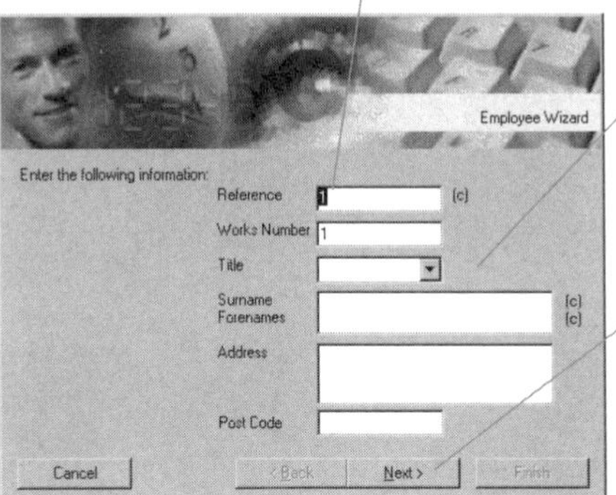

4 Enter employee's name and address details.

5 Click Next to continue to the next screen.

Use the drop down calendar button to select and enter dates quickly.

Click the Back button to check or change any details from previous screens.

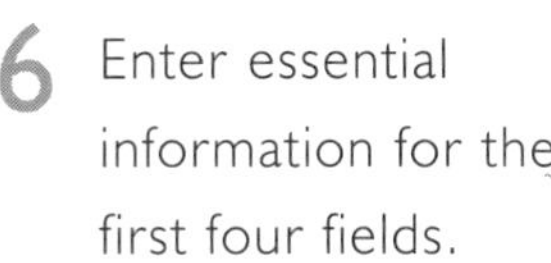

6 Enter essential information for the first four fields.

7 Select a Holiday and Pension Scheme here.

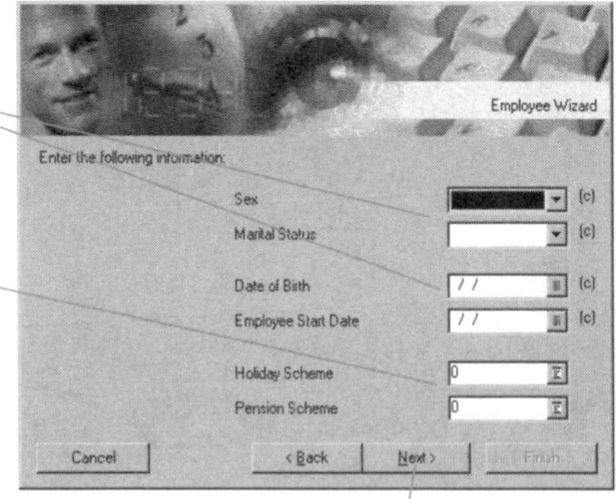

8 Click Next to continue.

P45 details may be entered using the YTD Values button from the Employee Record window.

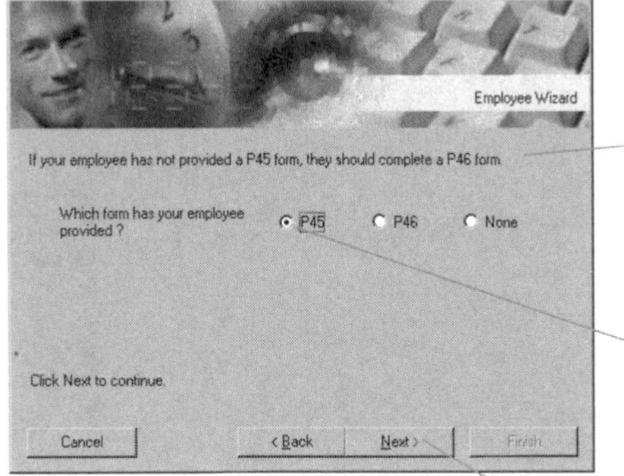

9 Follow instructions carefully before making your choice.

10 Click on the option you require, e.g. P45.

11 Click Next.

Press F1 for more information about tax codes and national insurance.

If you don't have a correct tax code for an employee ask them to fill in a P46.

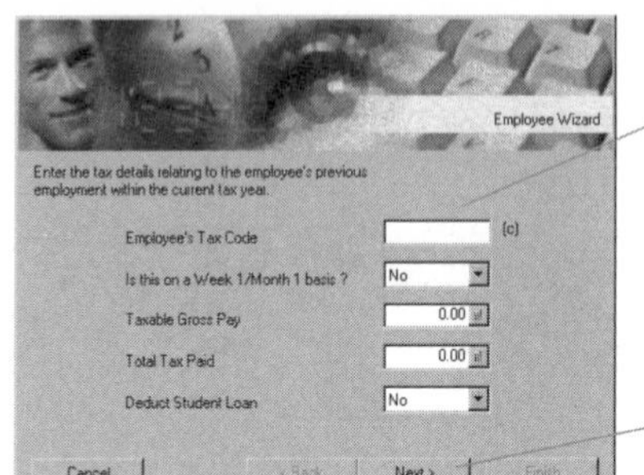

12 Enter any previous employment details here.

13 Click Next.

A National Insurance number must start with two characters, followed by six numbers and a final letter in the range A - D, for example, NW 12 34 56 A.

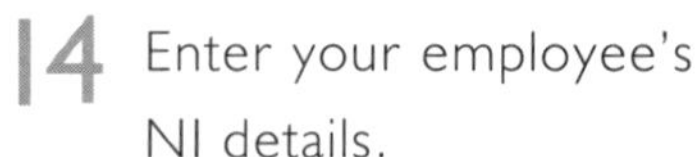

14 Enter your employee's NI details.

15 Click Next.

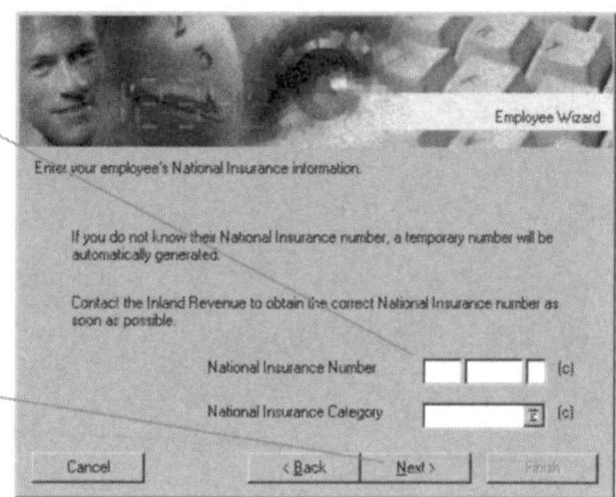

If you do not know an employee's NI number, Sage will generate a temporary one. Click Yes when prompted to do so.

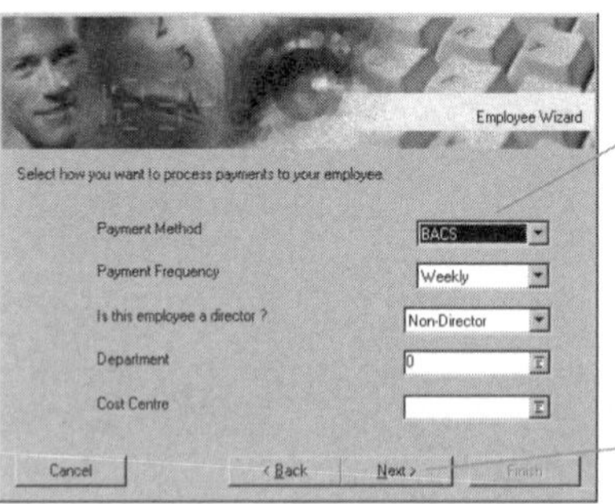

16 Select how you want to process payments to your employee.

17 Click Next.

Contact the DSS to obtain an employee's NI number.

18 Choose the payment type you require or click New to create a new payment type.

19 Click Next.

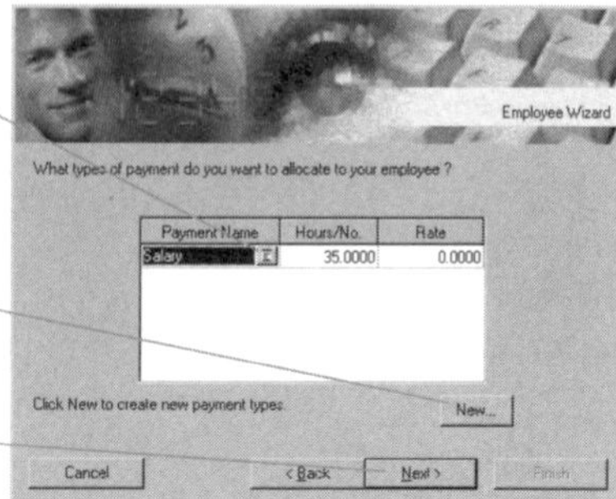

Use the New button to create a new deduction type.

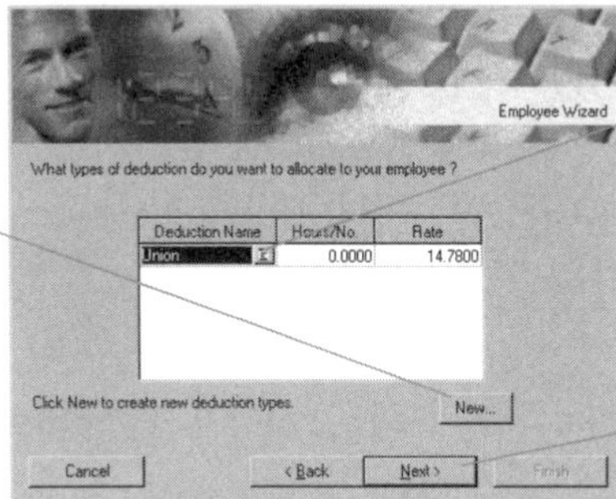

20 Choose your deduction type here, e.g., Union.

21 Click Next.

Remember that if an employee starts working for your company part way through the tax year you will need to enter the cumulative figures from their previous employment, shown on the employee's P45.

22 Select an Account Type and enter the details here.

23 Click Next.

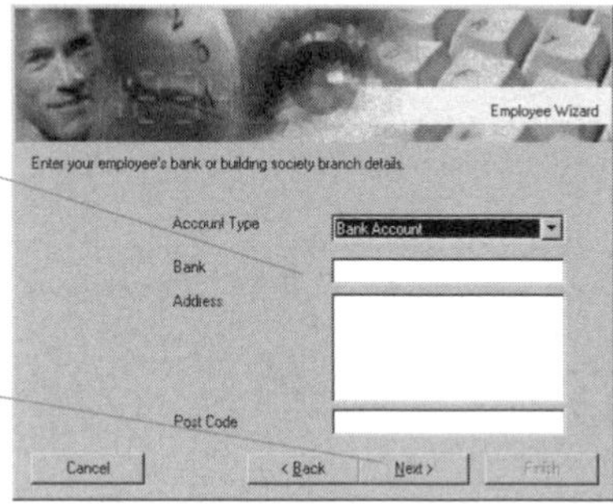

Account Number requires an eight-digit value. Where an account is less than eight digits, enter leading zeros before the number.

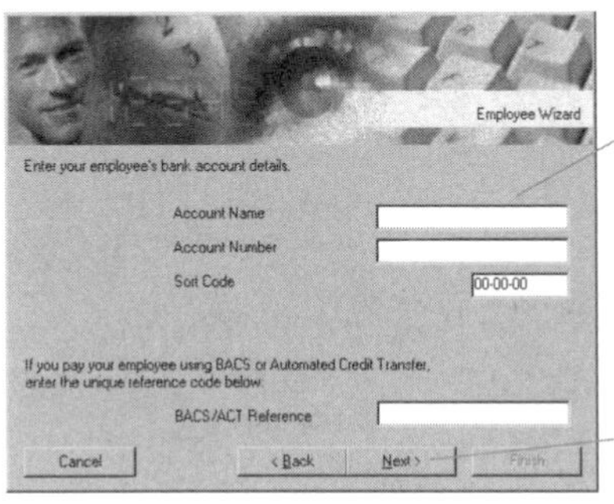

24 Enter bank or building society details.

25 Click Next.

Employee's bank details can be entered using the Banking tab within the Employee Record.

26 Click Finish to save the information you have just entered, else click Back to return to previous screens to make changes.

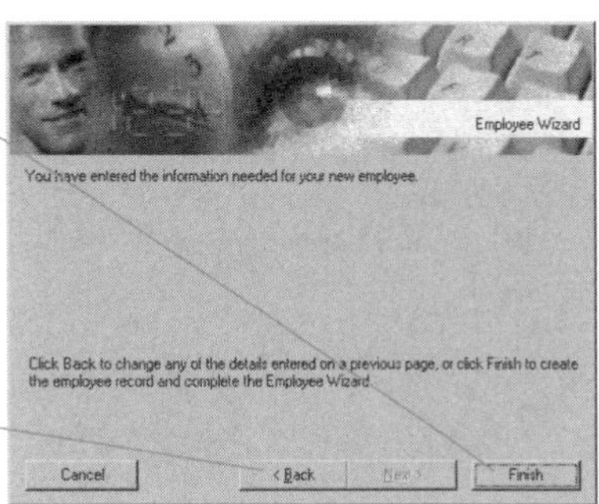

Quick New Employee Entry

It is essential to complete all fields labelled in blue, e.g.,Tax Code.

This method speeds up the process of creating new employee records by allowing you to enter all the basic employee information in one go, namely: personal details, bank, tax, national insurance and pay details. To add more information to an employee's record you need to follow some of the steps shown on page 61.

1. From the File menu click Quick New Employee Entry.

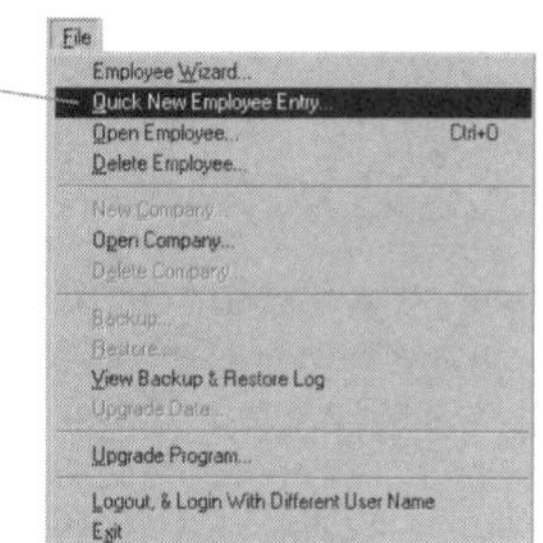

From the Sage Payroll desktop you can select and open an employee record by double clicking the appropriate record.

2. Enter employee's personal details here.
3. Select payment method and frequency

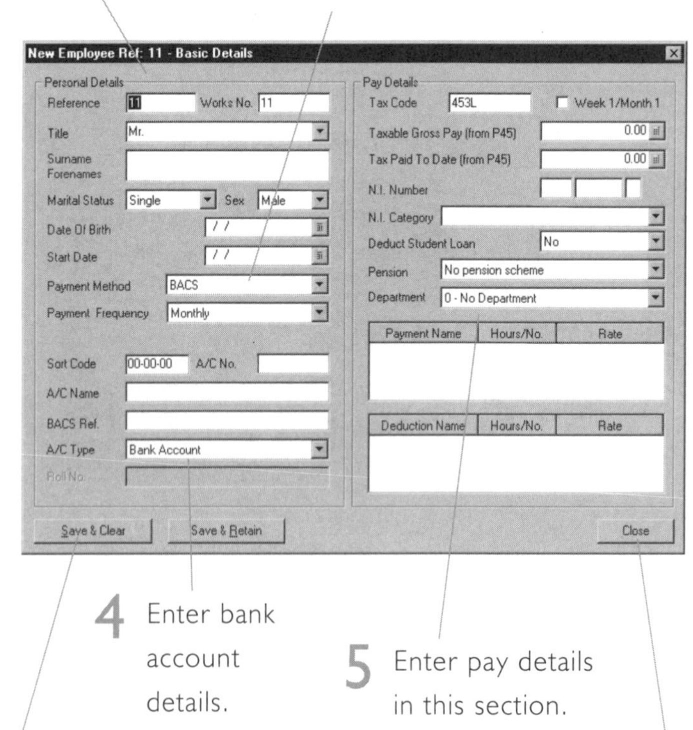

Within the Employee Record, click First, Previous, Next and Last to move between selected employee records.

4. Enter bank account details.
5. Enter pay details in this section.
6. Click here to save details and clear screen.
7. Click Close when finished.

To process a batch of employees with similar details click Save & Retain to keep some of the information on-screen.

Editing Employee Record Details

From the application toolbar, use the Clear and Swap buttons to select and deselect employee records.

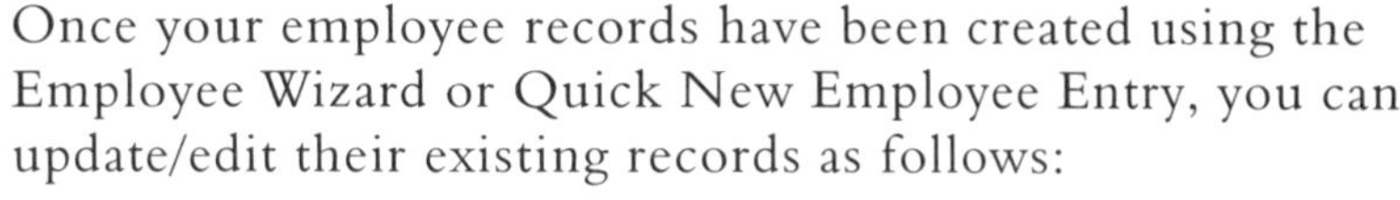

Once your employee records have been created using the Employee Wizard or Quick New Employee Entry, you can update/edit their existing records as follows:

1. From the Sage Payroll desktop select the employee you require from the employee list box and click the Employee Record button.

You cannot edit the employee's reference number. It is a unique number generated sequentially by the program.

2 Enter/edit employee's personal details here.

3 Click here to insert a scanned picture of your employee.

If access rights have been set up for your payroll users, the access level can be set up on their employee record here.

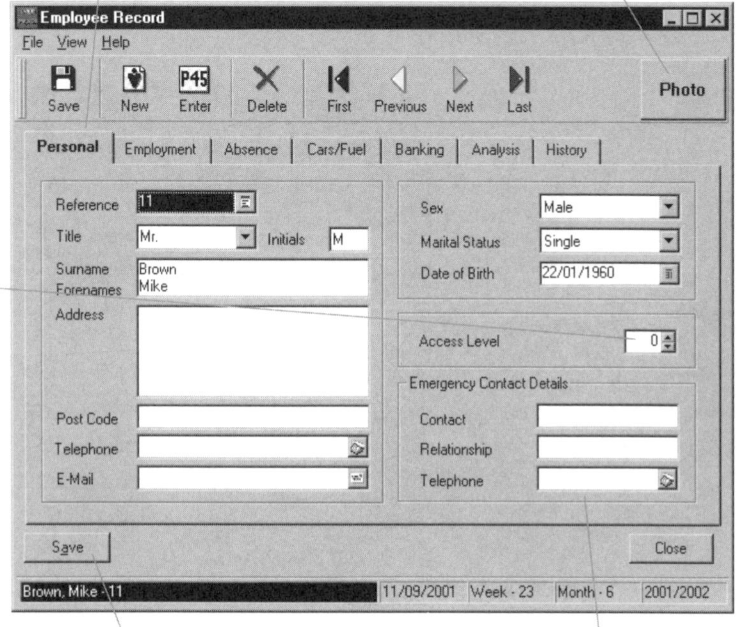

4 Enter Emergency Contact Details for your employee.

5 Click Save to record employee's personal details or Close to abandon changes.

Click the P45 button on the Employee Record toolbar to access the P45 Information Wizard.

Note: From the Employee Record detailed employment information is recorded. Previous payroll transactions can be viewed using the History tab, e.g., P11 information.

Use Sage Help Topics for additional information about entering tax and national insurance.

When an employee's employment details change, for example, change of tax code, the details can be amended as follows:

1 From the employee's record click Employment.

2 Click here to enter a new tax code.

3 Change NI Number here.

4 Check with Inland Revenue before placing an employee on a week/month 1 basis.

Only select the Manual NI Entry check box for national insurance after taking advice from the DSS.

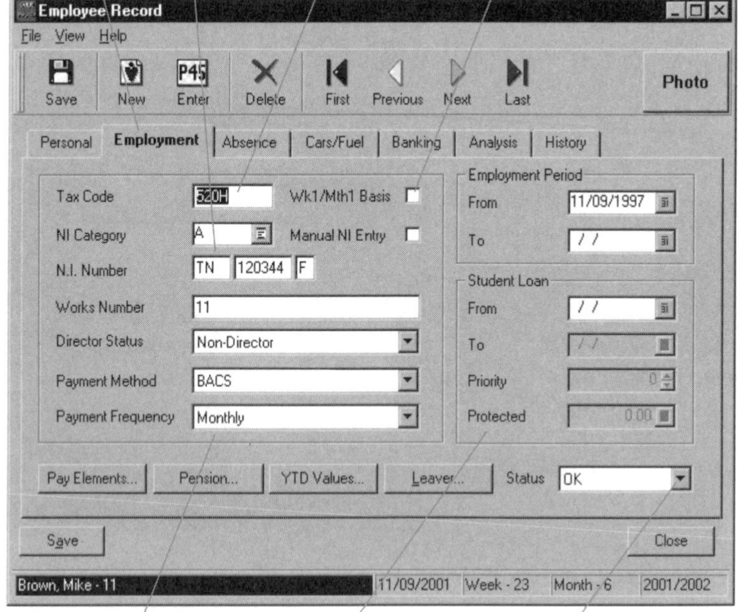

Once you have started processing, you cannot change the payment frequency on an employee's record.

5 Select your payment details here.

6 Enter any student related details here.

7 To place an employee On Hold or Trade Dispute click here.

8 Click Save to record employment details.

Let the Leaver Wizard help you process all your Leaver requirements.

Selecting Employee's Pay Elements

To open an employee's record, select the employee required and double click the left mouse button.

Before processing your payroll, your employees' payment details need setting up. Payments can range from hourly, daily, weekly to monthly. Where, for example, hours worked per week may vary, these entries can be left blank and set up during the payroll run. Follow the steps below to set up your pay elements:

1 From the employee's record click Employment, and then Pay Elements.

2 Click here for a list of payment types.

Use the New button to create a new payment type.

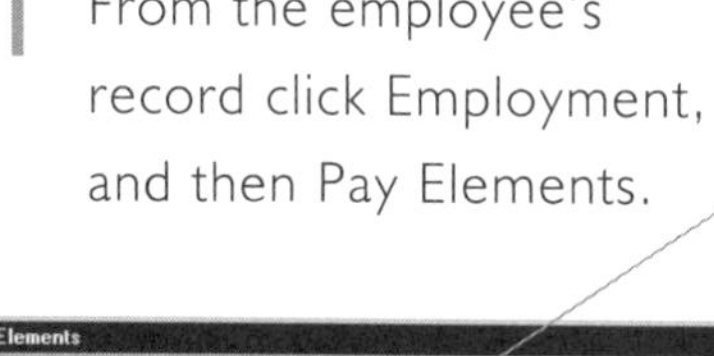

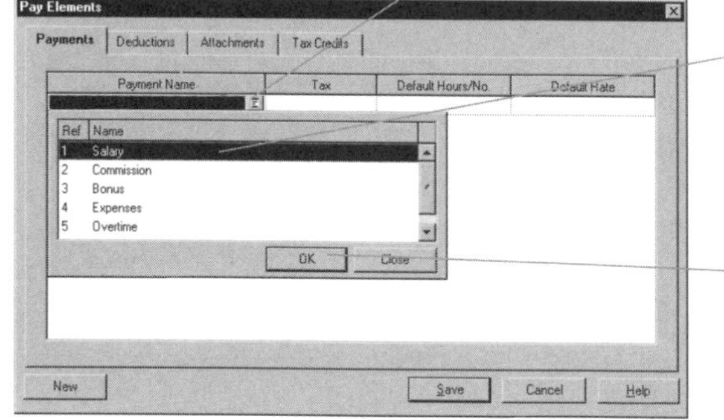

3 Choose a payment type.

4 Click OK and repeat if necessary.

If you enter an incorrect payment type for your employee, select the Payment Name, press F8 and click Yes to delete.

5 Pre or Post appears here automatically depending upon type of payment to be made.

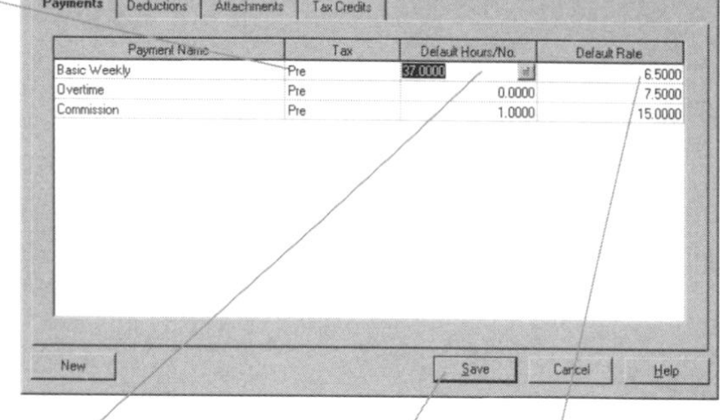

Pay Elements cannot be deleted if they contain a YTD value.

6 Enter default number of hours/units here, e.g. 37 hours.

7 Enter default rate/amount here, e.g., £6.50.

8 Click Save to record employee's payment details or Cancel to exit.

Entering P45 and YTD Details

Where an employee starts work part way through the tax year, their cumulative tax details may be entered using the Employee Wizard. See page 56.

The P45 details may be entered for each employee using the YTD Values button from the Employee Record window. To enter these details, do the following:

1 Click YTD Values from the Employment tab.

2 Enter the employee's previous employment figures here, i.e., Gross Pay for Tax and Tax Paid.

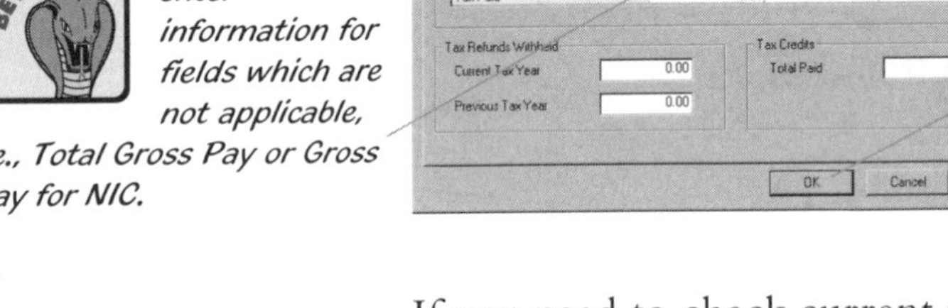

3 Click OK to save or Cancel to abandon.

Do not try to enter information for fields which are not applicable, i.e., Total Gross Pay or Gross Pay for NIC.

If you need to check current tax information for existing employees, do the following:

You can also enter YTD figures by clicking the P45 button from the Employee Record.

1 Click YTD Values from the Employment tab.

2 Previous and current tax details are displayed in the P.A.Y.E section.

3 Tax Refunds Witheld information displayed here.

4 Total Tax Credit Paid shown here.

5 Click OK to save changes or Cancel to abandon.

To begin using Sage Payroll part way through the current tax year use cumulative totals from your P11 deduction sheets .

To enter an employee's P45 details part way through the current tax year use the Tax and NIC tabs.

NIC

The NIC tab includes detailed information regarding National Insurance contributions paid during the current tax year as well as Director's Previous NI categories. To view employee's NI contributions do the following:

Select the employee you require from the employee list box before viewing or entering any new information.

1. Click NIC from the Year To Date window.

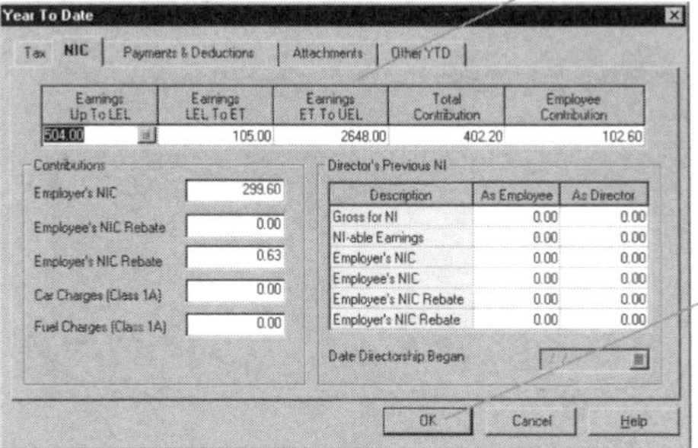

2. The NIC window shows details of NI Contributions paid for current tax year.
3. Click OK to return to Employee Record.

Payments & Deductions

Payments and Deductions information can be entered here manually for employees and updated later during processing.

Year to date values for employee's payments and deductions can be checked using the YTD Values button from the Employee Record window. To do this follow the steps below:

1. Click Payments & Deductions from the Year To Date window.

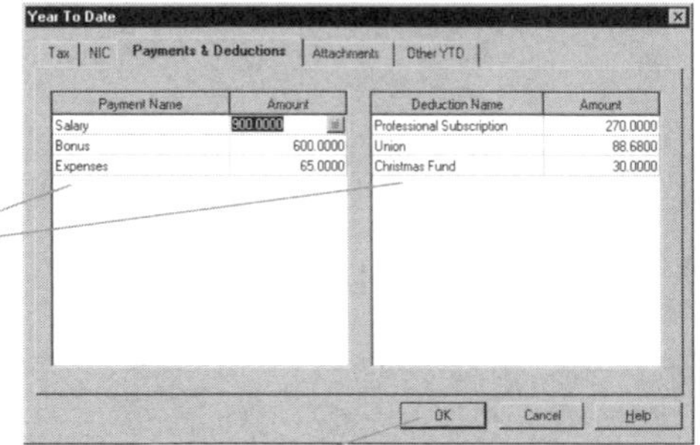

2. Year to date Payments and Deductions for this employee are displayed here.

Refer to chapter 7 for information about Payment of Employees.

3. Click OK to return to Employee Record.

The Attachments tab allows you to enter attachment values for the current tax year.

Attachments

This tab shows an employee's Attachment of Earnings payments after all other deductions for tax, pension, NI, etc. have been made. The Order Priority, any protected earnings and Admin Fee are also displayed here. To check your employee's attachments, do the following:

1. Click Attachments from the Year To Date window.

Refer to chapter 12 for information about setting up and processing your Attachment of Earnings.

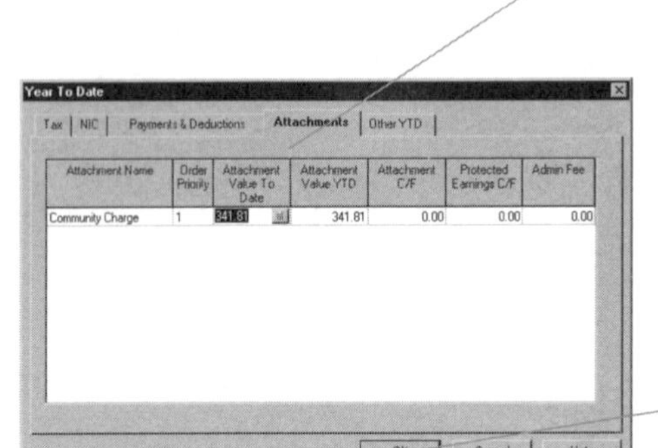

2. Any attachments set up for the employee for the current tax year are shown in this window.
3. Edit values if necessary.
4. Click OK to return to the Employee Record.

If you start using your Payroll program part way through the tax year, your employees' year to date cumulative totals can be taken from their P11 deduction cards.

Other YTD

Figures can be entered directly from your manual records regarding SMP, SSP, cash rounding carried forward, pension contributions, holiday pay and net pay. The example below shows an existing employee's Other YTD information. To view Other YTD follow the steps below:

1. From the employee's Year To Date window, click Other YTD.
2. Details can be viewed or recorded here.
3. Click OK to save or Cancel to abandon.

Once Other YTD figures are entered, they are updated by the system after each payroll run and will be cleared at year end.

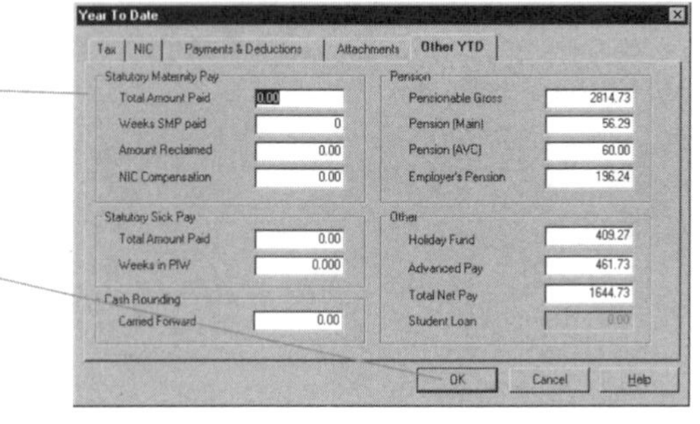

Assigning a Holiday Scheme

Use the Pattern tab, Qualifying Day box to select a working day pattern for your employee, e.g. for employees working Monday to Friday they would require the pattern NQQQQQN.

Once your holiday schemes have been set up using company settings, each employee can be assigned a holiday scheme. You will then be able to record staff holidays, the number of days taken, holidays accrued and where holiday entitlement has been exceeded.

To assign a holiday scheme to an employee do the following:

1. From the employee list box, select the employee you require.

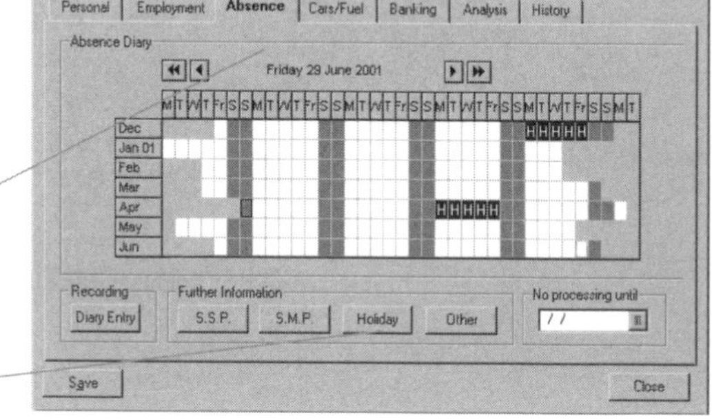

2. From Employee Record click the Absence tab.
3. Click the Holiday button.

For Qualifying Day Patterns N= Non-qualifying and Q= Qualifying.

4. Use Finder button to select holiday scheme required.
5. Any holiday carried over from the previous year is displayed here.

For more information about the holiday Accrual Details click the Payments tab.

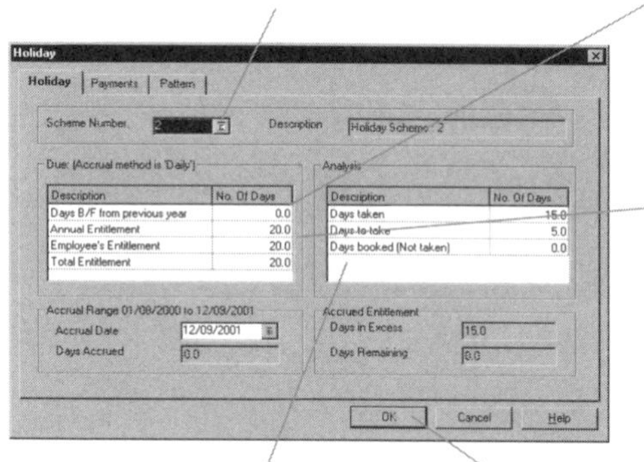

6. Holiday Scheme, Employee and Total entitlement details appear here.

Accrual Date displays the processing date entered when you started the Payroll program.

7. A breakdown of employee's holiday details is shown here.
8. Click OK to save and return to the Absence tab.

Recording an Employee's Holidays

Use the Calendar button to help you record holiday dates.

Once a holiday scheme has been set up for an employee, their holiday can be recorded on the Employee Record's Absence tab using the Diary Entry button. To record an employee's holiday follow the steps below:

When booking holidays, do not include weekends, normal days off etc. as this will reduce the employee's holiday entitlement.

1 From the Employee Record click the Absence tab.

2 Click Diary Entry to record holidays.

3 Click here to select Holiday

4 Select whether holiday is Taken or Booked.

Once holiday details have been saved, you can quickly see from the diary view when an employee is away on any holiday they may have booked.

5 Select AM or PM to record holiday as half or full day and enter dates.

6 You can enter any additional holiday information here.

7 Click OK to save holiday details or Cancel to abandon.

Refer to page 98 for information about advancing holiday pay.

Note: To quickly preview or print a range of Absence or Holiday reports for your employees use the Reports option from the main toolbar.

Recording Sickness

Half days are not applicable to SSP.

For more information about SSP for this employee click the S.S.P. button on the Absence tab.

Refer to chapter 9 when processing your SSP.

Refer to chapter 10 when processing your SMP.

Absences can be recorded by highlighting dates employee is absent. Click right button and enter details using pop up menu.

Recording absence through sickness for an employee is recorded using the Diary Entry button on the Absence tab of their Employee Record. Note that the AM/PM option is not available.

To enter your employee's sickness details

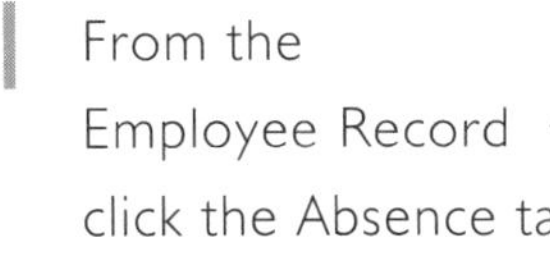

1 From the Employee Record click the Absence tab.

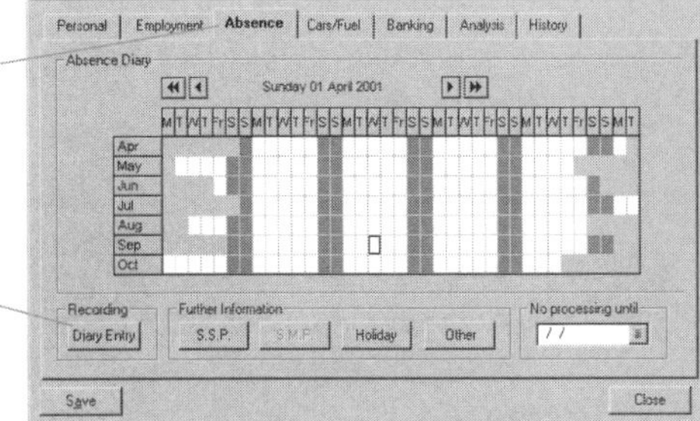

2 Click Diary Entry to record sickness.

3 In Absence Type select SSP.

4 Select absence type here.

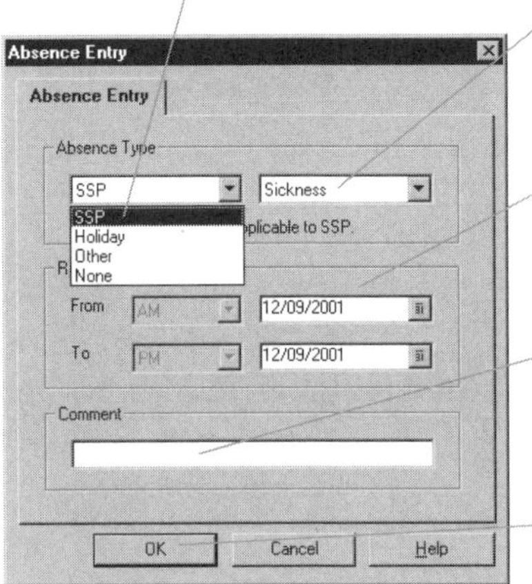

5 Enter dates for your employee's absence.

6 Add any additional information about sickness here.

7 Click OK to save changes or Cancel to abandon.

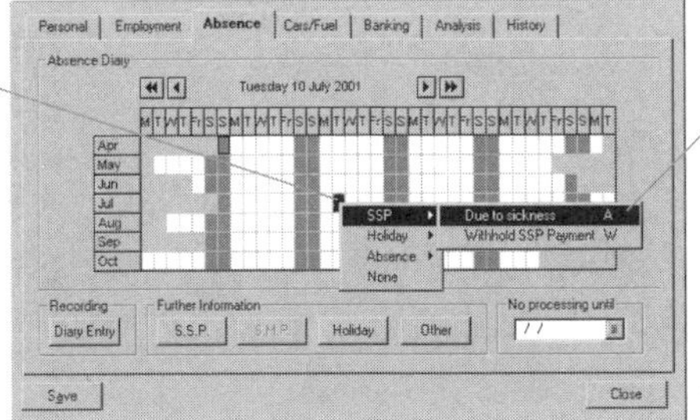

8 Method Two - use Absence tab to record all types of absence directly. See Hot Tip opposite.

Recording Other Types of Absence

Click Other on the Absence tab for a list of absence types and yearly analysis.

Besides recording absence for holidays and sickness, you may have to record absence for medical reasons, paternity leave etc. Sage provides a list of absence types for you to choose from. However, to enter another type of absence for an employee follow the steps below:

1. From the Employee Record click the Absence tab.

2. Click on arrows to select the year and month.

3. Click on a square to find correct date.

You can use the Diary Entry button on the Absence tab to enter different types of absences.

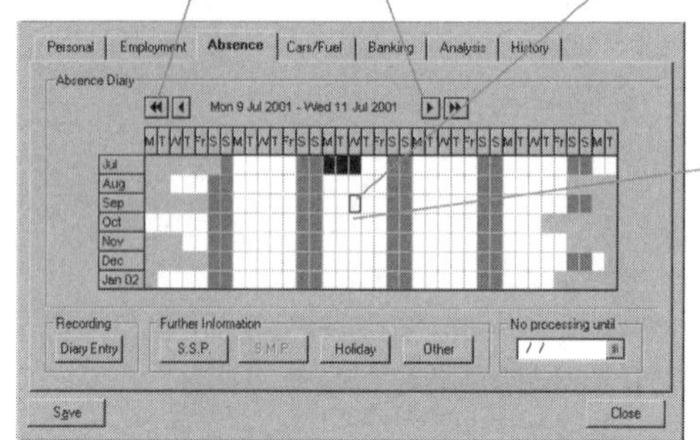

4. Use left mouse button and drag if you wish to highlight a range of dates.

5. Click right mouse button to select type of Absence.

An employee's absence can be viewed quickly using the Absence Diary screen. A fully coloured square indicates one day's absence whereas a half coloured square reflects a half day's absence, either AM or PM.

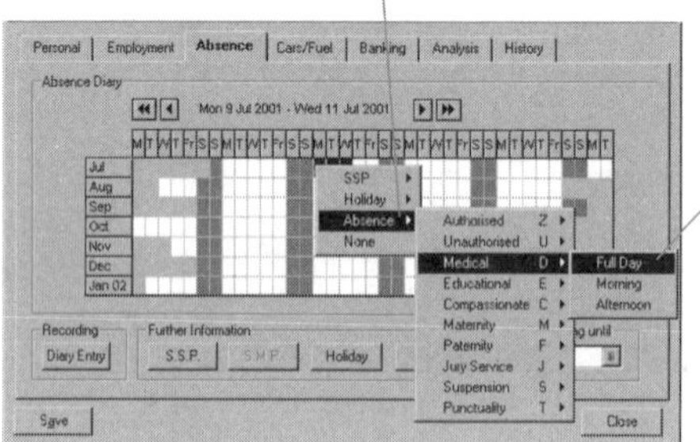

6. Select additional absence information here.

7. Add Comment if required in the Absence Information window.

8. Click OK to save.

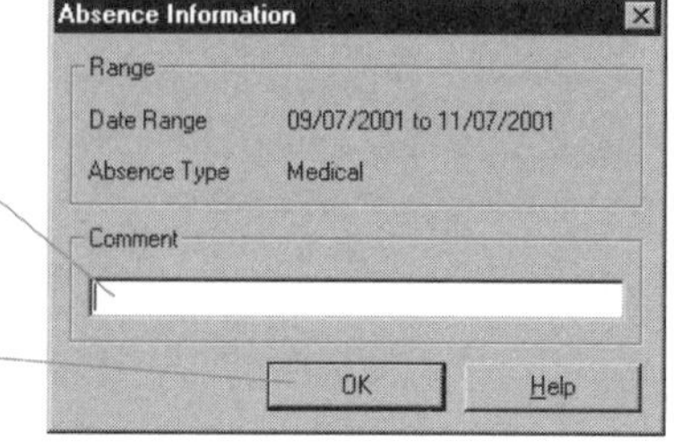

Recording Employee's Bank Details

You can enter up to 30 characters per line for fields Bank, Address and Account Name.

If you wish to to enter your employee's bank/building society details or amend existing information you can do this using the Banking tab on the Employee Record. To do this follow the steps below:

1 Select employee required and click the Banking tab on Employee Record.

2 Enter branch here.

3 Enter the branch's Telephone and Facsimile details.

4 Select Account Type here.

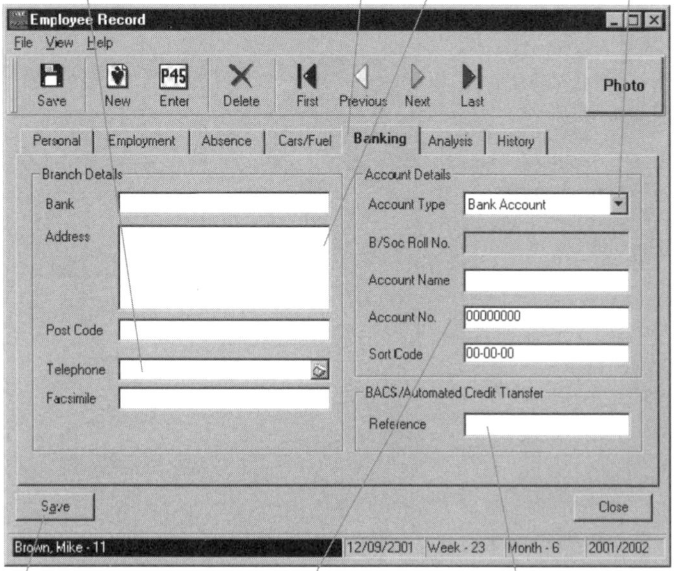

Where Account No. is less than eight digits, insert leading zeros, e.g. 00123456.

You must complete bank account details if you pay the employees by credit transfer.

B/Soc Roll No. is only needed for building society accounts.

5 Enter Account details here.

6 If you pay by credit transfer enter reference here.

7 Click Save to record bank details.

Avoid unnessary use of punctuation for Account Name, e.g., commas or full stops.

Note: If your computer modem & telephone share the same line you can ring the bank/building society using the Phone button at the side of the Telephone box, then pick up your phone to talk to them.

Company and Employee Analysis

Departments, Cost Centres and Employee Analysis first need setting up using the Analysis tab from Company Settings.

For businesses who wish to use departments, cost centres and employees for analysis purposes this can be achieved by setting up their individual Employee Record. To enter this information follow the steps below:

1 Select employee required and from the Employee Record click the Analysis tab.

2 Click here to select a Department.

3 To select a Cost Centre click here.

There are three types of Employee Analysis. You can customise them to your own business needs. On this example Union Member and Job Title have been set up.

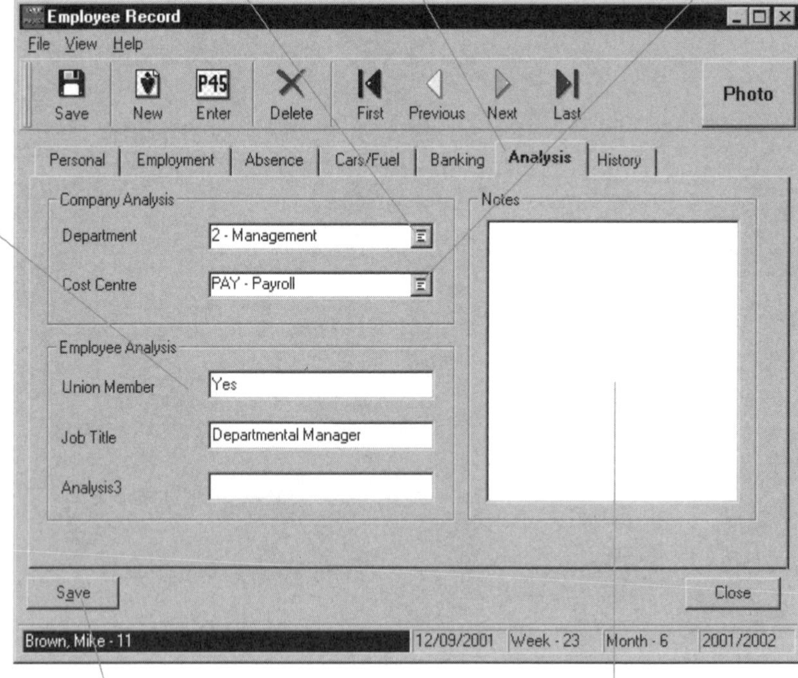

It is always useful to store a scanned photograph of your employee with their record card, especially in the case of larger businesses, for identification purposes.

4 Enter any information you wish to keep with your employee's record.

5 Click Save to record new details or Close to return to Payroll desktop.

Viewing Employee's Payment History

The History tab does not display any brought forward values.

To obtain a quick overview of your employees' payment history details, use the History tab from the Employee Record to provide you with this information. To view an employee's payment history do the following:

1 Select employee required and, from the Employee Record, click on the History tab.

After processing your employee's payroll, their payment details will appear on the History tab.

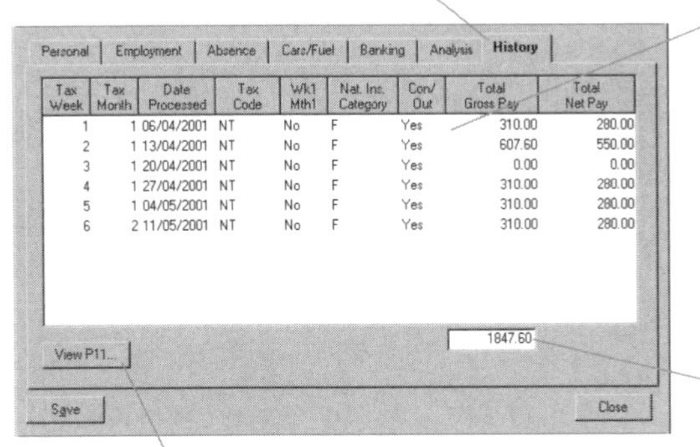

2 You can view each payment processed for your employee here.

3 Total Gross Pay appears here.

You can view employee history payment details, but you cannot edit any of this information.

4 Click here to view NI contributions or click Close to return to the Payroll desktop.

5 In the View P11 window, click Help for an explanation of payment terms etc.

The View P11 button provides employees' P11 information, i.e., National Insurance, PAYE (1) and PAYE (2).

6 Click here to preview PAYE details or click Close to return to History tab.

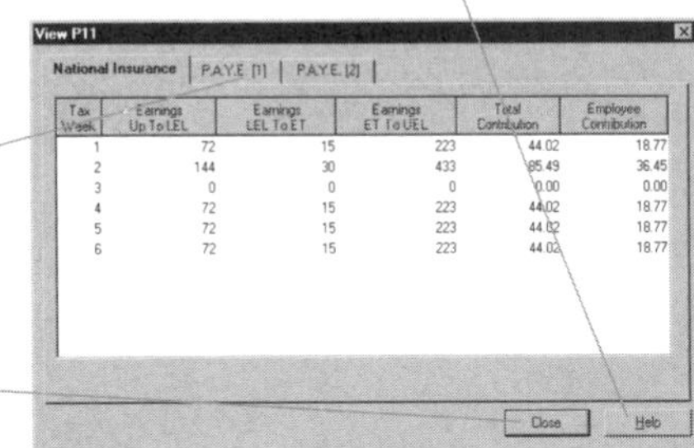

Note: A P11 NIC Deduction Card shows information relating to standard earnings, total NI contributions, and employee and employer contributions for an employee. It also includes totals for any SSP and SMP.

From the Payroll toolbar, Reports option, Employee section you can print a P11 Deduction Card (NIC Details) and a P11 Deduction Card (PAYE Details) for your employees.

7 You can view details here of any tax paid by an employee for each tax period as well as an up to date figure.

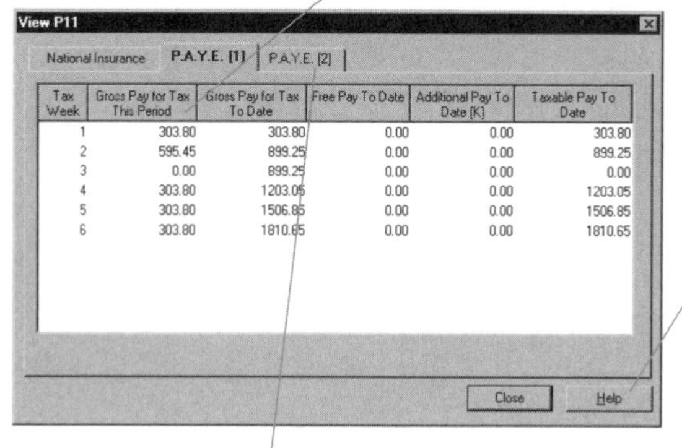

Tax Week	Gross Pay for Tax This Period	Gross Pay for Tax To Date	Free Pay To Date	Additional Pay To Date [K]	Taxable Pay To Date
1	303.80	303.80	0.00	0.00	303.80
2	595.45	899.25	0.00	0.00	899.25
3	0.00	899.25	0.00	0.00	0.00
4	303.80	1203.05	0.00	0.00	1203.05
5	303.80	1506.85	0.00	0.00	1506.85
6	303.80	1810.65	0.00	0.00	1810.65

8 Click Help button for explanation of payment terms.

9 Click this tab to view further details about tax and tax credits or click Close to close the View P11 window.

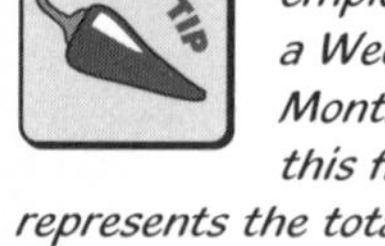

If your employee is on a Week 1 or Month 1 code this figure represents the total tax due to date from when the selected employee started working for you. It does not include cumulative values from any previous employment.

10 This figure shows the total (cumulative) amount of tax paid by the selected employee, from the start of the tax year.

11 Details of any Tax Credits.

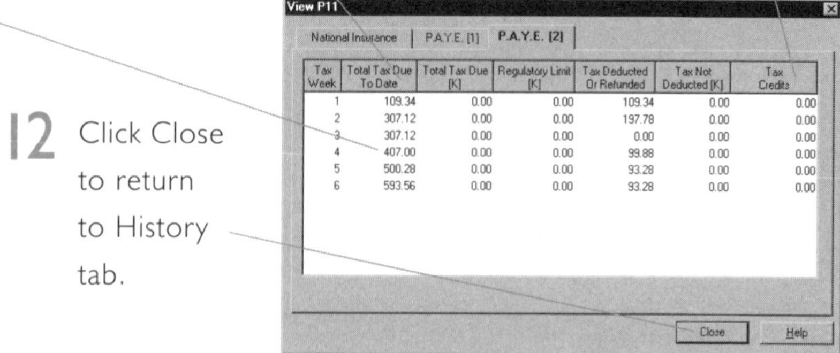

Tax Week	Total Tax Due To Date	Total Tax Due [K]	Regulatory Limit [K]	Tax Deducted Or Refunded	Tax Not Deducted [K]	Tax Credits
1	109.34	0.00	0.00	109.34	0.00	0.00
2	307.12	0.00	0.00	197.78	0.00	0.00
3	307.12	0.00	0.00	0.00	0.00	0.00
4	407.00	0.00	0.00	99.88	0.00	0.00
5	500.28	0.00	0.00	93.28	0.00	0.00
6	593.56	0.00	0.00	93.28	0.00	0.00

12 Click Close to return to History tab.

Note: The P11 PAYE deduction card shows an employee's payments and deductions of PAYE within the current tax year for each payment period. Totals for pay and pay adjustments to date are also included.

Cars, Fuel & Class 1A NIC

This chapter shows you how to set and maintain company car details and record the fuel they use. You will learn how to enter Class 1A National Insurance contributions liable by the employer for employees who are provided with a car and fuel for both business and private use.

Covers

Chapter Six

Cars and Fuel Records

Let the New Car Wizard guide you through the stages of setting up your new car records.

In the 1991 budget, legislation was introduced making employers, not employees, liable for national insurance contributions on the value of company cars and the fuel they use. Directors and employees need to be earning over a specific figure per annum (including expenses and any benefits) before the employer is liable for NIC payments on the value of the company car and fuel provided to them. This is what is referred to as Class 1A National Insurance contributions.

Class 1A NIC is paid one year in arrears and will appear on the Form P32 Employer's Payment Record in month 3 of the following year, for example, Class 1A NIC due for a car used in tax year April 2001 to March 2002 will show on the P32 in June 2002, i.e. month 3.

To calculate the amount of liability due scale rates are applied which refer to the age of the car, its original market value, its engine capacity, number of business miles, Carbon Dioxide (CO2) emissions, etc.

Details for each employee provided with a company car are recorded on the Cars/Fuel tab of the Employee Record. Once this information has been entered the program will automatically calculate the Class 1A NIC liability using the current legislation rates.

Preparing to set up your new car records checklist

Before creating your new car records you will need:

- The car registration number
- Its make and model
- The engine capacity
- List price of the car
- Date the car was first registered
- Date the car was first used
- Type of fuel or power used (i.e., petrol, diesel, etc.)
- CO2 emissions (Note: All cars registered from the 1 January 1998 are required by law to be supplied with details of their CO2 emissions. Cars registered after 1 November 2000 will have the CO2 emissions figure recorded on the Vehicle Registration Document V5).

Refer to the Payroll Library Help system for more information about legislation governing Class 1A NIC for company cars.

Creating New Car Records

Sage Payroll automatically calculates the field Adjusted Annual Mileage, where an employee starts using the car part way through the tax year, or where the car is unavailable for use for a period of time during the tax year.

Once you have followed the checklist on page 76 and have collated all your information together you can now begin setting up your new car records by following the steps below:

To set up your new car records

1 Select your employee record and click the Cars/Fuel tab.

2 Click New Car button to bring up the New Car Wizard.

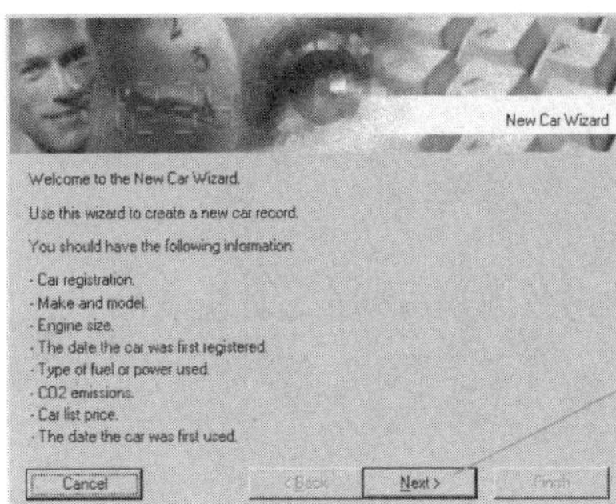

3 Click Next to continue.

For new cars, the CO2 emissions are shown on the registration document.

4 Enter the car details here.

5 Click here for a list of fuel options and select the appropriate one.

6 Enter CO2 emissions.

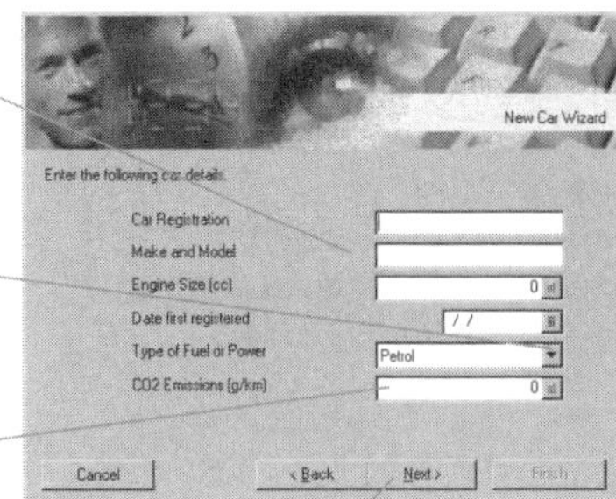

7 Click Next to continue.

The Remove Car Wizard, activated by clicking the Remove Car button on the Cars/Fuel tab, will allow you to keep a car record without removing the mileage information, or delete all of the details about the specified car.

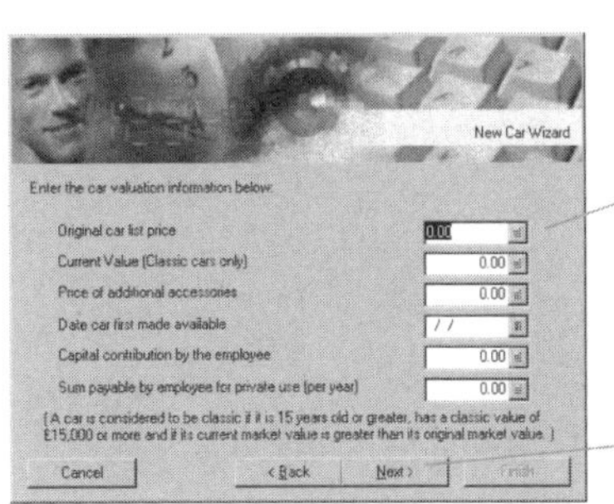

8 Enter the car valuation information in this screen.

9 Click Next to continue.

Accessories include car items such as car stereos, sun roofs etc.

10 Tick here if fuel is provided for the employee's private use.

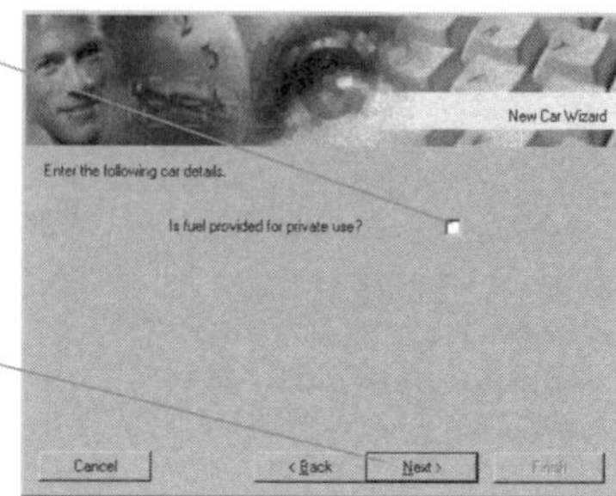

11 Click Next to continue.

Accessories of a value of £100 or more will be added to the Car List Price before the car benefit is calculated by the program.

12 If applicable, enter when the employee stopped using the car.

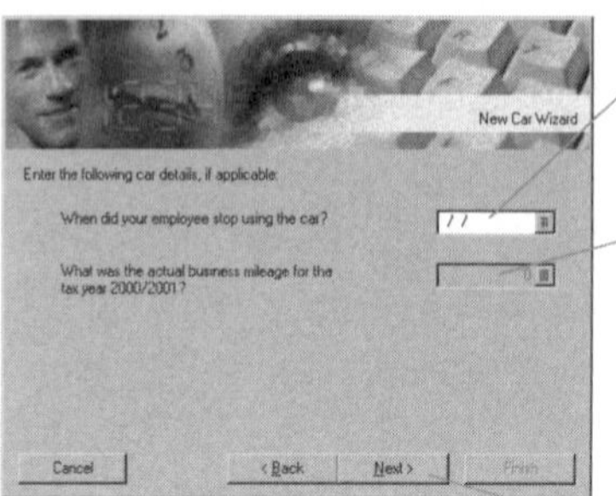

13 If you entered a tick in Step 10, enter the actual business mileage for the appropriate year.

14 Click Next to continue.

A car is considered as classic if it is 15 years old or more and has a classic value of £15,000 or more and if the current market value is greater than the original market value.

15 Check here that the new car information you have entered is correct. If not, use the Back button to return to the appropriate screen and make the necessary amendments.

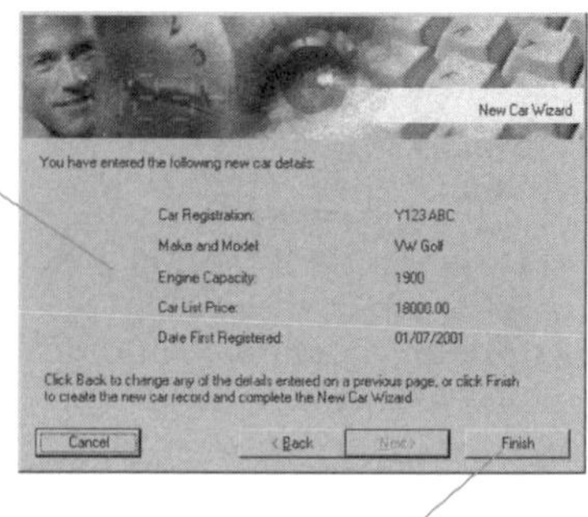

Classic accessories are assumed to be part of the classic car price.

16 If the details are correct, click Finish to create the new car record.

Removing Car Details

The occasion may arise when you need to remove mileage details, but retain the car record, or delete all details about a certain car. Sage Payroll lets you do this through the Remove Car Wizard.

Use the Enter Mileage button to view the Employee Mileage Log.

To remove an employee's mileage details

1. From the Cars/Fuel tab click Remove Car to bring up the Remove Car Wizard, then click Next.

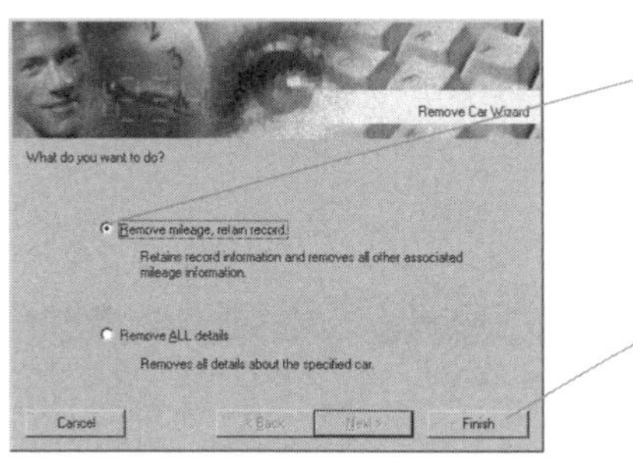

2. Click here to remove mileage only, but retain all other record information.

3. Click Finish to complete the action and return to the Cars/Fuel tab.

When you remove the car mileage for a selected car you should note that the Mileage Log details are also blanked.

To delete all car details

1. From the Cars/Fuel tab click Remove Car to bring up the Remove Car Wizard, then click Next.

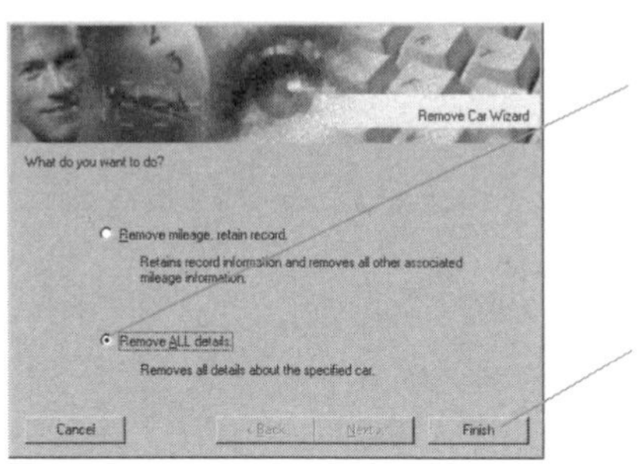

2. Click here to remove all details about the specified car.

3. Click Finish to complete the action and return to the Cars/Fuel tab.

Note: Sage Payroll will automatically prompt you if a P46 (Car) form is required when you select the Remove ALL details option and click Finish.

Entering Mileage Records

The total for Business Mileage may be entered at the year end.

Having set up your employee car details, you now need to keep an accurate record of the mileage covered. Sage Payroll will then use this information to calculate the Class 1A NICs.

Remember that mileage records will normally be recorded in the current tax year but the Class 1A NICs on company cars are calculated using the annual mileage for the previous tax year.

To enter mileage records do the following:

1 Using the Cars/Fuel tab on your employee's record card click Enter Mileage.

2 The Employee Mileage Log appears.

When you need reports containing information about car details, mileage and Class 1A NIC, these are available within the Reports option, Cars & Fuel section.

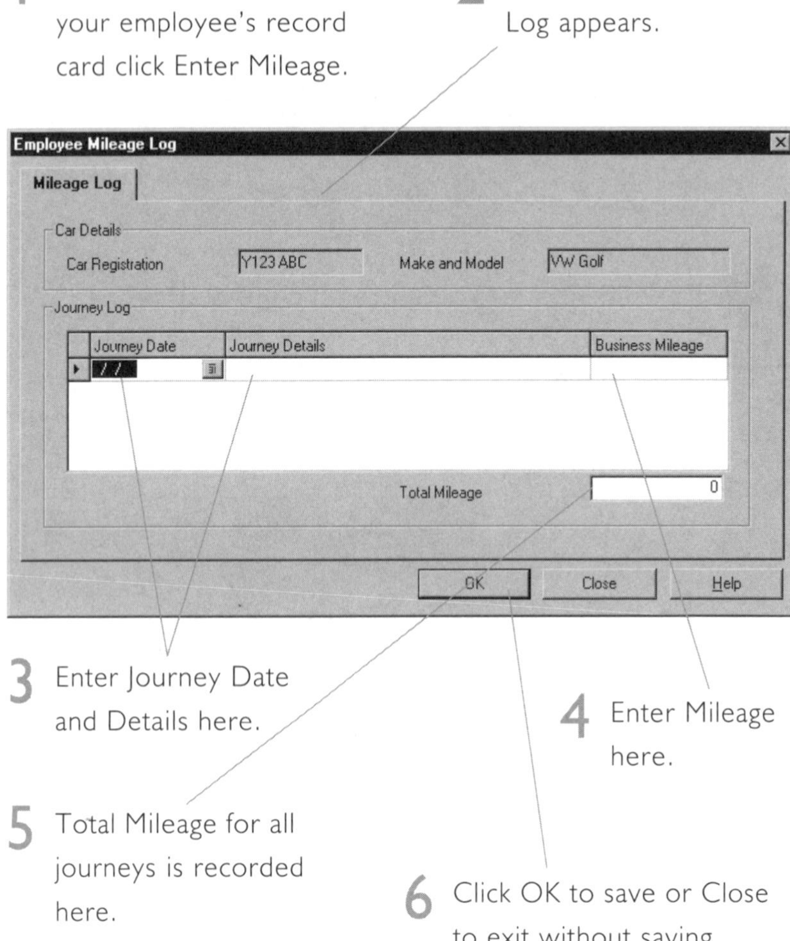

3 Enter Journey Date and Details here.

4 Enter Mileage here.

5 Total Mileage for all journeys is recorded here.

6 Click OK to save or Close to exit without saving.

You must keep accurate and up-to-date records of all business mileage details.

Entering Class 1A NIC Details

For more information about Class 1A NICs contact your local Inland Revenue (Contributions) office.

Employers who provide a car to an employee for both private and business use as well as providing fuel for the vehicle are liable for payment of Class 1A NIC contributions. However, the employee is not liable to make any payments.

These Class 1A NIC details are set up within the employee record as follows:

To enter your Class 1A NIC details

1. Using the Cars/Fuel tab within your employee's record click on the Class 1A NIC button.

The standard charge for fuel is based upon the engine capacity of the car and the type of fuel, either diesel or petrol.

2. The Class 1A NIC window appears.

3. Standard Charges display automatically once the mileage record has been created.

If a car is unavailable to an employee for 30 days or more you need to enter the number of days within the Other Days Unavailable field, for example, cars off the road and in for repair after an accident.

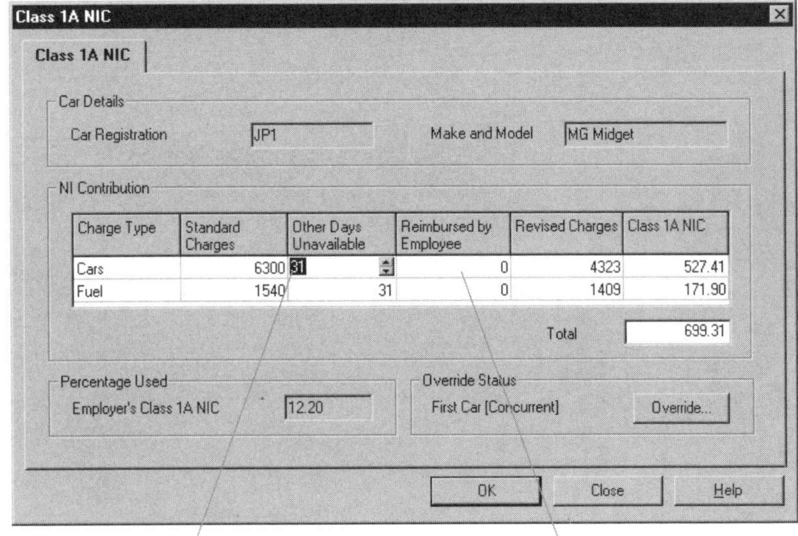

4. Enter Other Days Unavailable, if applicable.

5. Enter any contributions paid by the employee for payment of fuel and/or use of the car.

An employee may have more than one car assigned to them. If the employee only has one car, First Car: Yes,[Non Concurrent] appears next to the Override button. If the employee has more than one car, the highest mileage is determined by the program. The car with the highest mileage appears as 1st Car (Concurrent) whilst the car with the second highest mileage appears as 2nd Car (Concurrent).

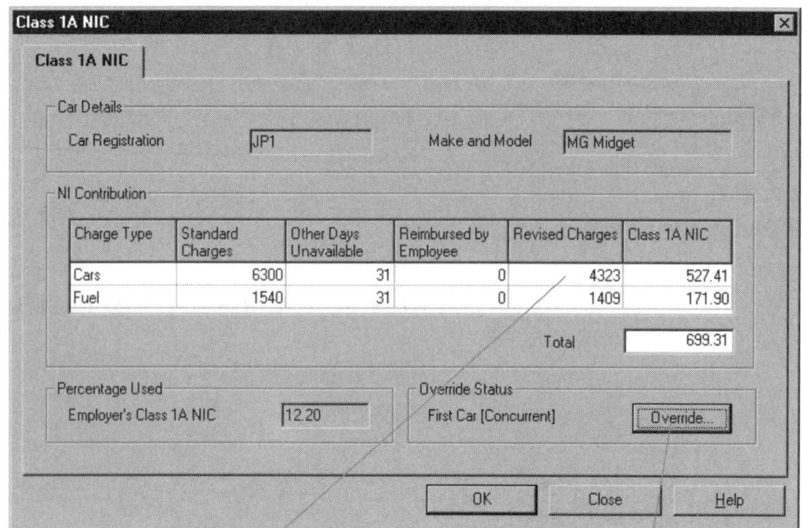

6 Note here revised scale charges after applying any reimbursements or days unavailable.

7 If the employee has more than one car record, click the Override button if you need to change Override Status.

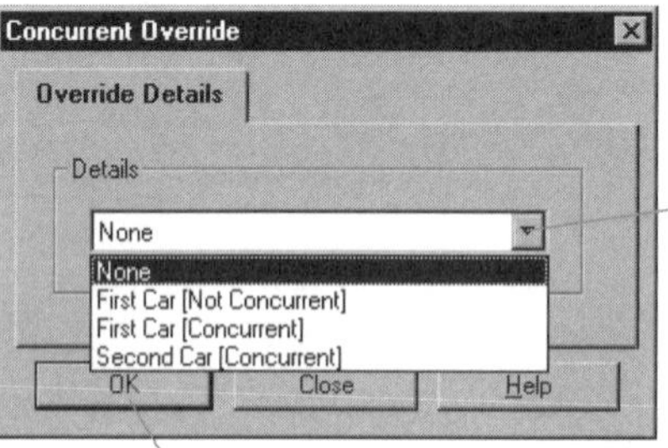

8 Select the relevant details from the drop down list.

If a car is unavailable and the exact dates are not known, the program's calculation in respect of First Car/Second Car status may need to be overridden.

9 Click OK to save the Override changes and return to the Class 1A NIC window.

10 When all changes have been made, click the Close button to save the Class 1A NIC details.

Payment of Employees

Chapter Seven

This chapter shows you how to process different payment types for your employees (e.g., monthly, weekly) and by different methods (cheque, cash, BACS etc.). You will learn how to enter the hours and rate of pay for your hourly paid staff. Sick pay, maternity pay, deductions, attachments, manual pension payments and advancing holiday pay are also covered in this chapter.

Covers

Processing your Payroll

Use the Criteria button to select which payment period and payment method you wish to process.

Once your employees' records and payment types have been set up you are ready to process your payroll and pay your employees.

You will have employees with different payment types, for example, some will require paying weekly, others fortnightly and some four-weekly or monthly. Different methods of payment can also be set for your employees and include cash payment, cheque, BACS and credit transfer.

When entering payments a warning message will appear if the payroll has already been updated for this period.

Where employees are hourly paid you can enter the number of hours they work, which will be multiplied against the rate to calculate the gross amount.

Whilst preparing your payroll, you will need to check if any sick pay, maternity pay or holiday pay needs including. Attachments and deductions may also be applied to some of your employees.

Parts 1 & 2 of the Payment Summary Report must be printed BEFORE updating the payroll, whilst part 3 needs printing AFTER the update.

Once all the information has been processed, pre-update reports must be printed and checked for any discrepancies before the records are actually updated. This Payment Summary consists of three parts, namely: two pre-update and one post-update report.

Part 1 – gives a payroll summary for the period being processed

Part 2 – gives a National Insurance summary

Part 3 – gives a Year To Date summary

Refer to chapter 4, (page 48) for setting up the Nominal Link.

After the payroll has been processed, you may need to use the Nominal Link to update your Sage accounts data. There may be leavers to deal with and P45s to produce. The P32 Employers Payment Record will need submitting to the Inland Revenue.

Initially, it is useful to follow the payroll checklist opposite to remind you of the different procedures that contribute to the processing of your payroll.

Payroll Processing Checklist

Reset Payments Wizard will not reset any Global payments or deduction types.

Before processing your payroll you might find it useful to work through the checklist below:

- Check that government legislation has not changed. Amend if necessary.
- Create any new employee records.
- Note any changes to your employees' pay rates.

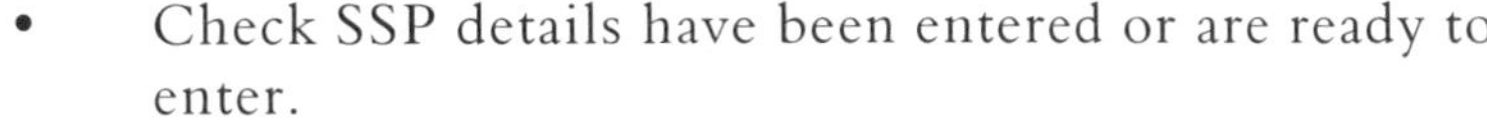

- Check SSP details have been entered or are ready to enter.

Use Pre-update Reports from the Payroll stacked toolbar, Summary section to preview/print your Payment Summary (Parts 1 & 2).

- Have details of any holiday payments to make.
- Set up any court order details relating to your employees.
- Check the previous payroll date has been updated.
- Enter your payroll processing date.
- Reset Payments (where applicable).
- Enter your employee payments, deductions, attachments and tax credits.

Updating your records also updates the P11 information.

- Print your pre-update Payment Summary report. Check and correct any mistakes–reprint.
- Print payslips, cheques etc.
- Print all reports you may require.
- Make a pre-update backup copy to floppy disk.

To print your P32 Employers Payment Summary report, select Reports from the Payroll toolbar then choose Period End from the tree view.

- Update the records.
- Update your accounts program via the Nominal Link (optional).
- Deal with any leavers and produce their P45s.
- At the month end print the P32 report to show payments due to the Inland Revenue.

Payroll Processing Date

The payroll processing date is used to calculate the tax week or tax month.

It is important to check the processing date before you start to process your payroll. The date is normally the day you pay your employees, e.g., if you pay your employees on a monthly basis, the processing date may be the last working day of the month.

This date calculates the tax week or month and determines the amount of NI contributions and tax etc. you deduct from your employees' pay. To change the Process Date do the following:

Changing your process date is also available by selecting the Change Process Date option from the Payroll Stacked toolbar.

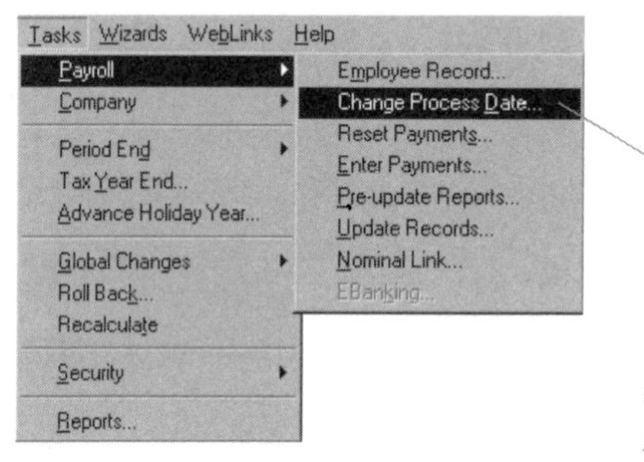

1 From the Payroll toolbar click Tasks, select Payroll and then Change Process Date.

2 Use the Calendar button to change your process date.

Always check you have the correct process date. It can be entered when you start the program.

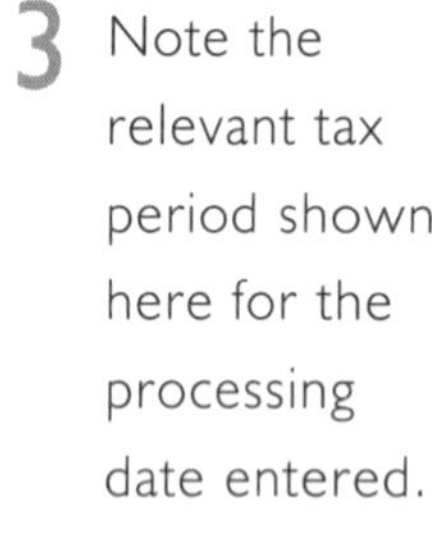

3 Note the relevant tax period shown here for the processing date entered.

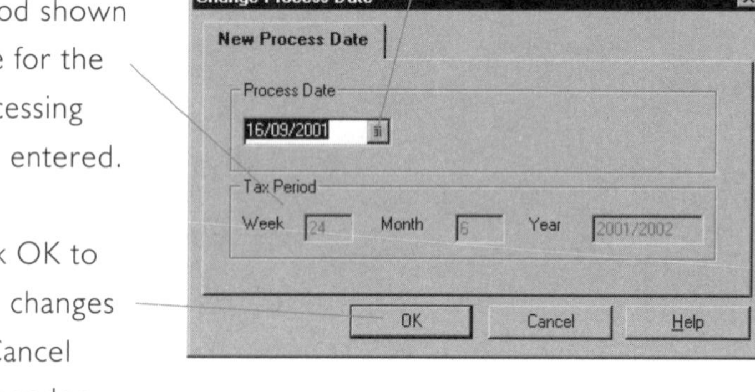

4 Click OK to save changes or Cancel to abandon.

If you move between different companies the program will prompt you to check the processing date.

Note: If you have changed the Process Date to a new date to allow you to process your payroll in advance, say, it is important to remember to change it back to the correct date before performing any other tasks.

Resetting Payments

Only the Hours/No. Values for fixed payment types can be reset by the Reset Payments Wizard.

Before entering new payments for the current payroll period, it may be necessary to clear certain payment details from your employees' records for the last period.

An example of this is where the number of overtime hours varies from week to week. However, the rest of the payroll details can remain the same. To reset your employees' payments do as follows:

Global Payments contain values which apply to all employees so you cannot use the Reset Payments Wizard to change them.

1 From the Payroll stacked toolbar click Reset Payments.

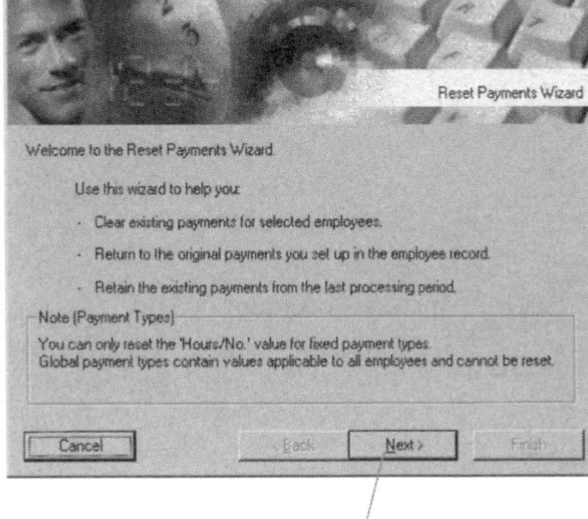

2 Click Next to continue.

The Reset Payments Wizard is available from the Payroll toolbar using the Wizards option.

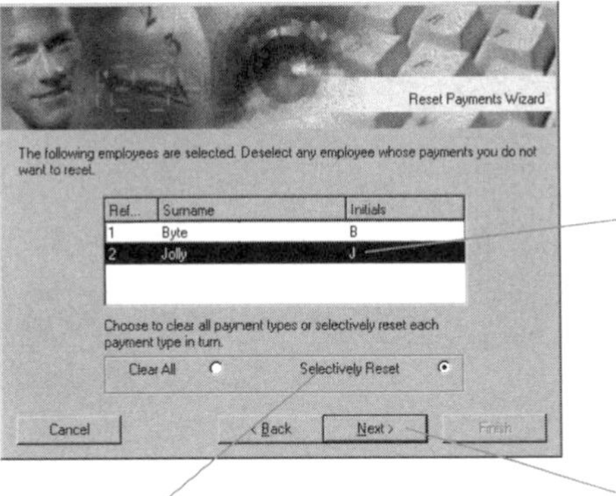

3 Deselect any employees whose payments do not need changing.

4 Click here to Selectively Reset each payment in turn, else Clear All to clear all payments in one go.

5 Click Next to continue.

Just click Cancel to exit the Reset Payments Wizard.

From this screen you can reset all values for all payments OR check through each individual payment. From the drop down lists you can then decide whether to retain, clear or use default settings.

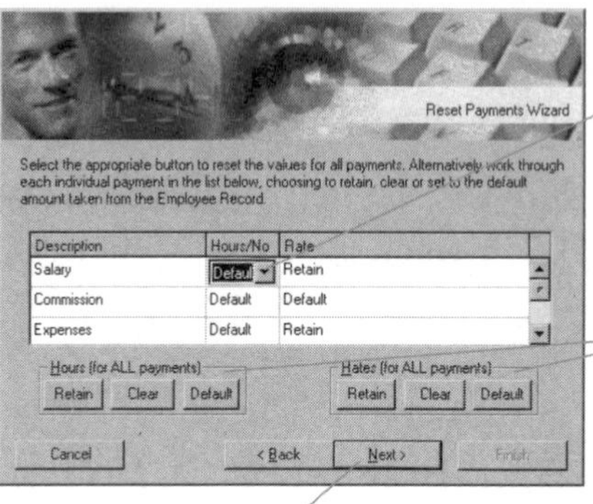

6 For individual payments, choose an option from the drop down list.

7 Set Hours and Rates (for ALL payments) as appropriate here.

8 Click Next to continue.

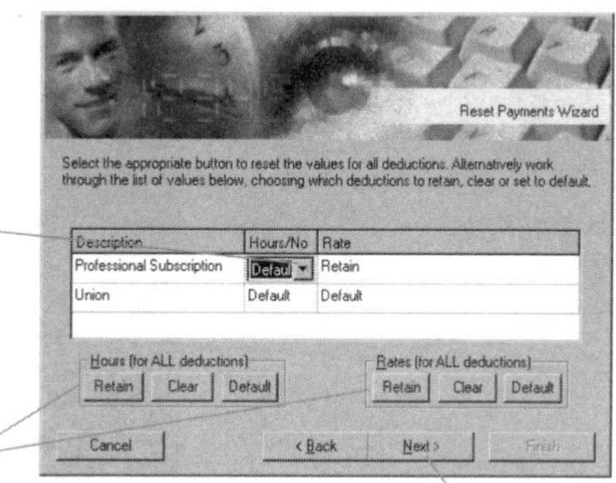

9 Individual deductions can be reset here.

Use the vertical scroll bar to view all your payment types.

10 ALL deductions can be reset from here.

11 Click Next to continue.

12 Click here to reset values from this list.

Click the Back button to view existing payments settings and make changes where necessary.

13 Click Finish to save changes and return to the Payroll desktop.

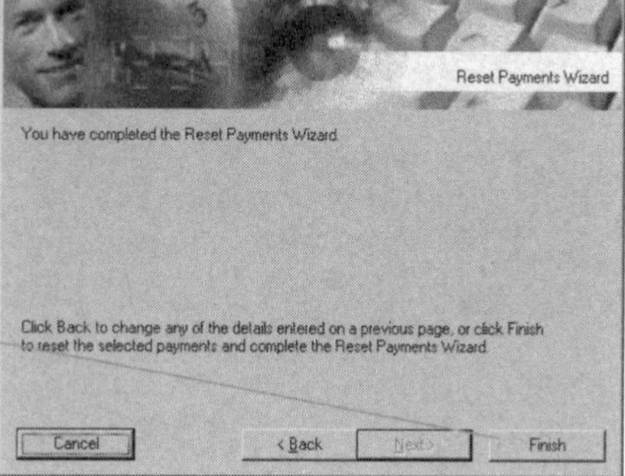

Processing your Payments

Any Payment Names you assigned to your employee appear automatically on the Payments tab.

Payment information is entered using the Enter Payments option from the Payroll stacked toolbar. This payroll information is then used for automatically generating your employees' net pay. To process your payments do as follows:

1 From the employee list box, select the employees you wish to process.

The Tax field displays whether the payment is pre tax or post tax.

2 From the Payroll stacked toolbar click Enter Payments.

3 If a default number of hours is not set up, enter your employee's hours here.

You cannot change the default hours for a global payment type.

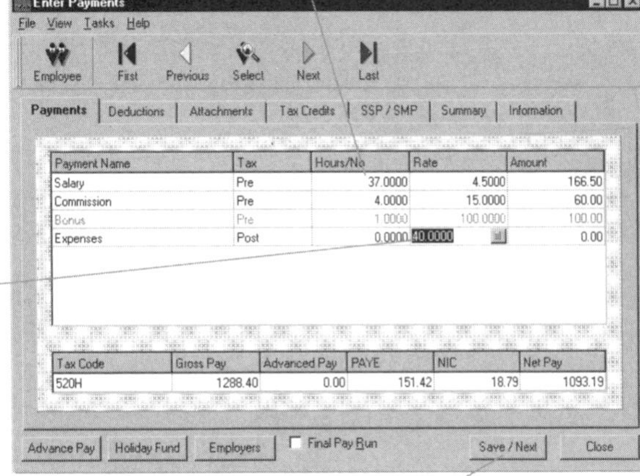

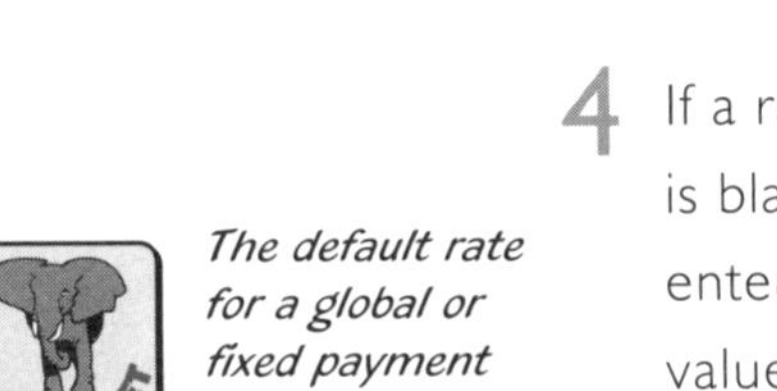

4 If a rate is blank enter a value here.

The default rate for a global or fixed payment type cannot be changed.

5 Carefully check all information is correct.

6 To save and move to next record click Save/Next button, else Close to return to the Payroll desktop.

Use the Select button to produce an employee list for entering payment information.

Note: Before leaving this record, you may find it convenient to check other details, e.g. SSP/SMP etc.

Processing your Deductions

If a default number has already been set up for the deduction type in the Hours/No field it appears automatically.

To process deductions for your employees, the information needs to be entered using the Deductions tab from the Enter Payments window. Commonly used deductions include union fees/professsional fees, health schemes, recreation activities, etc. Chapter 12 shows you how to set up deductions for both your Company and your employees. To process your deductions follow the steps below:

1 From the Enter Payments window click Deductions.

For a global deduction type you cannot change the default hours.

2 Deduction types previously assigned to an employee appear.

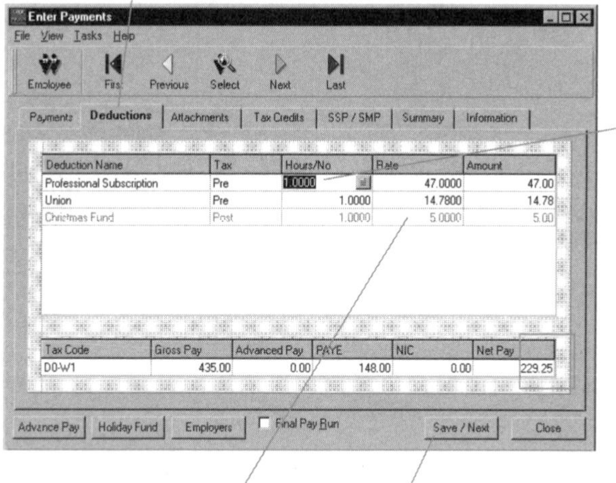

3 Enter the number of hours or deduction payments here.

If you have entered a default rate or amount for the field Rate it appears automatically.

4 Enter the deduction rate for the deduction type in this column.

5 Carefully check that all Deductions entered are recorded accurately for the selected employee.

You cannot change the default rate for global or fixed deduction types.

6 Click here to Save and move to the next record (if more than one employee was initially selected) or click Close to return to the Sage Payroll desktop.

Processing Attachments

You cannot edit the information in the Name field as this is stored on the Employee Record.

Sage Payroll will process these attachments of earnings automatically for those employees liable for these deductions. To process these attachments follow the steps below:

1 From the Enter Payments window click Attachments.

2 Details of any Attachments set up on the employee's record are shown.

The Amount/ Percent field shows if the attachment is to be calculated as a percentage of the employee's wages or as a fixed amount.

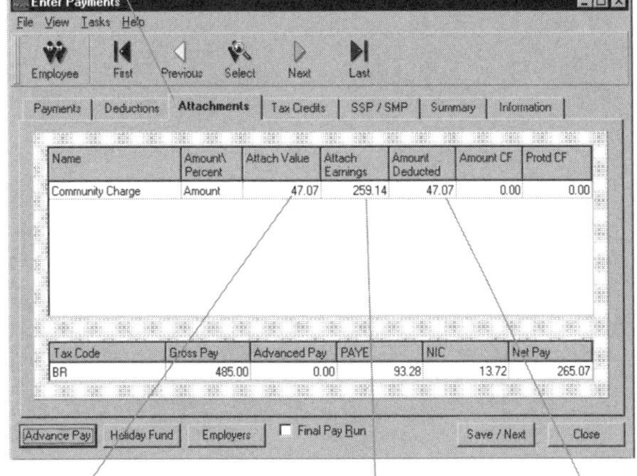

3 To add a new attachment to this list you need to return to the Employee Record.

For the Attach Value field you need to enter an exact amount for a Child Support Attachment, but for a Council Tax attachment, you need to enter a percentage.

4 This shows amount being deducted.

5 The earnings from which the attachment is deducted are show here.

6 Note actual amount deducted, which takes into account any protected earnings.

7 Click Save/Next to save and move to next record or Close to return to the Sage Payroll desktop.

Use horizontal scroll bar to view all attachment details.

Note: If the whole amount is unable to be processed for this period, the Amount CF field shows the value carried forward to the next period. The Protd CF field shows any protected earnings which are also carried forward.

Processing Tax Credits

Refer to chapter 13 for more information about Tax Credits.

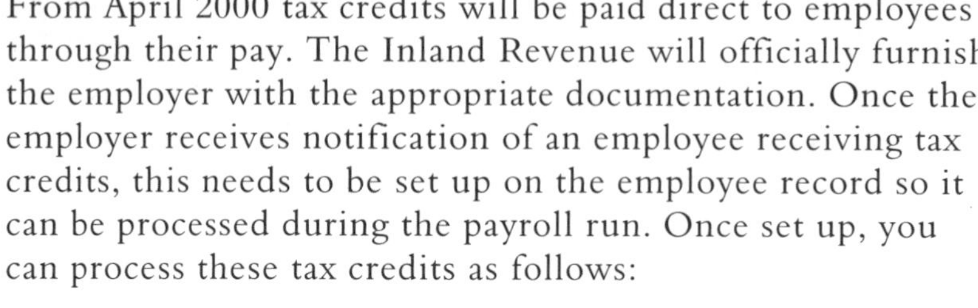

From April 2000 tax credits will be paid direct to employees through their pay. The Inland Revenue will officially furnish the employer with the appropriate documentation. Once the employer receives notification of an employee receiving tax credits, this needs to be set up on the employee record so it can be processed during the payroll run. Once set up, you can process these tax credits as follows:

To enter Tax Credits for your employees, you need to set this up on their Employee Record. To do this select the Employment tab, Pay Elements button and then Tax Credits tab.

1 From the Enter Payments window click Tax Credits.

2 Details of any Tax Credits set up on the employee's record are shown.

3 Note duration of payments for tax credits.

4 Number of days between First Date and Last Date is inclusive.

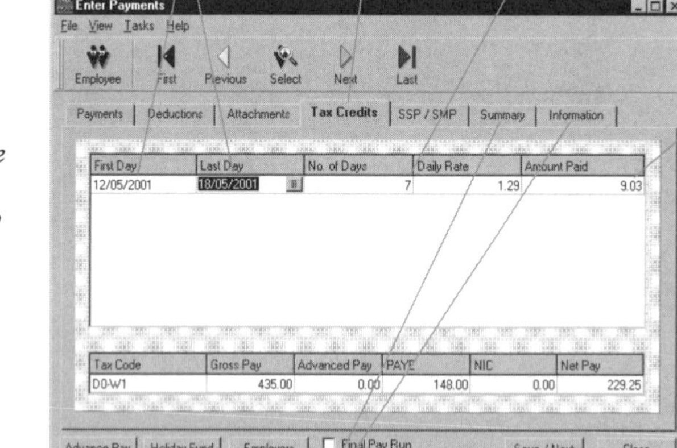

5 This shows the number of days multiplied by the Daily Rate.

Use Employee button to quickly return to an employee's record.

6 To view tax credit information for this employee click the Summary and Information tabs.

7 Click here to save and move to next record.

To record Tax Credit Funding and Tax Refund Received, select the Tax Credit tab from Company Settings.

Note: First Date is the first day payments start in the current pay run and Last Date is the last date for these payments. Both cannot be before the 'effective from' date, or after the 'effective until' or 'stop' date.

Statutory Sick Pay

Refer to chapter 9 for details about processing SSP.

Recording an employee's absence through sickness is carried out using the Absence tab's Diary Entry button. This is available on their Employee Record or when you are processing their payroll within the Enter Payments window. To enter an employee's sickness details whilst processing the payroll do as follows:

1 From the Enter Payments window click the SSP/SMP tab.

Click S.S.P. button for additional information.

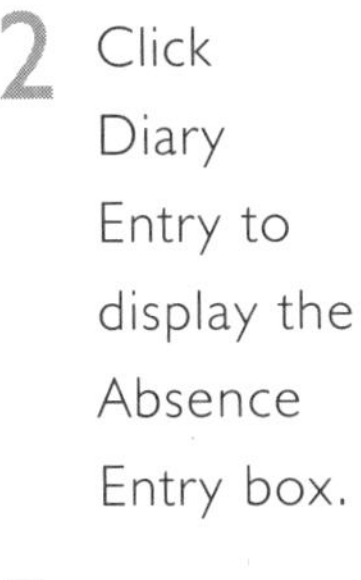

2 Click Diary Entry to display the Absence Entry box.

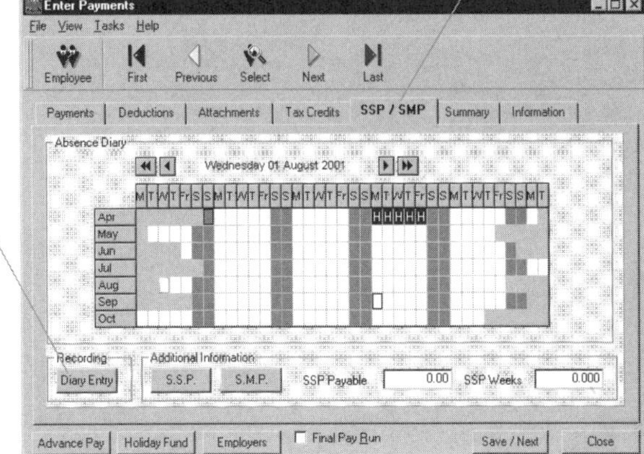

The types of absence you record for SSP are Sickness or Withhold.

3 Click here to select SSP.

For additional information about sickness and SSP Legislation refer to Sage Payroll's Help Topics option.

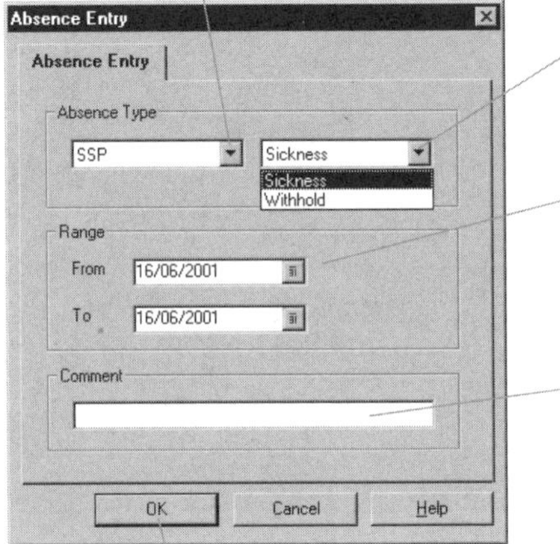

4 Select type of absence from here.

5 Enter dates for your employee's absence.

6 Add any additional information about sickness here.

You cannot record half days for Absence due to Sickness.

7 Click OK to save changes and return to SSP/SMP window. Note: the Absence Diary will now be updated with the new sickness details.

Statutory Maternity Pay

Refer to chapter 10 for details on processing SMP.

Sage Payroll will calculate the correct figures for any employee who is eligible for SMP. The correct information needs entering using the SSP/SMP tab as shown below. To enter your SMP dates do the following:

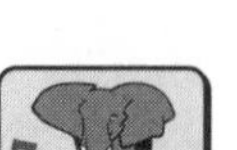

EWC is the term describing the expected week of confinement, which begins on a Sunday.

1 From the Enter Payments window click the SSP/SMP tab.

2 Click here to open the employee's SMP window.

3 Click on the Dates tab.

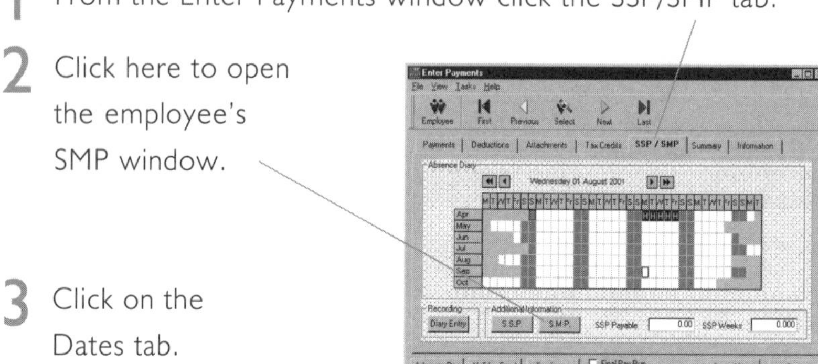

The baby's arrival date needed for the Expected On (EWC) field is normally found on the Mat B1 maternity certificate.

4 Enter date baby is due.

5 Click here on receipt of Mat B1 maternity certificate or other medical evidence of arrival date.

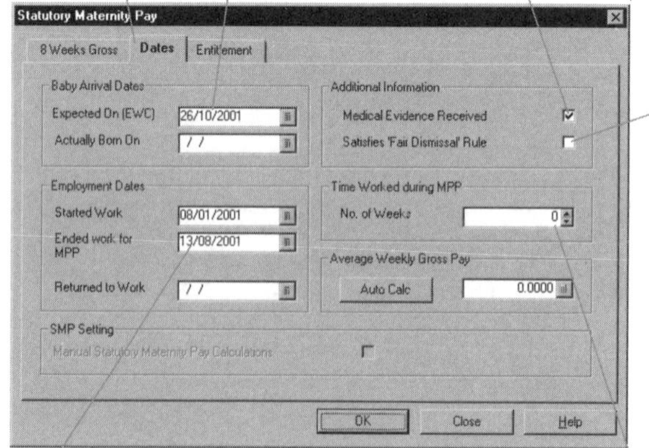

6 If an employee is fairly dismissed by the employer click here.

If an employer fairly dismisses an employee, SMP regulations state they may still receive SSP.

7 Enter the date when your employee will leave to start her maternity leave.

8 If employee has worked during MPP, enter number of full or part weeks here.

You will only be able to check SMP entitlement with Sage Payroll from the first processing date after maternity pay period (MPP) starts.

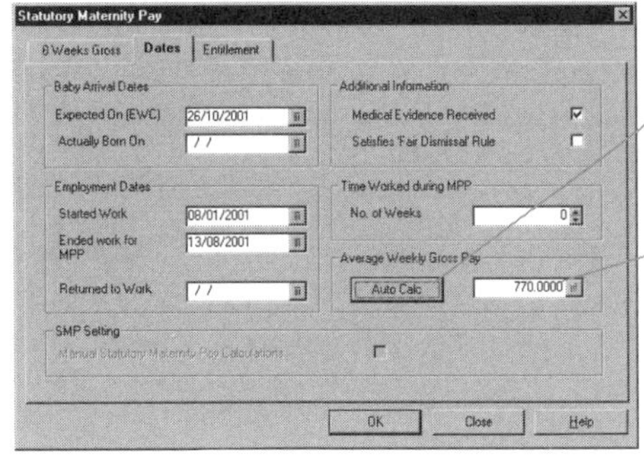

9 Click here to calculate Average Weekly Gross Pay OR enter figure manually here.

10 Click here to view Entitlement for employee.

If your employee works during MPP, she loses entitlement to SMP for the weeks she works.

11 These dates appear automatically.

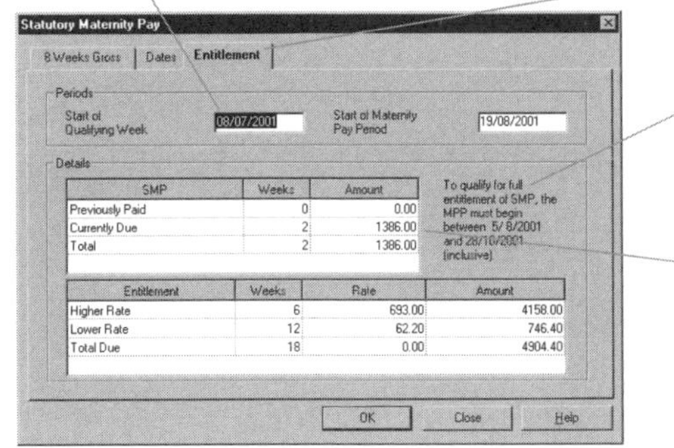

12 Note qualifying entitlement details.

13 Total amount of maternity pay due shows here.

If you have not selected the Manual Statutory Maternity Pay Calculations check box, you need to manually enter SMP payments for your employees when processing your payroll, for example, when you start using the Payroll program part way through the tax year.

14 Click here to view 8 Weeks Gross, 8 Weeks Average, Payments included in calculation and Last Payment details.

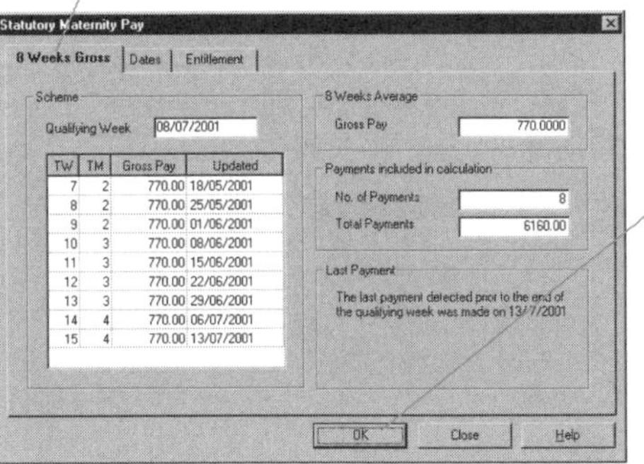

15 After checking figures are correct click OK to save any changes or Close to exit.

Note: Actually Born On field for baby's date of birth and mother's Returned to Work details can only be completed once the event has happened.

Viewing Summary and Information

If an employee is receiving SSP or SMP you may want to make their payments up to their normal wages/salary. To do this, click the MakeUpBasic button on the Summary tab.

Sage Payroll lets you view together both your payments and deductions for a selected employee. This is available using the Summary tab from the Enter Payments window as follows:

1 From the Enter Payments window click the Summary tab.

2 Current Payments and Deductions appear here.

3 Click here to view Employers National Insurance and pension contributions.

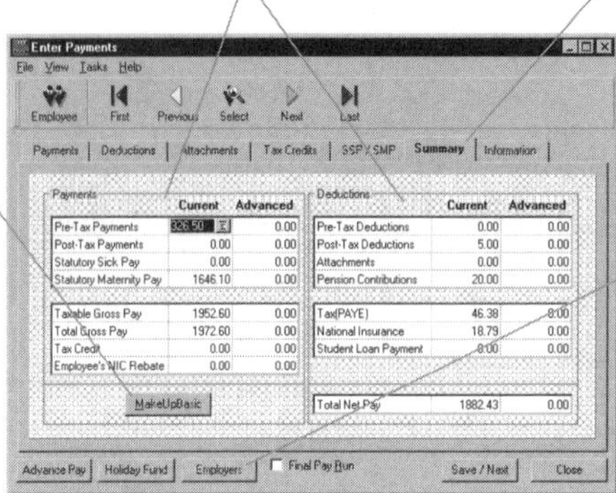

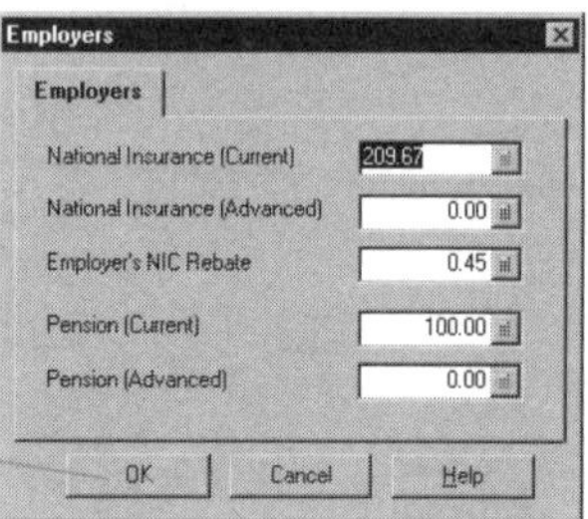

4 Click OK to return to Summary tab.

It is recommended to use the MakeUpBasic button for your hourly paid staff. To manually adjust and make up a normal wage to take account of any SSP/SMP can be tedious and time consuming.

5 To view an itemised breakdown for an employee's Income Tax, National Insurance, SSP/SMP, Pension, Student Loans, Tax Credits, Attachments and Holiday Fund select the Information tab.

6 Click each folder in turn to view details.

7 Click here to save and move to next record or Close for Payroll desktop.

Use the Previous, Next and Last buttons to move between your selected employees.

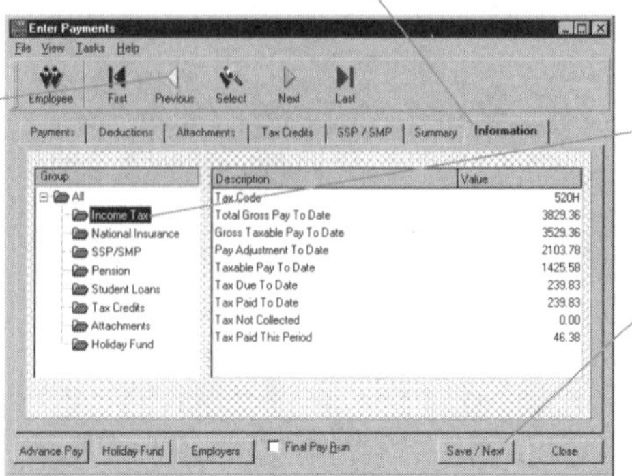

Manual Pension Payments

Before entering your pension payments manually you must set up a pension scheme which is Fixed, with no default amount or percentage entered.

Manual pension contributions need processing as part of your normal processing routine. The Pension Scheme will need setting up first and named, for example, Manual Entry, then the scheme will need applying to the relevant employee.

Each time the payroll is updated the Pension's YTD figures will accumulate. To enter an employee's pension manually do the following:

1. From the Enter Payments window click the Summary tab.

Pension Schemes are set up using Pensions Schemes from the Company stacked toolbar.

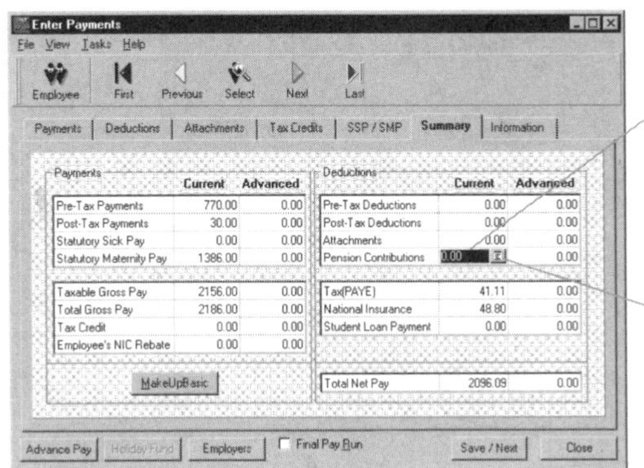

2. Note: If no contributions made, this is currently zero.

3. Click here to enter the Pension Contributions.

You cannot enter Additional Voluntary Contributions when processing pensions manually.

4. Enter your employee's pension details here for the current processing period.

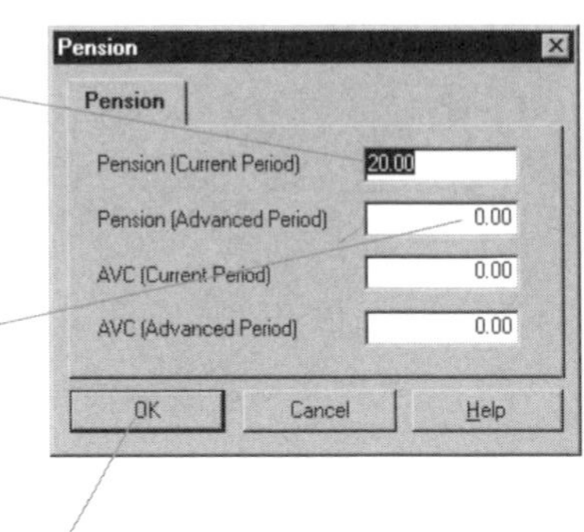

5. Enter any holiday pension contributions if you are paying your employee any holiday pay during this processing period.

If using a contracted out pension scheme run the Minimum Payments to COMPS report to check payments for each payroll run.

6. Click OK to save or Cancel to abandon and return to the Summary tab.

Advancing Holiday Pay

When you advance an employee's holiday pay, Sage Payroll will automatically flag them as being on holiday. This avoids them being accidentally processed again during the holiday period.

To record an employee's holiday pay in advance use the Advance Pay button from the Enter Payments window. This method ensures your employee's tax is calculated correctly over the whole holiday period instead of on a lump sum payment. To do this follow the steps below:

1 Click on the Advance Pay button at the foot of the Enter Payments window for your selected employee.

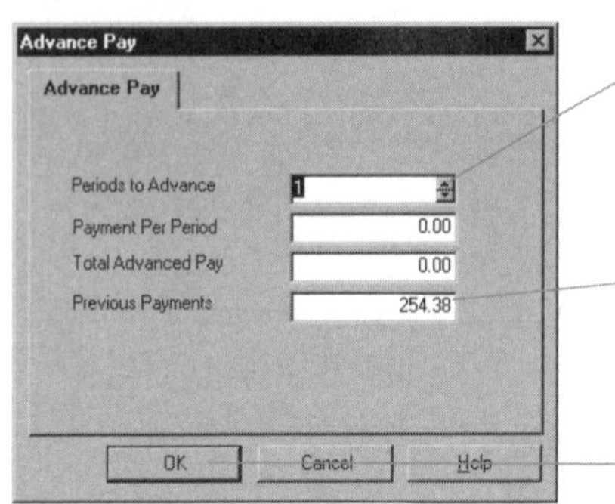

2 Enter number of payment periods you wish to advance, e.g. 1.

3 Any previous advanced pay is shown here.

4 Click OK.

When entering information into the Periods to Advance field, weekly paid staff need the number of whole weeks they will be on holiday and monthly paid staff need a whole month period entering.

5 Enter relevant payment information here.

6 Remember to enter any Deductions, Attachments or Tax Credits.

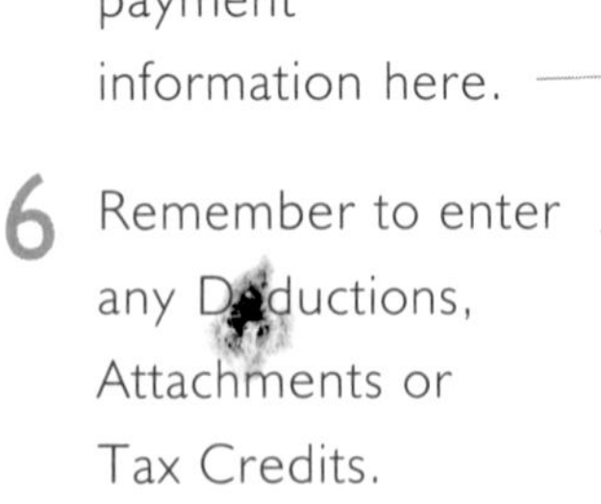

7 Click OK to save.

Advancing holiday pay applies only to full weekly or monthly periods not single days.

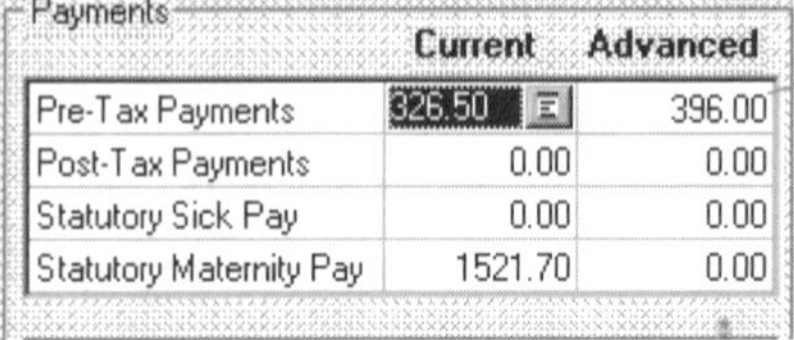

Payments

	Current	Advanced
Pre-Tax Payments	326.50	396.00
Post-Tax Payments	0.00	0.00
Statutory Sick Pay	0.00	0.00
Statutory Maternity Pay	1521.70	0.00

8 Click Summary tab on Enter Payments window to confirm the holiday pay entered.

Processing Requirements

This chapter shows you how to produce your pre-update reports so you can check payment details before updating the payroll. Taking backups, correcting errors, processing leavers, restarting employees with the company and placing employees on hold are all explained. You will also learn how to print the P32 Employers Summary Report and are taken through the procedure for correcting processing errors.

Covers

Chapter Eight

Printing Pre-update Reports

Use the Summaries button from the Enter Payments window when you want to generate pre-update reports.

Once processing is complete you must produce your pre-update reports. Several pre-update reports are available for you to use after entering the payment details, for example, payment summary, attachment of earnings summary and update records check report. These reports will help you check payment details before updating the payroll.

To run payroll reports

Use the Reports button from the Application toolbar to provide additional reports, for example, Company, Legislation and Year End.

1. Select from the employee list employees required for pre-update reports.

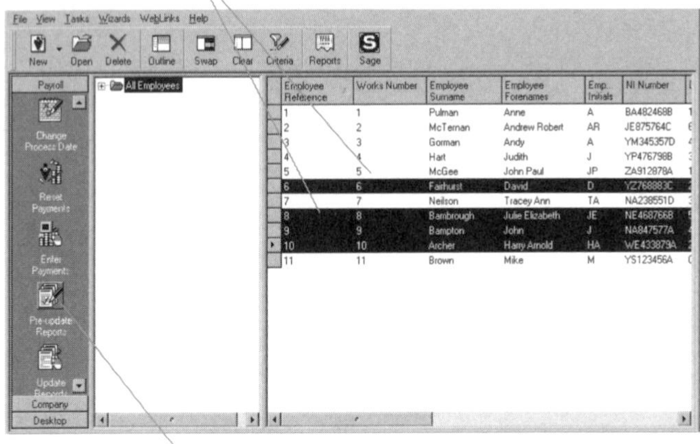

Within Pre-update Reports, the reports are grouped into sections: Payslips, Cheques, BACS, Analysis, Summary and User Defined.

2. Click Pre-update Reports from the Payroll stacked toolbar.
3. Select the type of report you require from the tree view.

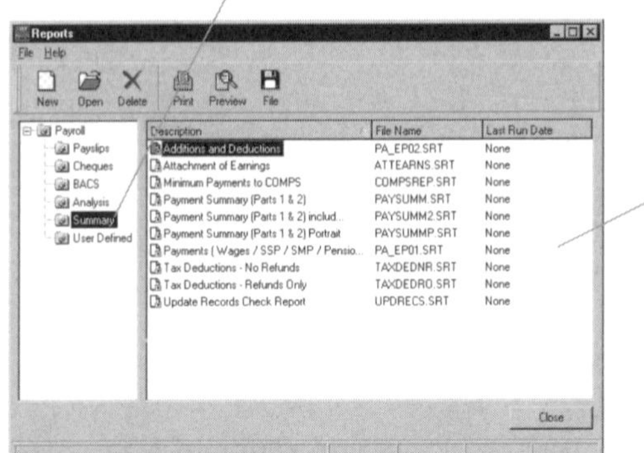

4. The list view contains different reports for each section .

Use the Print button if there is no need to preview a report first.

A report can be saved as a (.SRD) file for preview later. However, the data saved with the file is that as at the time of saving.

5 Select the layout you require.

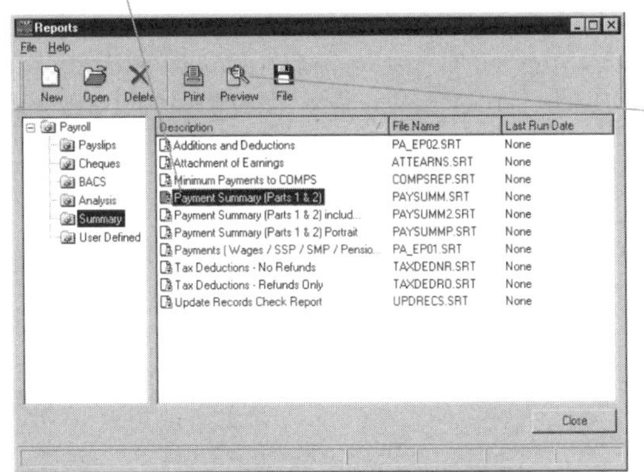

6 Click Preview from the application toolbar.

Check the Payment Summary carefully for discrepancies before updating your records to avoid having to make corrections later.

7 A preview of the report appears on-screen.

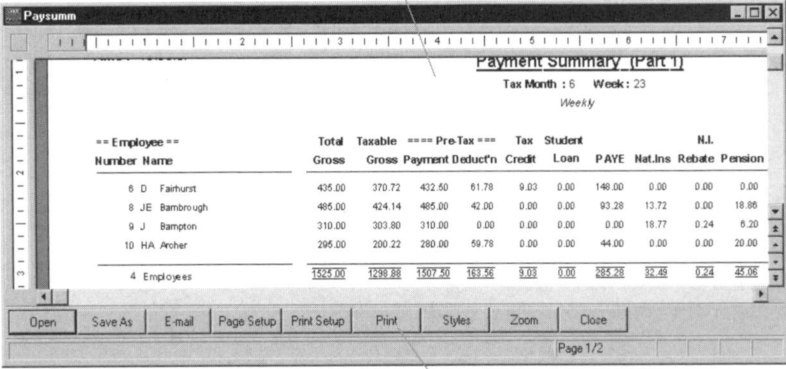

Use the Zoom button to help you display the report at different percentages, in Page width or Full page view.

8 If you require a hardcopy, click the Print button else click Close.

9 Click OK from the Print dialog box unless you need to set up your printer, in which case select Printer or Setup first.

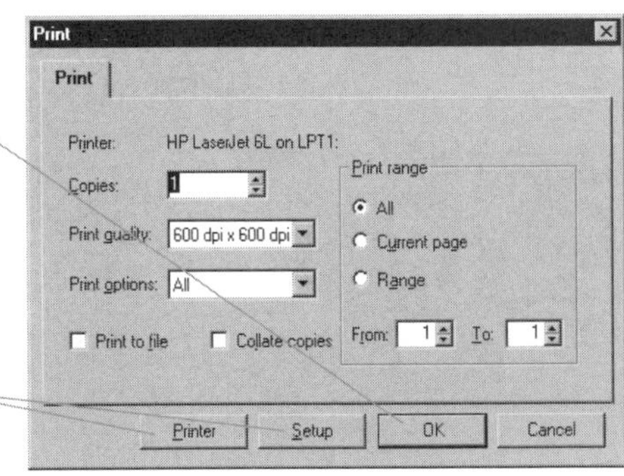

Once you have printed your pre-update reports, you need to make a pre-update backup. See page 102.

Updating your Records

Make a backup whilst using the Update Records Wizard.

After printing pre-update reports and making a pre-update backup it is time to update the employees payment records. The Update Records Wizard will update the cumulative totals, add the current processing period to the P11 deduction cards and maintain historical information. Even the backup is handled by the wizard.

The Backup Wizard allows you to select which files you wish to backup. Data Files is selected as the default setting.

To make a backup

1. From the Payroll stacked toolbar click Update Records.

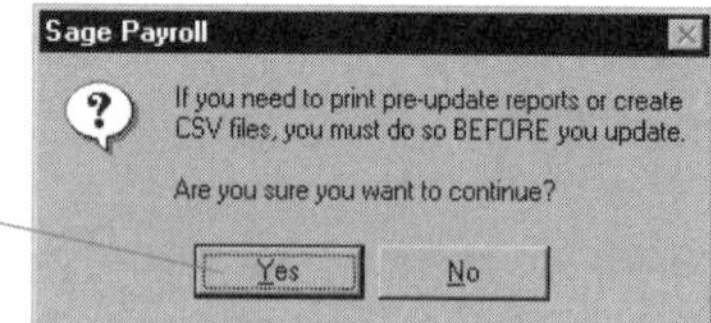

2. Click Yes to close the reminder and continue.

Sage backs up all data files into one file. The filename consists of the word SAGE followed by the tax week, the tax year and a file extension, for example, SAGE2301.001 = Tax Week 23, Tax Year 2001/2002.

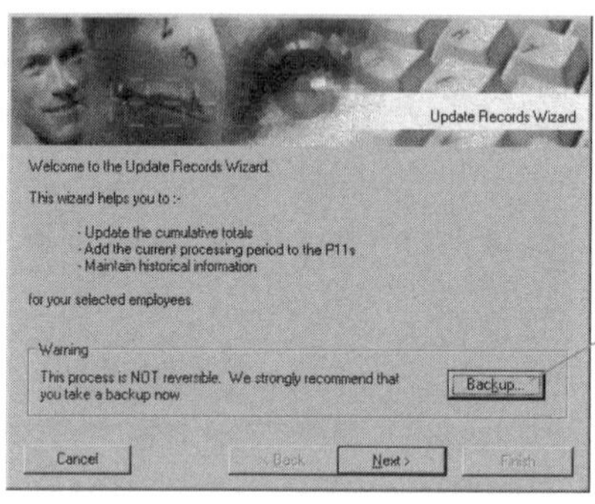

3. On the Update Records Wizard opening screen click the Backup button.

4. The next window shows any previous backups and the path where they are stored. This is the path chosen when you took your first backup and is where subsequent ones will be stored.

After updating your records, you must make a post-update backup.

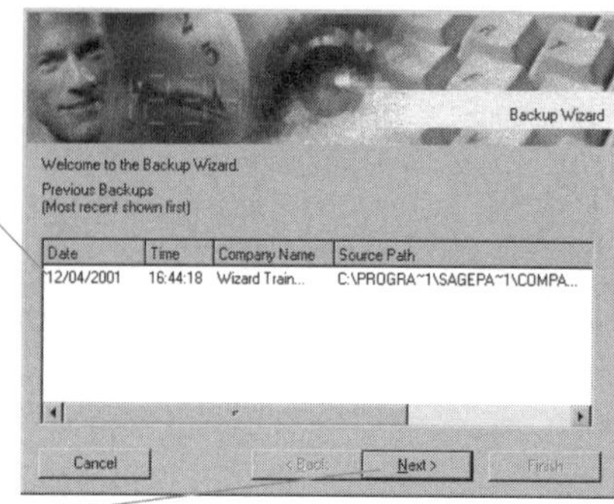

5. Click Next to contiue.

Clearly label your security backup disks to avoid corrupting or deleting important information.

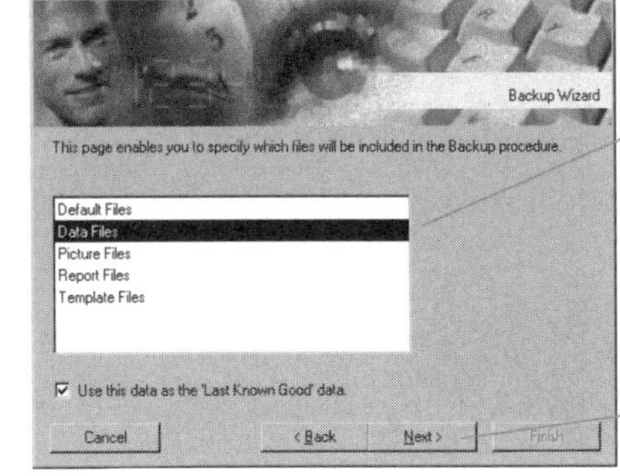

6 Select which files are to be included in the backup. Data Files is the default selection.

7 Click Next to continue.

If records have already been updated and they contain errors, the only way to remove incorrect details is to restore a backup of the data files.

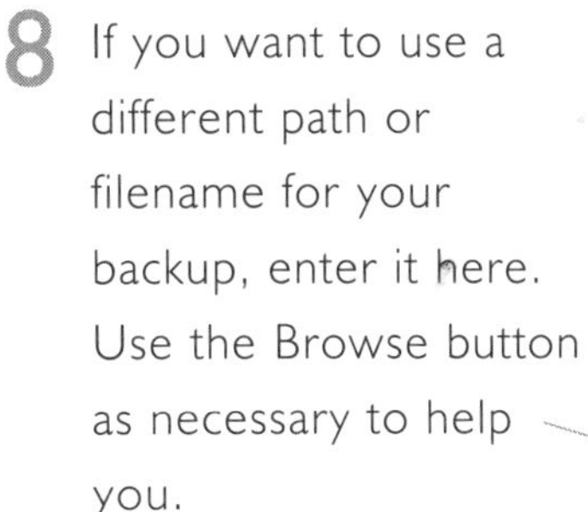

8 If you want to use a different path or filename for your backup, enter it here. Use the Browse button as necessary to help you.

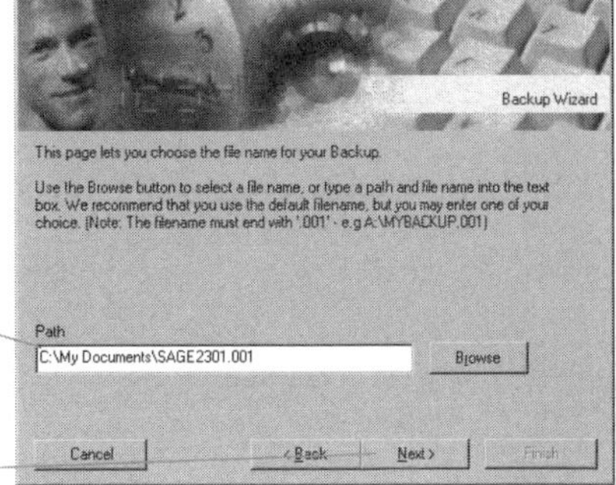

9 Click Next to continue.

Refer to chapter 16 File Maintenance about making backups and restoring data.

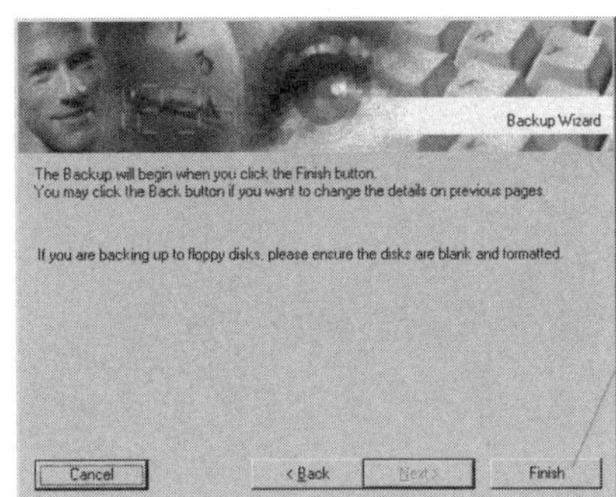

10 Click Finish to create the backup. Remember to have sufficient blank floppy disks available if you are going to backup to Drive A.

If a backup is restored, all payroll frequency types that have been run since the last backup was taken will need to be run again.

11 Backup progress displays here.

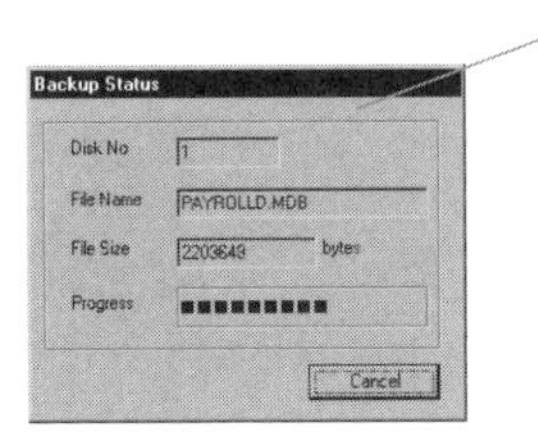

12 Click OK to close.

Check that all processing details on the Update Records Wizard are correct before continuing with the update, for example, all employees have been updated for the previous period.

Updating your records

1. The Update Records Wizard displays information about employees to be updated.

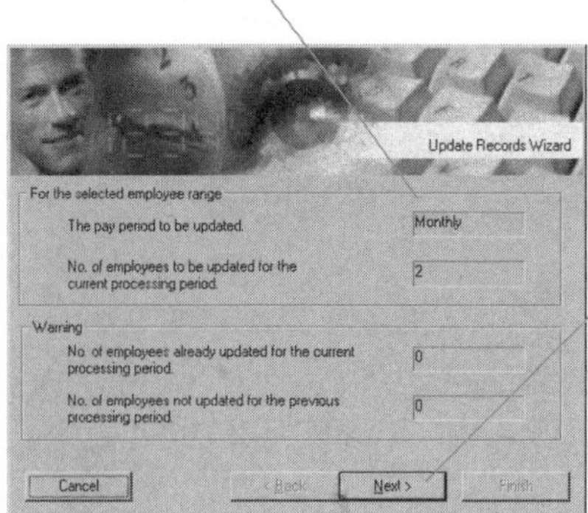

2. Click Next to continue if all details are correct or Cancel to exit.

3. Note Employees' Payroll being recalculated.

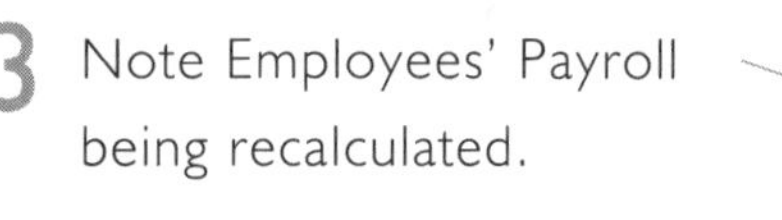

The Previous column indicates whether or not an employee record was updated for the tax period immediately before this one.

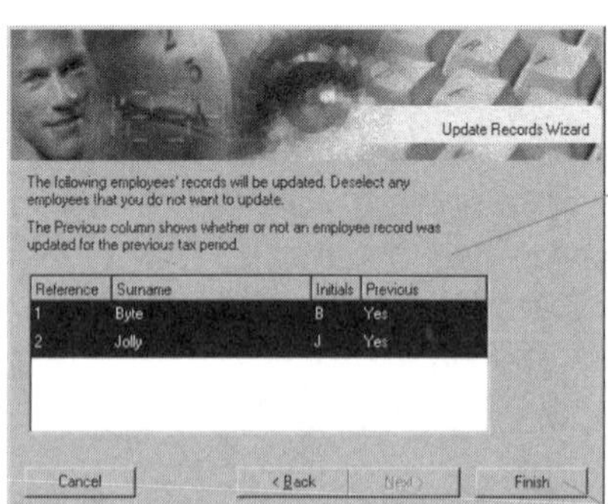

4. A list of employees' records to be processed is displayed. Deselect any records not required.

5. Click Finish to update records.

Let the Nominal Link Wizard guide you through posting your payroll payments directly to your accounts program.

6. Click OK to close the update complete prompt and return to the Payroll desktop.

Posting Nominal Link Payments

Your nominal link settings must be configured before using the Nominal Link.

Once you have updated your payroll, you use the Nominal Link Wizard to process your payroll postings to your accounts data. Also see page 53.

1 Go into your accounts program, i.e., Sage Line 50, and make a backup of your accounts data. This is because posting nominal link payments is not reversible, so if you make a mistake you can at least restore your accounts data and try again.

The Nominal Link can only post one payment type at a time, i.e., monthly, weekly.

2 From the Sage Payroll desktop, click here to list Payment Period type.

3 You cannot process weekly and monthly staff at the same time, so select the required Payment Period here.

To configure your nominal codes, select Nominal Settings from the Company stacked toolbar.

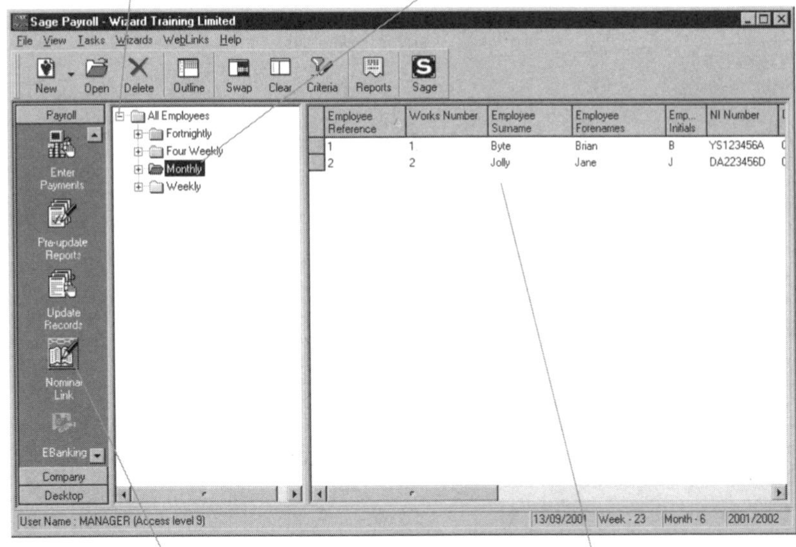

The Nominal Link can only be posted after the payroll has been updated.

4 Employees' details appear in the list view.

5 Click Nominal Link from the Payroll stacked toolbar.

Ensure you have a backup copy of your accounts data before using the Nominal Link Wizard.

6 The Nominal Link Wizard appears, ready to guide you through the stages of posting your payments to the your accounts data.

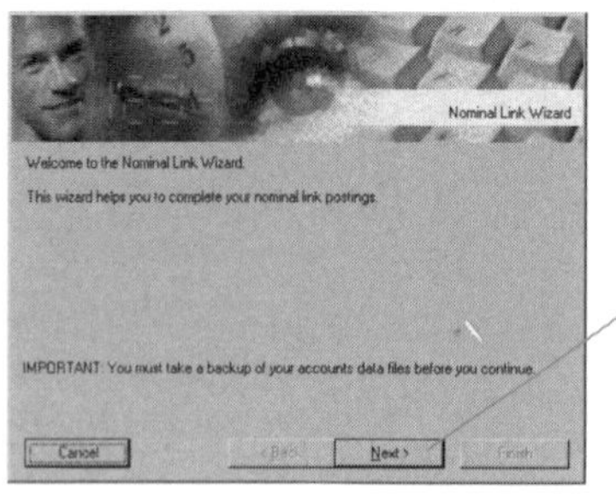

7 Click Next to continue.

If you have difficulty setting up the Nominal Link, always check that you have set up the correct nominal codes in the Analysis tab of the Nominal Link Settings window (see page 49).

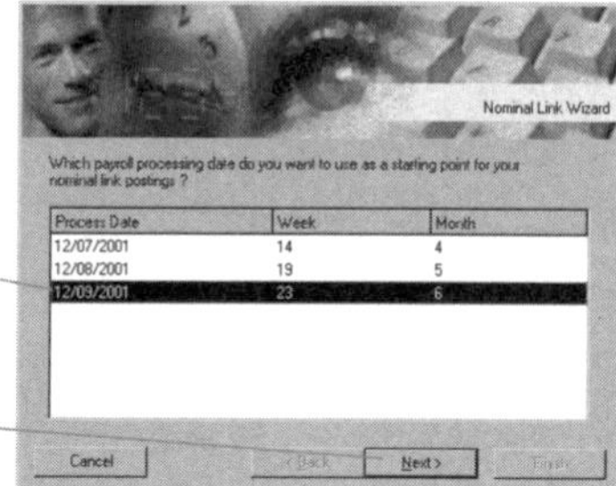

8 Select the process date you require.

9 Click Next to continue.

10 Check information is correct. Use Cancel button if you need to make any change, else click Next.

You will only be given the option of choosing a company if you are using Sage Line 50 multi-company and have more than one company set up.

11 If you have Sage Line 50 multi-company, select the company here, else go to step 12.

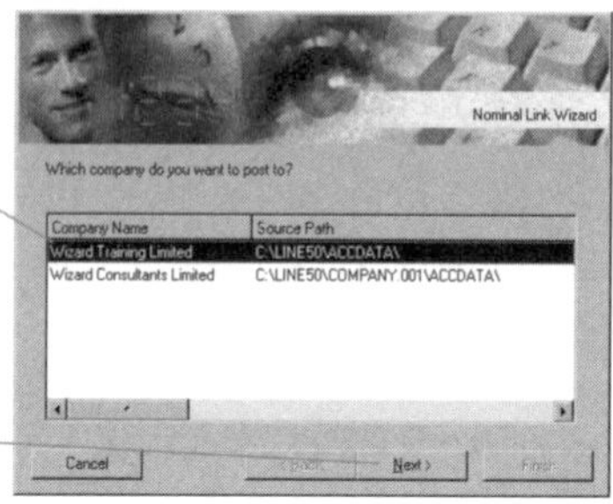

12 Click Next to continue.

It is advisable to print a list of payroll transactions for checking purposes before updating your accounts package.

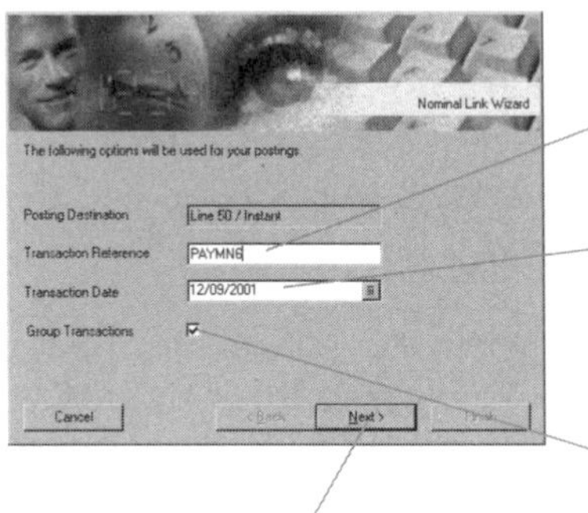

13 Enter a reference here.

14 Process date appears here automatically but another date may be specified.

15 Click here to group nominal codes, or deselect to produce a list of nominal code values for each individual employee.

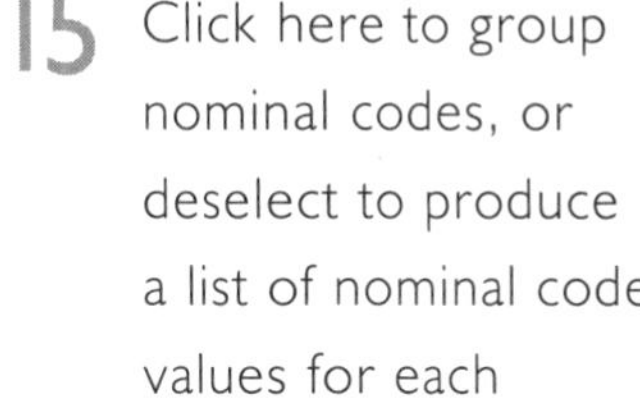

16 Click Next to create a posting file.

Once you have selected Finish the transactions will be added to the audit trail within your Sage accounts package.

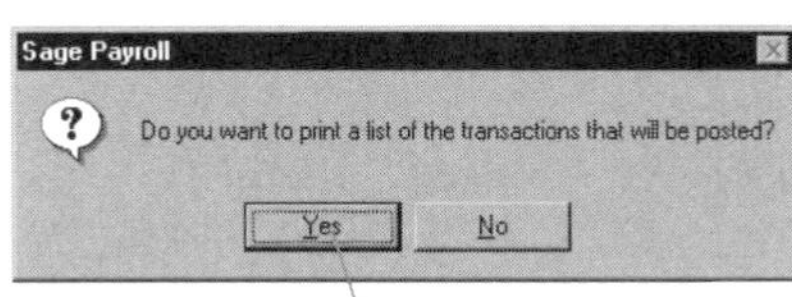

17 Click Yes to print transactions.

18 Then click Print and Close.

If there are discrepancies in the posting information a posting will be made to the Mispostings nominal account.

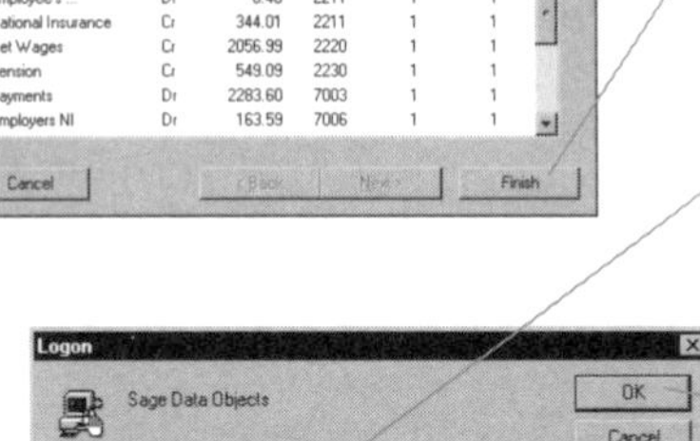

19 Click Finish to post transactions to your accounts program.

20 Enter your accounts Logon Name and Password here.

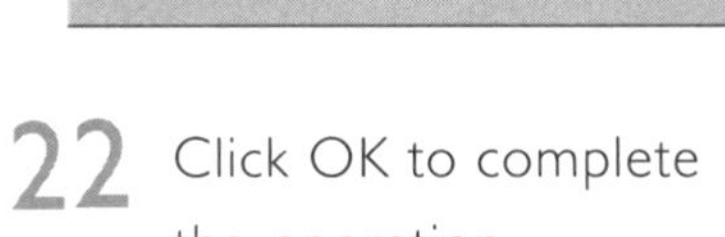

21 Click OK to perform the postings.

22 Click OK to complete the operation.

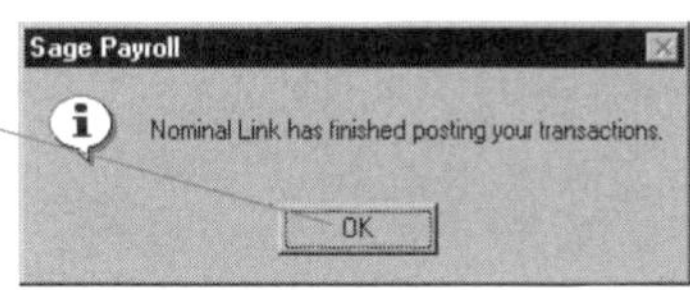

Processing Leavers

An employee must have been included in their final payroll run before they are marked as a leaver.

Employees who have left the company can be marked as leavers after their final payroll payment has been updated. Their employee record will remain on the system until all the Year End procedures have been completed, unless they have a company car.

For leavers with company cars, their details must be retained on the payroll for an additional tax year. This information will be required for Class 1A NIC calculations as explained in chapter six. To mark an employee as a leaver do the following:

Use the Leaver Wizard to produce an employee's P45 and P11 forms.

1. From the Payroll desktop list view, select the Employee Record for the employee you wish to mark as a leaver.

2. Click the Employment tab.

Where an employee's status is changed to a director, the leaving date should be the final payroll run date as a non-director.

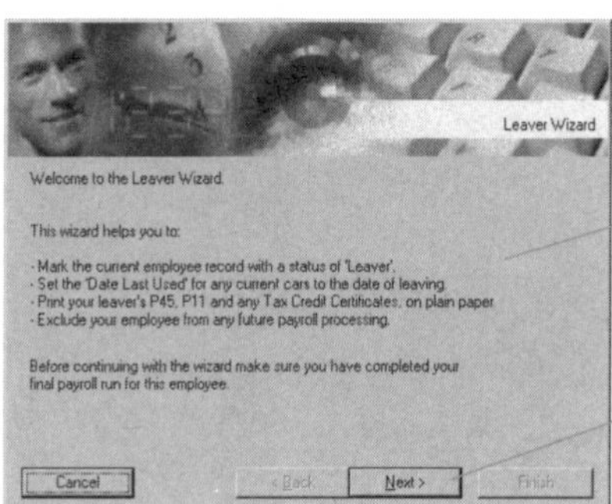

3. Click the Leaver button to start the Leaver Wizard.

4. Click Next to continue.

The employee list displays an employee's Status.

5. Check the details and amend the Leaving Date as necessary.

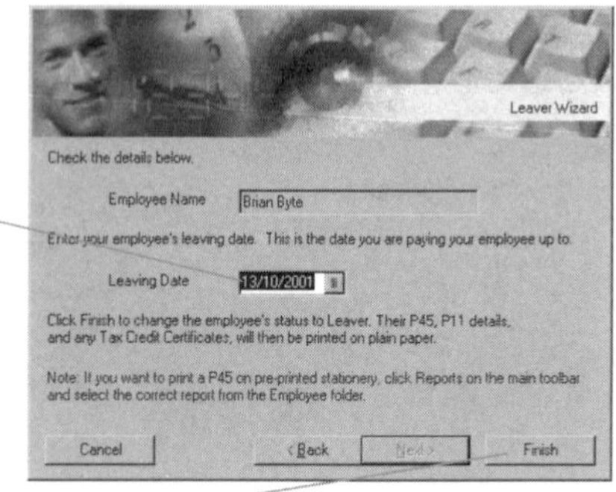

The Leaver button on the Employment tab appears in grey for leavers.

6. Click Finish to change the employee's status to 'Leaver'.

The Print window appears three times to print out the P45, P11 (NIC Details) and P11 (PAYE Details).

7 The Leaver Wizard now takes you through the process of printing out all the relevant documents, one at a time.

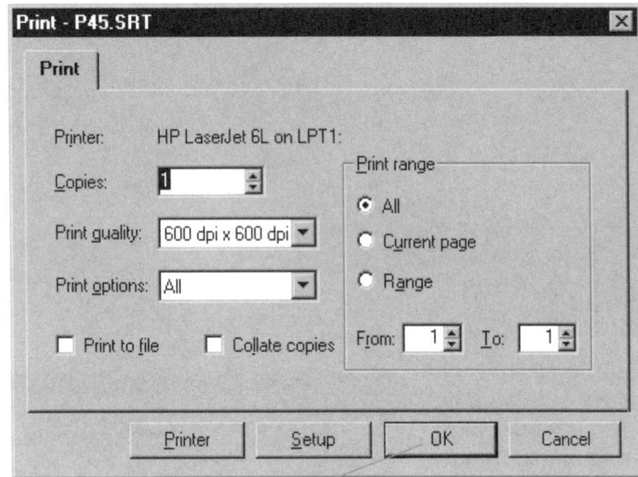

The P45 details report is a guide to help you write out by hand a leaver's P45. It is NOT an acceptable substitute for a P45 form. However, if you require a computer printed P45 use the Reports icon from the main Payroll toolbar, and run the P45 report from the Employee section.

8 Click OK to print the leaver's P45 details.

9 On the next print window, click OK to print the leaver's P11 details (NIC).

10 On the third print window, click OK to print the leaver's P11 details (PAYE).

11 Click OK to return to the Payroll desktop.

To print the P45 report

1 Click Reports from the Application toolbar.

2 From the Employee section select the report required and click the Print button on the application toolbar.

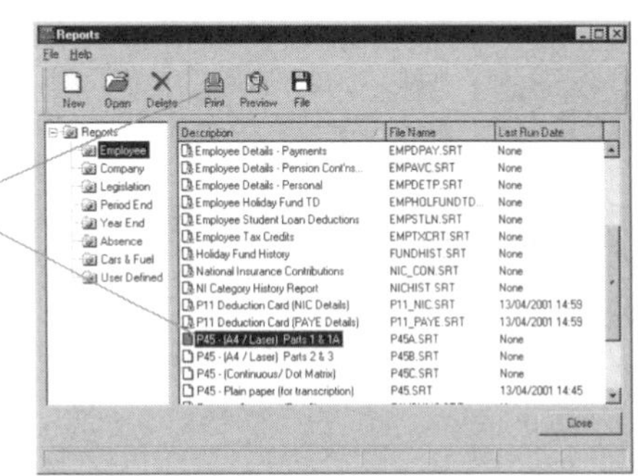

When printing out a P45 report you need to check you have selected the correct stationery and printer type.

P32 Employers Summary Report

Refer to Sage Payroll's Help system for information about Payment to the Collector of Taxes.

When the payroll processing has been completed and the payslips and P45s have been distributed, the P32 Employers Summary report must be printed.

To print the P32 Employers Summary Report:

1. From the Application toolbar click Reports to bring up the Reports window.

2. Select Period End.

3. Select the P32 Employer's Payment record.

4. Click Print.

Payment to the Collector of Taxes can be made in several ways, e.g., cheque, BACS etc. A receipt for payment is not usually issued so it is important to keep a copy of the cheque etc. as proof of payment in case payment is lost in the post, banking system etc.

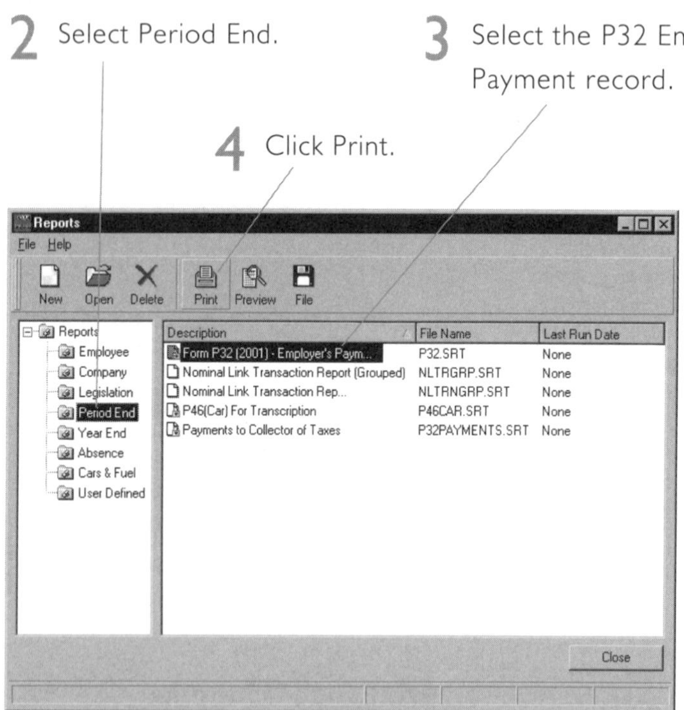

Use the Employee Wizard to create a record as you would with a new employee.

5. Enter From and To Tax Month here.

6. Click OK to continue.

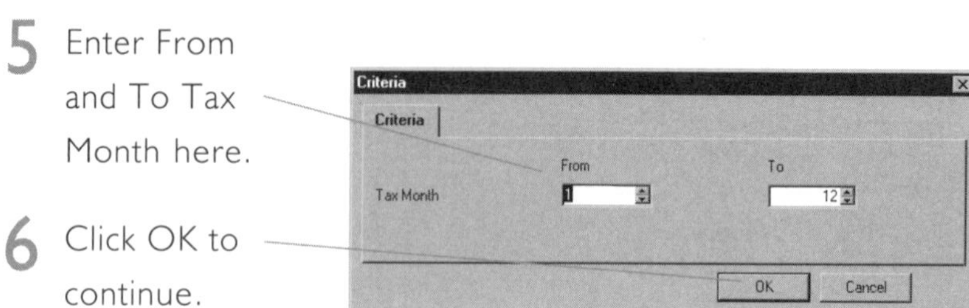

7. Click OK to print out the P32 report.

Changing Payment Frequency

The start of a new tax year is a good time to carry out any payment frequency changes.

If you wish to change the frequency of an employee's pay, for example, monthly instead of weekly, in Sage Payroll V7, simply do the following:

1 Make sure you have posted all outstanding payment transactions for the employee you are about to change.

2 From the Payroll desktop list view, select the Employee Record for the employee you wish to change payment frequency for.

When you mark an employee as a leaver and re-create their details, this means the employee will have two records. At the year end only one P14 per employee can be submitted. The second P14 must be used, which records the cumulative values carried forward.

3 Click the Employment tab.

4 Click here for a list.

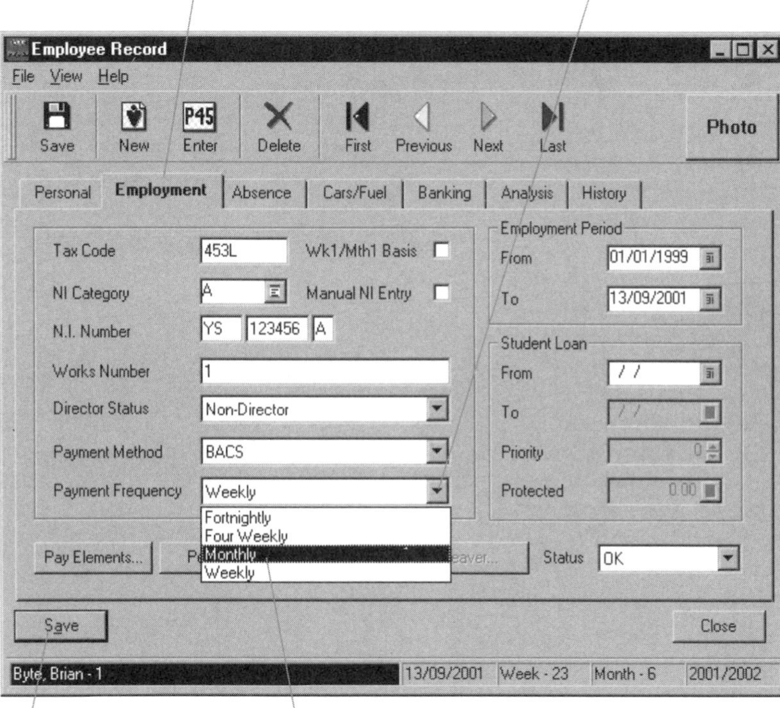

5 Select new frequency.

6 Click Save.

7 Click Yes to confirm.

Sage Payroll

Are you sure you wish to change this employee's Pay Frequency ?

Yes No

You must cross out the first record on the P35 and amend the totals.

Changing to Director Status

Where an employee is flagged as a Director their NIC is calculated on a yearly, cumulative basis, and not on a weekly or monthly basis as it is with other employees.

Sage Payroll lets you change an employee's status to Director at any time during the tax year. Simply do the following:

1 Open the relevant employee's record.

2 Click the Employment tab.

3 Click here for a list.

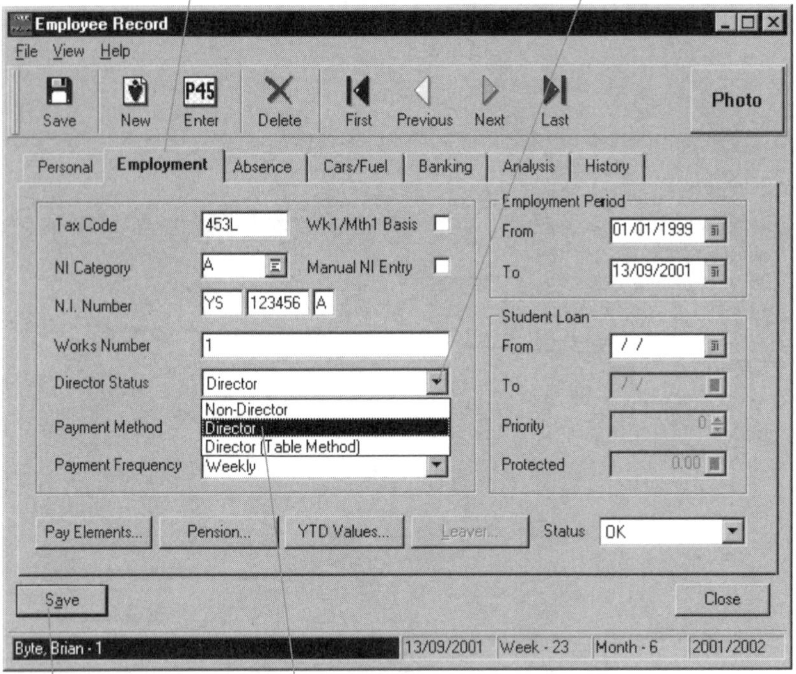

Directors can elect to pay NIC period to period, the same as other employees. To do this, choose Director (Table Method) for Director Status. At the year end, or if the director leaves part-way through a tax year, the NI contributions must be recalculated on a year to date basis. Sage Payroll automatically calculates this for you at the year end, or when you set the Final Pay Run flag for a director who is leaving your company part-way through a tax year.

4 Select relevant Director Status.

5 Note Date Directorship Began prompt.

6 Click OK.

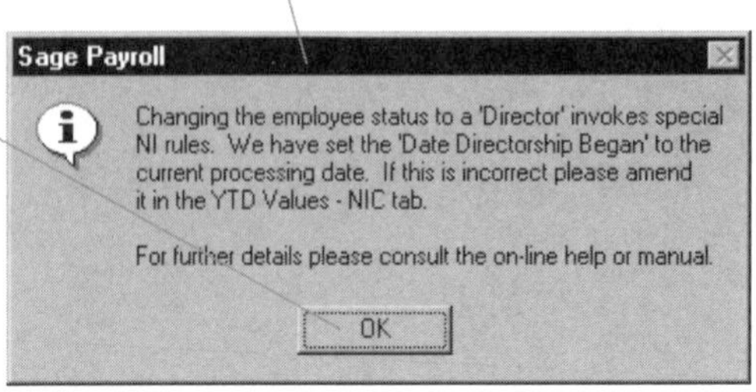

7 Click Save.

Refer to the Sage Help or the Sage Payroll User Guide for additional information about directors.

The Date Directorship Began is automatically set to the current processing date. If the date the actual directorship began is different, you can change it on the Year To Date NIC tab. To do this:

1. On the Employee Record, click the YTD Values button.
2. Click the NIC tab.

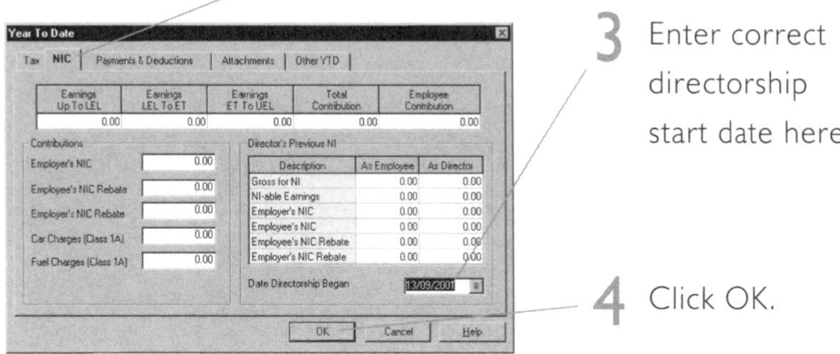

3. Enter correct directorship start date here.
4. Click OK.

Simply deselect the On Hold check box on the Employee Record to include your employee in the payroll processing routine again.

To place employees on hold

The Sage Payroll program provides the facility to place employees on hold, for example, if an employee is employed on a casual basis but not working for you at the moment. To temporarily exclude them from the payroll processing routine, they need to be placed on hold and then taken off hold when they return to paid work.

Where employees leave your company and return within the same tax year, they must be added to the payroll as a new employee. You cannot reactivate their old employee record.

1. Select the employee's Employee Record.

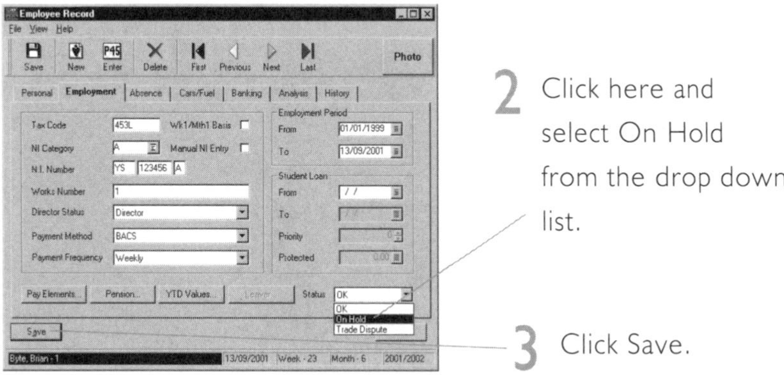

2. Click here and select On Hold from the drop down list.
3. Click Save.

Correcting Errors with Roll Back

The Roll Back Employee Wizard is irreversible so always take a backup before you use it.

Sage Payroll enables the user to correct processing errors for one or more employees. The employee's basic record and car mileage details will not be affected, but all histories, absence records (SSP and SMP and holiday), cumulative values and update records will be amended. To use the Roll Back Employee Wizard do the following:

1. Click Roll Back from the Tasks menu.
2. Click here to first make a backup.

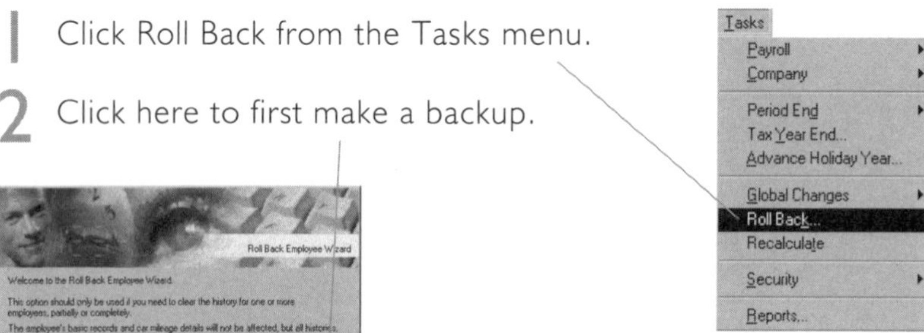

If you have made any changes to your employee's payment details, use the Recalculate option from the Tasks menu to recalculate the payroll for the selected employees for the current process date.

3. Click Next.

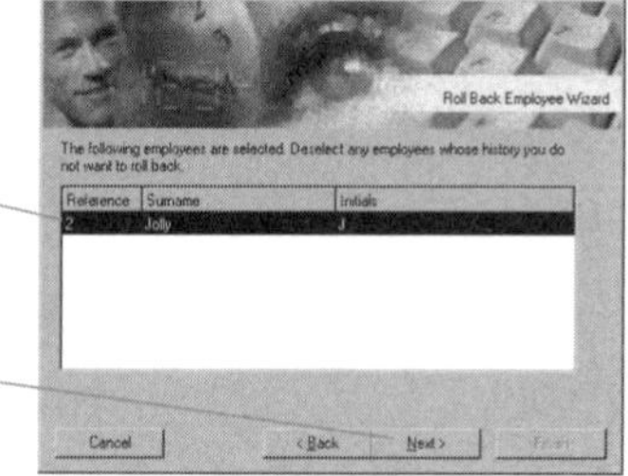

4. Make sure only the relevant employee is selected.
5. Click Next.

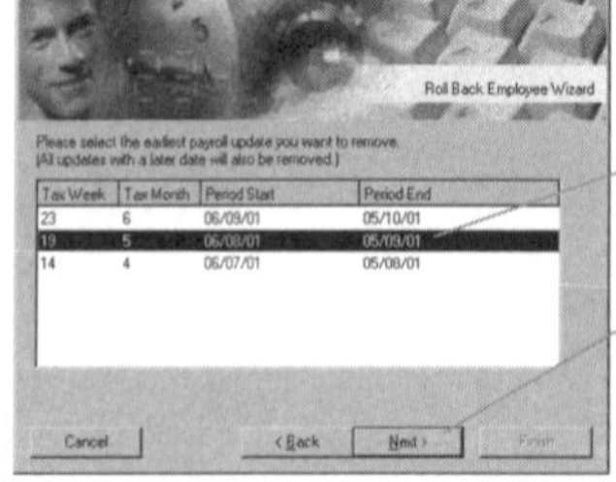

6. Choose Date to remove.
7. Click Next.

8. Click Finish.

After a rollback, reprocessed periods MUST be reconciled with actual employee payments, returns sent to the IR and postings made to your accounts.

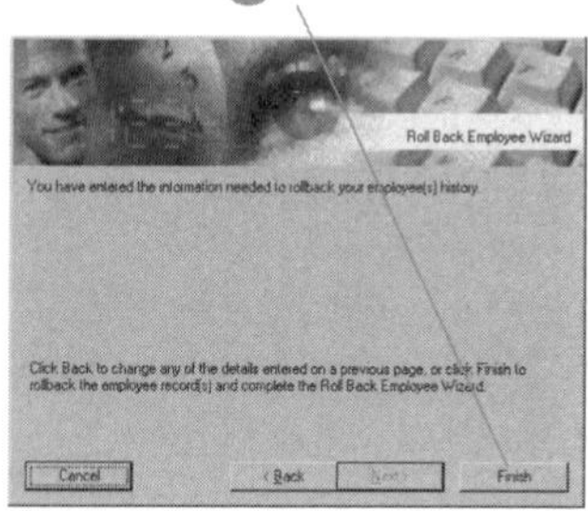

To use Recalculate

1. Select employee record and click Recalculate from Tools menu.
2. Click Yes to confirm.

Statutory Sick Pay

Chapter Nine

This chapter shows you how to set up and maintain your employees' Statutory Sick Pay. You will learn how to enter an employee's SSP details and view their automatically calculated SSP 8 Weeks Gross Pay. This chapter also includes tips to help solve problems you may experience while trying to calculate and process your SSP payments.

Covers

Introduction to Statutory Sick Pay

From 6 April 1986 employers have been responsible for paying Statutory Sick Pay (SSP) to employees who are ill for a period up to 28 weeks.

To be eligible for SSP the employee's average weekly earnings must be above the lower earnings limit for National Insurance Contributions (NICs). The average weekly earnings are calculated from the previous eight weeks' pay.

You need to be familiar with the following SSP terms.

PIW = Period of Incapacity for Work of four or more continuous calendar days (PIWs can be linked)
QD = Qualifying Day
WD = Waiting Day

SSP qualifying conditions

The majority of employees are eligible for SSP providing they meet the following criteria:

- An employee must be over 16 and under 65 years of age.
- The employee must be sick and absent from work for a minimum of four consecutive days (this includes holidays, weekends and any other day which the employee is not normally expected to work).
- The employee's average gross pay for the eight weeks immediately prior to the first day of sickness mustbe equal to or greater than the NI lower earnings limit for weekly paid employees.
- SSP is not payable for the first three qualifying days of the period of sickness. These days are known as Waiting Days.
- Where an employee has two PIWs with 56 or less days between the end of the first PIW and the start of the second PIW, the two PIWs are said to be linked and count as one continuous PIW. The employee then does not need any further Waiting Days before SSP starts.
- Employees are entitled to a maximum of 28 weeks SSP within one period or two linked PIWs.

A linked PIW is eight weeks or 56 days.

If a period of sickness is linked the employee must be absent for no less than four consecutive days to receive SSP for the waiting days.

SSP Checklist

Refer to your Sage Payroll Help for more information about linking PIWs.

Employers have certain responsibilities. These include establishing if an employee is eligible for SSP, the correct SSP is paid for up to a maximum of 28 weeks and that appropriate tax and NI deductions are paid. The Inland Revenue requires that the following SSP records be kept.

For employers who operate SSP, records must include:

- Dates of sickness lasting at least four days.
- All payments of SSP.

Agency Workers/ Contract Workers are not eligible for SSP as they are normally employed on a limited contract of employment. The contract ends when this person, for whatever reason is no longer available for work. Where a person is employed on a short term contract, for three months or less, they are not covered by the SSP scheme.

For employers who do not operate SSP, they must record:

- First and last day that SSP liability arises.
- Number of weeks and days of SSP entitlement.
- Number of SSP qualifying days.

To help you through the stages of processing your sick pay, work through the checklist below:

- Are Qualifying Day Patterns set up?
- Has the employee been absent for four or more days in a row?
- Has a notice of sickness been received?
- Is the employee eligible for SSP?
- Are the absence days qualifying days?
- Check the employee's last eight weeks average earnings. They must not be less than the lower earnings limit for NI to qualify for SSP.
- Check whether the employee has had an earlier period of absence within the last eight weeks. If so, the two PIWs may link.
- Decide which are the qualifying days for SSP.
- Process the SSP at the same time as you process an employee's normal earnings.

When unsure about an employee's SSP entitlement, contact your local Inland Revenue (Contributions) Office.

Employee's SSP Qualifying Days

Qualifying days need setting up BEFORE you process SSP.

Qualifying days are days agreed between the employer and employee. These days are normally when the employee is contractually required to be available for work, for example, Monday to Friday.

Once the days are agreed, a qualifying pattern needs allocating to each employee identifying the qualifying days for SSP entitlement. To set up your qualifying days do the following:

The SSP qualifying patterns are set up on the Absence tab of the Company Settings window from the Company stacked toolbar.

More than one qualifying pattern can be assigned to an employee, for example, if they are a shift worker and have different work patterns.

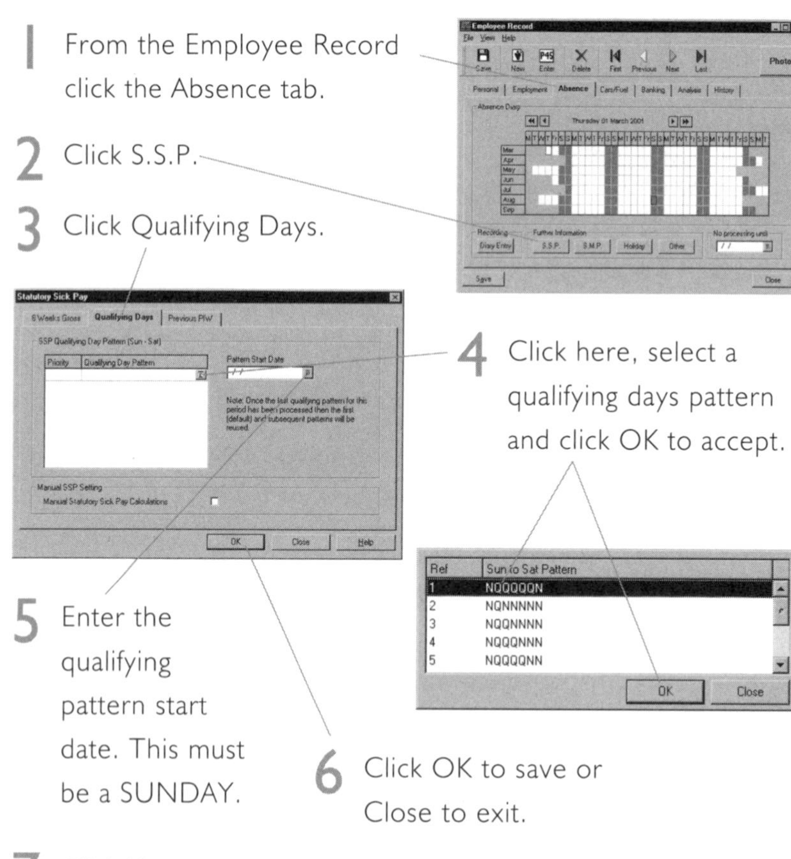

1. From the Employee Record click the Absence tab.
2. Click S.S.P.
3. Click Qualifying Days.
4. Click here, select a qualifying days pattern and click OK to accept.
5. Enter the qualifying pattern start date. This must be a SUNDAY.
6. Click OK to save or Close to exit.
7. Click Yes to confirm changes or No to return to the Qualifying Days screen.

The first qualifying pattern becomes effective again after all other available patterns have been used.

SSP 8 Weeks Gross Pay

When recording previous sickness you must: 1 - enter gross pay received prior to the previous sickness, 2 - enter PIW date and 3 - record payments made to the employee in the eight weeks prior to that date. SSP can then be calculated providing qualifying conditions are met.

To be eligible for SSP an employee's average weekly earnings must be above the lower earnings limit for NICs. Average weekly earnings are calculated by Sage Payroll from the previous eight weeks pay. To view an employee's SSP 8 weeks gross pay do the following:

1. Select your employee, and from their Employee Record click the Absence tab.
2. Click the S.S.P. button.
3. Note details of Tax Week, Tax Month and Gross Pay are displayed here.
4. This example shows the first absence date for an unlinked PIW.
5. Note your employee's 8 Weeks Average Gross Pay is calculated for you.

The Start of PIW field is the first date of an unlinked PIW. It must be a minimum of four consecutive days' illness and not linked to an earlier period of sickness.

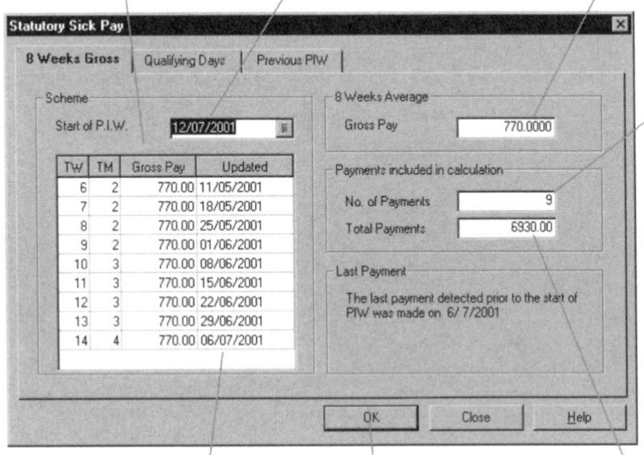

6. Number of payments up to the PIW are shown here.
7. Total value for payments made within the eight weeks.
8. These dates show when the payroll records were last updated for each tax week.
9. After checking the figures click OK to return to the Absence tab.

To quickly record an employee's absence use the Employee Record, Absence tab, Diary Entry button.

Recording Current Sickness

Half days are not applicable to SSP.

Absence through sickness for an employee is recorded using the Diary Entry button on the Absence tab of their Employee Record. Note that the AM/PM option is not available because half days do not count for SSP. To enter your employee's sickness details, follow the steps below:

For more information about SSP for this employee click the S.S.P. button on the Absence tab.

1 From the Employee Record click Absence tab.

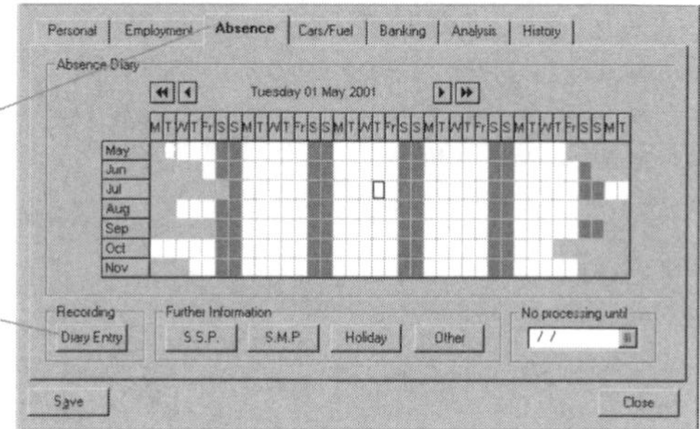

2 Click Diary Entry to record sickness.

To run a detailed report about SSP absence click Reports from the Payroll toolbar and select Absence, Detailed SSP Analysis.

3 In Absence Type select SSP.

4 Further details can be selected here.

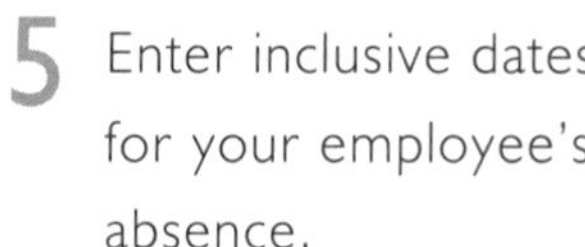

5 Enter inclusive dates for your employee's absence.

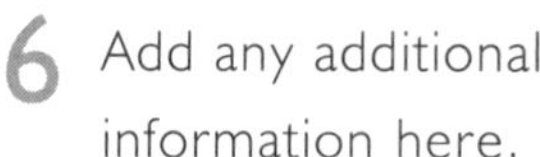

6 Add any additional information here.

7 Click OK to save changes or Cancel to abandon.

Check the Summary tab to view your employee's employee's SSP.

Absences can also be recorded by highlighting dates, clicking right mouse button and entering details from pop-up options.

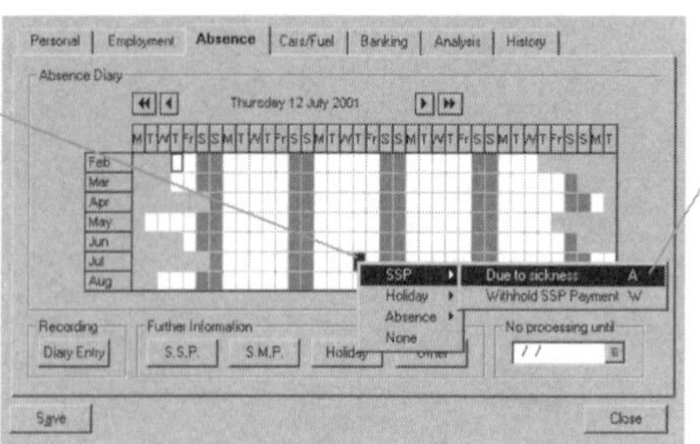

8 Method Two - use the Absence tab to record all types of absence directly. See Hot Tip opposite.

Entering SSP Manually

BEFORE you enter your employee's SSP manually you must select the Manual Statutory Sick Pay Calculations check box on the Qualifying Days tab.

If an employee has just started work with your company, the previous eight weeks' pay must be entered manually into the Gross Pay field before Sage Payroll can automatically calculate SSP.

For occasions where you need to enter an employee's SSP manually, do the following:

1 Select your employee, and from their Employee Record click the Absence tab.

2 Click the S.S.P. button and select Qualifying Days.

3 Click here to enter SSP details manually.

4 Click OK to save and return to the Absence tab.

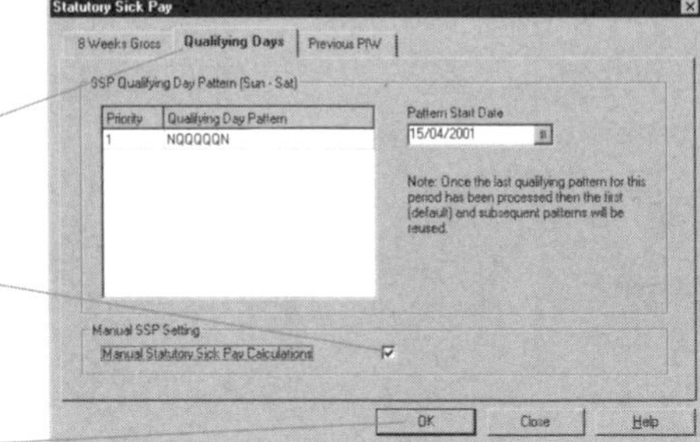

5 Click Close and Yes to return to the desktop.

6 To enter your employee's sick pay manually, click Enter Payments from the Payroll stacked toolbar.

7 Select SSP/SMP tab.

8 Click S.S.P. button.

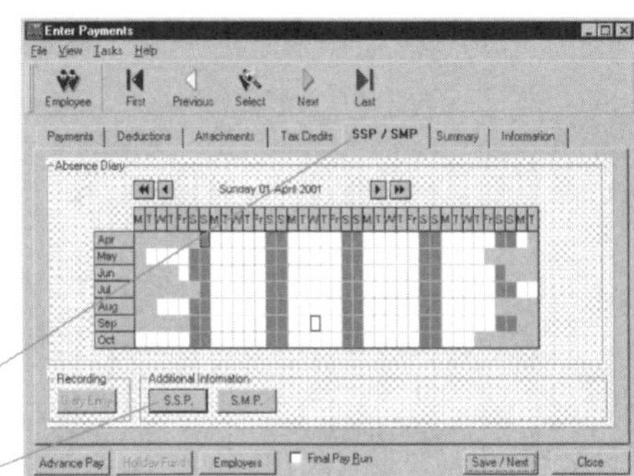

The SSP Diary Report is useful for viewing absence details in table form and provides the employee's Qualifying Day Pattern and PIW Linkage Records.

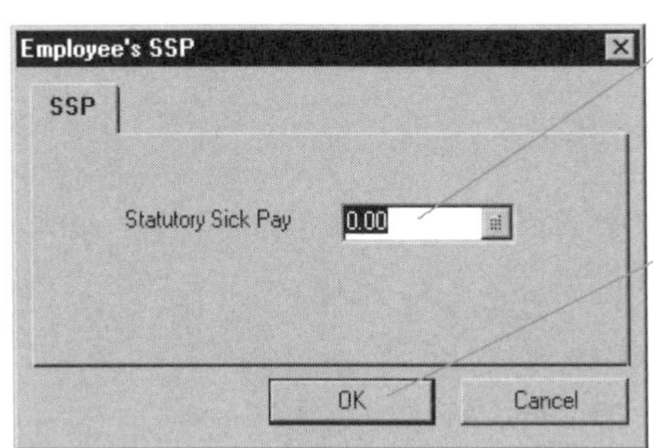

9 Enter your employee's SSP figure here.

10 Click OK to save changes and return to the SSP/SMP window.

SSP Calculation and Recovery

Ask the Inland Revenue for copies of 'Employer's Quick Guide to PAYE and NICs' and further guides to PAYE and NICs.

As Government Legislation often changes, it is important that you ensure all your manual and computerised information is accurate and up to date in order to produce the correct figures when processing your payroll.

It is important to understand how certain information is calculated. Below are a couple of examples which show you how to manually calculate SSP and work out any SSP to reclaim.

To manually calculate the amount of SSP due

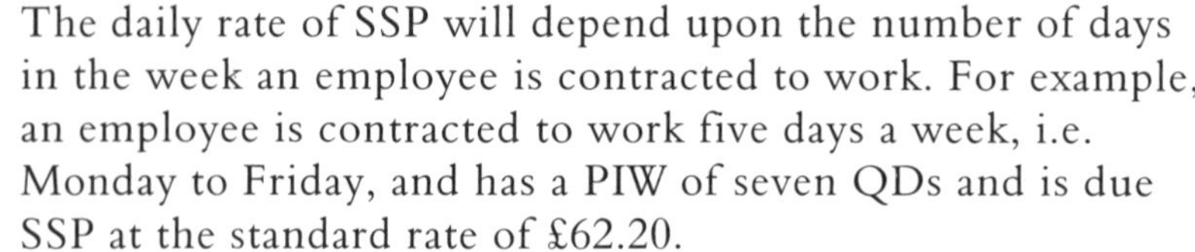

The daily rate of SSP will depend upon the number of days in the week an employee is contracted to work. For example, an employee is contracted to work five days a week, i.e. Monday to Friday, and has a PIW of seven QDs and is due SSP at the standard rate of £62.20.

You must record any SSP Funding from the Inland Revenue to compensate for any tax refunds paid to employees. Use the SSP/SMP Funding tab from Company Settings.

The SSP payable is calculated as follows:

1) 7 QDs less 3 WDs = 4 QDs for which SSP is payable

2) Daily rate of SSP is calculated as £62.20 ÷ 5 = £12.44

3) SSP payable is £12.44 × 4, the 4 QDs after the 3 WDs

4) SSP payable = £49.76.

To recover SSP

To check if you can reclaim any SSP you need to calculate 13% of your company gross NIC for the relevant tax month. If the amount of SSP you paid in this month is higher than the 13% figure, you can claim the difference, for example:

The P32 report details information about any SSP recovery. These details are also reported at Year End using the P35 Form.

13% of £1000 gross NIC = £130

If 2 weeks SSP was paid @ 62.20 a week = £124.40

Therefore, £5.60 can be recovered.

(Note: the SSP weekly rate was £62.20 as at 1 April 2001.)

SSP Handy Tips

For an employee who works Monday to Friday, the Qualifying Pattern should read NQQQQQN. N is a non-qualifying day and Q is a day the employee works.

There may be times when your SSP is not calculating properly, for example, when an employee has the incorrect qualifying pattern set up. Other reasons include the length of absence may be insufficient for the second PIW; sickness may not have been entered, where appropriate, on non-qualifying days, e.g., weekends; an employee's earnings may be below the lower earnings limit for National Insurance; the employee's 8 weeks gross pay has not been entered; the wrong sickness date is entered accidentally.

The following information shows you how to quickly check and resolve any SSP problems.

To check the employee has the correct qualifying pattern

Check that Pattern Start Date is at least the Sunday prior to the first day of sickness.

1. From the employee's Absence tab, click S.S.P.

2. From the Qualifying Days tab check your employee's qualifying pattern is set correctly.

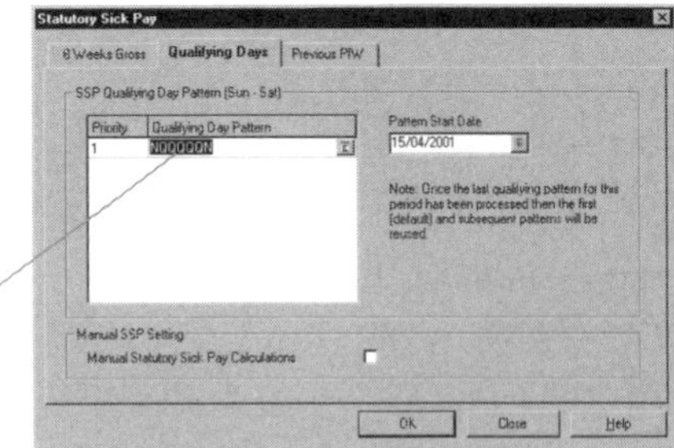

Use SSP Diary Report to quickly view and check absence details.

To check Linked Periods of Incapacity for Work

1. From the Absence Diary check that your employee's second PIW's absence length is four or more consecutive days.

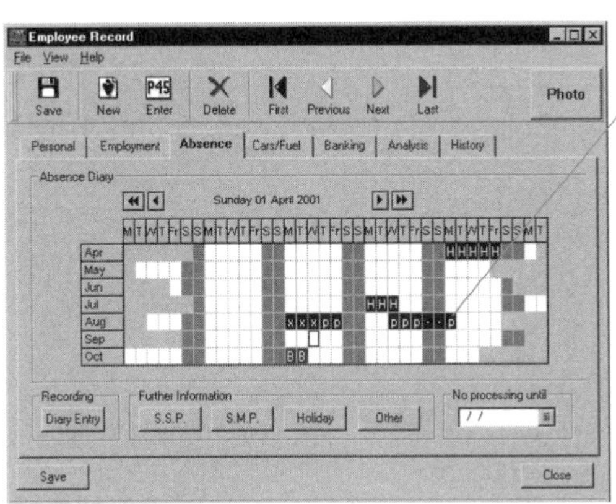

To view an employee's previous PIW, select their Employee Record, Absence tab, S.S.P button and click Previous PIW.

Entering sickness on non-qualifying dates where appropriate ensures that ongoing periods of SSP link correctly.

To check and enter average earnings

1 Using the 8 Weeks Gross window from your employee's record enter sickness start date.

2 Press TAB and enter previous 8 weeks gross pay here.

3 Ensure that this figure is greater than the lower earnings limit.

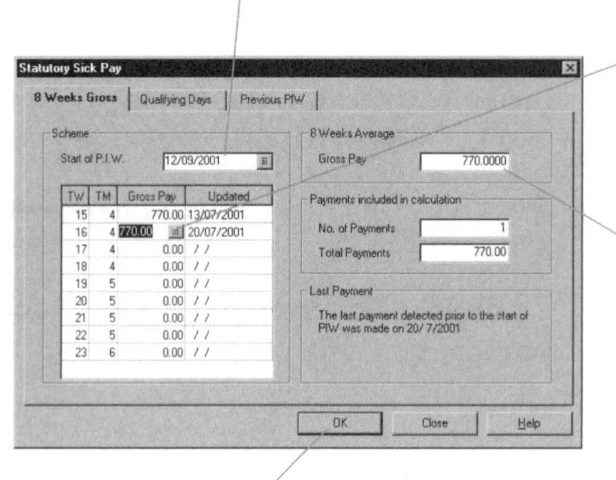

4 Click OK to close.

The warning message 'Average Earnings Too Low' appears after entering SSP dates in the Absence Diary because the employee earns below the lower earnings limit for NI or the 8 weeks gross pay for this employee has not been entered.

To delete the wrong sickness dates before update

1 Select the incorrectly entered dates from your employee's Absence Diary

2 Click right mouse button and select None from the drop-down list.

3 Click left mouse button to accept change.

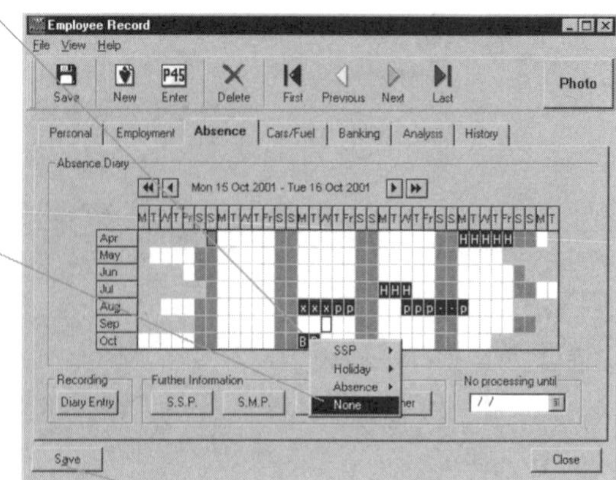

4 Note the entry is now cleared.

5 Click Save.

Delete wrong dates by selecting Diary Entry and choosing None.

Statutory Maternity Pay

This chapter shows you how to enter Statutory Maternity Payments, view any SMP entitlement, check your employee's SMP 8 weeks gross pay and enter an employee's SMP manually. The chapter finishes with some SMP tips.

Covers

Chapter Ten

Introduction

Refer to Sage Payroll Help for additional information about SMP.

In 1987 a Statutory Maternity Pay scheme was introduced to provide expectant mothers with maternity pay for a maximum of 18 weeks. Payment is based upon the employee's average earnings calculated from the eight weeks' pay immediately before the Qualifying Week and is automatically calculated for you by Sage Payroll.

Familiarise yourself with the following five SMP terms:

SMP queries, not relating to the Payroll program should be directed to the local Department of Social Security.

EWC = Expected Week of Confinement. This week starts on a Sunday

QW = Qualifying Week. This is 15 weeks before the week the baby is due. A woman has to have been employed for 26 weeks before the QW to be eligible for SMP

MPP = Maternity Pay Period (max. of 18 weeks)

MLP = Maternity Leave Period (max. of 14 weeks)

EML = Extended Maternity Leave. This can be up to 29 weeks after the birth.

To view SMP Legislation Settings select Government Legislation option from Company stacked toolbar, then SMP Rates.

To help you determine whether an employee is entitled to SMP check through the following list.

SMP Qualifying Conditions:

- Average earnings must be above the lower earnings limit for National Insurance.
- Employee must have been continuously employed for at least 26 weeks immediately before the QW.
- Notice must be given of the date when her MPP is due to start at least 21 days beforehand.
- Has medical evidence been given of the date her baby is due within three weeks of the start of her MPP?
- Employee must still be pregnant at the 11th week before the baby is due, or have had her baby by then.
- Employee must have stopped working for you.

The employee must satisfy all six conditions to qualify for SMP, whether or not she wishes to return to work after the baby's birth.

SMP Processing Checklist

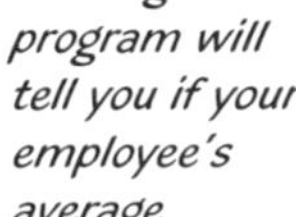

The Sage program will tell you if your employee's average earnings are too low to claim SMP.

When getting ready to process any SMP payments use the checklist below to help you:

- Does your employee meet all the qualifying conditions?
- Have you received medical evidence from your employee, including the date the baby is due?
- Your employee needs to give notice of the date her MPP is due to start at least 21 days beforehand.
- Has your employee been continuously employed by you for 26 weeks before the qualifying weeks?
- Check that your employee's last eight weeks' average earnings are not less than the lower earnings limit for National Insurance.
- Calculate your employee's qualifying week and enter it onto the system using the SMP tab.
- Has the employee now stopped working for you?

The qualifying week is the week commencing the Sunday prior to the 15 weeks before the baby is due (Expected Week of Confinement). Sage Payroll automatically records this date from the EWC date you enter in the SMP dates tab.

To manually calculate the amount of SMP due to an employee follow the example below:

An employee's average weekly earnings in the Qualifying Week are £200. A higher rate of SMP is calculated as 90% of average weekly earnings:

i.e. 90% x £200.00 = £180.00

This higher rate of SMP is payable for six weeks:

i.e. 6 x £180.00 = £1,080.00

Lower rate of SMP then payable for remaining 12 weeks:

i.e. 12 x £62.20 = £746.40

Therefore, the total SMP payable is:

£1,080.00 + £746.40 = £1,826.40

The higher rate of SMP is payable for six weeks and the lower rate of SMP is then payable for the remaining 12 weeks.

Entering Maternity Pay Details

Refer to chapter 7 for information about processing an employee's SMP.

To ensure your employee receives the correct amount of Statutory Maternity Pay, it is important that the correct dates are recorded. To enter your employee's details once all the information is available, follow the steps below:

1. Select your employee, and from their Employment Record, click Absence, then S.M.P. button.

The baby's arrival date needed for the Expected On (EWC) field is normally found on the Mat B1 maternity certificate.

2. From the Statutory Maternity Pay window click Dates tab.

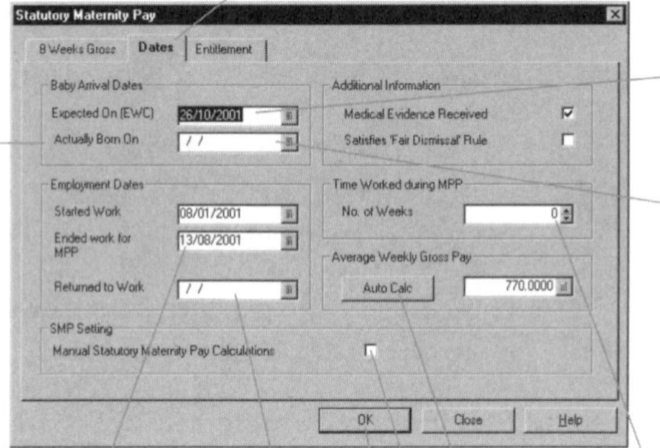

3. Enter date baby is due.

4. When known, enter baby's actual date of birth.

EWC is the term describing the Expected Week of Confinement, which begins on a Sunday.

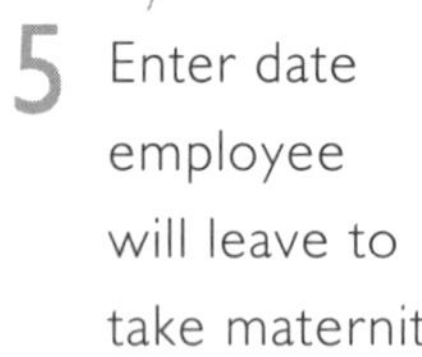

5. Enter date employee will leave to take maternity absence.

6. Enter this date once employee has returned to work.

7. If employee has worked during MPP, enter number of full or part weeks.

8. Auto Calc will generate Average Weekly Earnings.

9. Click here only if you need to enter employee payments manually.

10. Click OK to save.

If an employee is fairly dismissed by her employer she can still qualify for SMP. Tick the Satisfies 'Fair Dismissal' Rule check box if this applies.

Note: When you next process your payroll, the employee's SMP will be calculated and be displayed on the Summary tab of the Enter Payments window.

Viewing SMP Entitlement

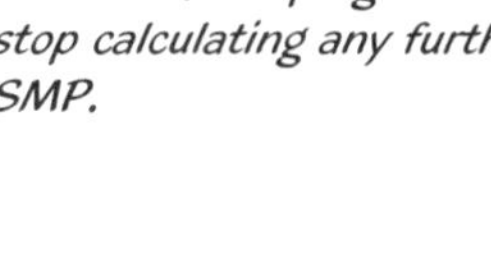

Once an employee has received her full SMP entitlement of 18 weeks, the program will stop calculating any further SMP.

The Entitlement tab displays information about an employee's Statutory Maternity Pay. It details the start of the employee's maternity pay period, the total SMP entitlement and the sum amount currently due. To view SMP entitlement do as follows:

An employee's cumulative values for SMP are stored with the Employee Record, YTD Values and are updated during payroll processing.

If you are processing an employee's payment, you can view their SMP entitlement by clicking the S.M.P. button from the SSP/SMP tab within Enter Payments.

1. From your selected Employee Record, select the Absence tab and then click the S.M.P. button.

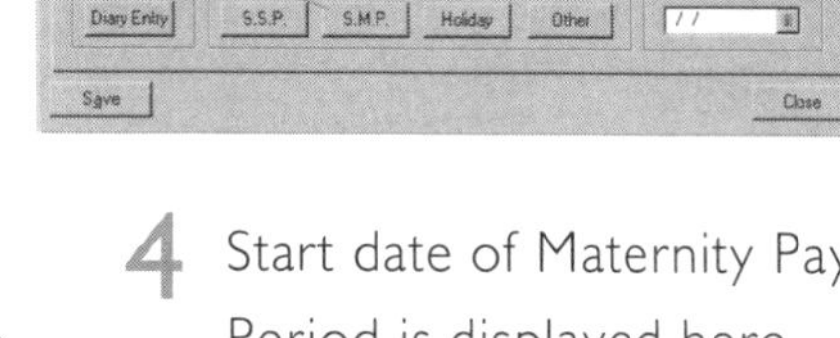

2. Select the Entitlement tab in the Statutory Maternity Pay window.
3. Note the first Sunday of the Qualifying Week appears here.
4. Start date of Maternity Pay Period is displayed here.

Statutory Maternity Pay

8 Weeks Gross | Dates | **Entitlement**

Periods

Start of Qualifying Week: 08/07/2001 — Start of Maternity Pay Period: 19/08/2001

Details

SMP	Weeks	Amount
Previously Paid	0	0.00
Currently Due	5	3465.00
Total	5	3465.00

To qualify for full entitlement of SMP, the MPP must begin between 5/8/2001 and 28/10/2001 (inclusive).

Entitlement	Weeks	Rate	Amount
Higher Rate	6	693.00	4158.00
Lower Rate	12	62.20	746.40
Total Due	18	0.00	4904.40

OK | Close | Help

5. SMP payment details shown here.
6. Note the Entitlement, i.e., number of Weeks, Rate and Amount, is calculated for you by Sage Payroll.
7. This figure is the total amount of SMP the employee is entitled to.
8. Click OK to return to the Employee Record.

Employee's SMP 8 Weeks Gross Pay

Qualifying Week is 15 weeks before the week the baby is due. A woman has to have been employed for 26 weeks before the QW to be eligible for SMP.

Once the employee's SMP dates have been entered, Sage Payroll uses these dates to automatically calculate the Statutory Maternity Pay entitlement. The program also establishes the employee's entitlement by checking and using the employee's 8 weeks gross pay figures. To check an employee's SMP 8 weeks gross pay do the following:

1 Open the Employee's Record.

2 Click on the Absence tab.

3 Click the S.M.P. button to bring up the Statutory Maternity Pay window. The 8 Weeks Gross tab will be selected by default.

Sage Payroll automatically enters gross earnings from previously processed payrolls.

4 The date of the first Sunday in the Qualifying week appears here.

5 Gross average weekly payments are displayed here.

The field TW (tax week) is displayed in ascending order and includes eight tax weeks up to and including the Qualifying Week.

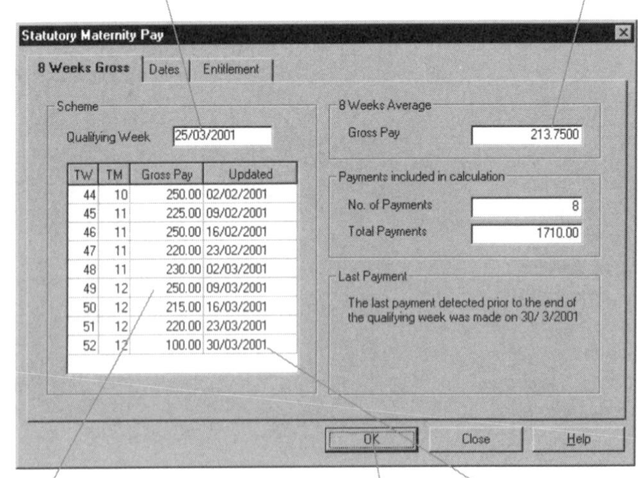

TW	TM	Gross Pay	Updated
44	10	250.00	02/02/2001
45	11	225.00	09/02/2001
46	11	250.00	16/02/2001
47	11	220.00	23/02/2001
48	11	230.00	02/03/2001
49	12	250.00	09/03/2001
50	12	215.00	16/03/2001
51	12	220.00	23/03/2001
52	12	100.00	30/03/2001

If the employee is paid monthly, the tax month (TM) is displayed as well as the tax week.

6 This window displays the total gross pay for each tax week/month for the eight tax weeks up to and inclusive of the Qualifying Date.

7 Note date of last payroll update.

8 Click OK to return to Absence window.

Entering Maternity Pay Manually

When entering maternity pay manually for your employee, you must always select the Manual Statutory Maternity Pay Calculations check box on their Employee Record BEFORE processing any payments.

When you need to enter your employee's maternity pay manually follow the steps below:

1 Select your employee and from their Employee Record, click the Absence tab.

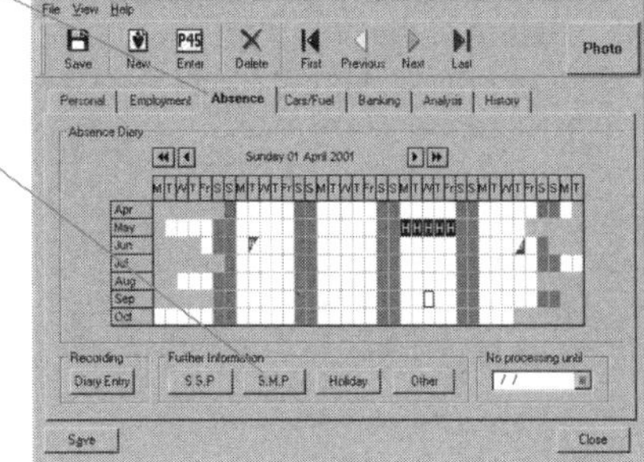

2 Click the S.M.P. button to bring up the Statutory Maternity Pay window.

3 Select the Dates tab.

4 Check that all the relevant fields are completed and tick boxes are checked accordingly.

If the payroll program is being used for the first time you can manually enter the 8 weeks gross pay prior to the Qualifying Week to satisfy the employee's entitlement to SMP, for example, are employee's average earnings more than the current NI lower earnings level?

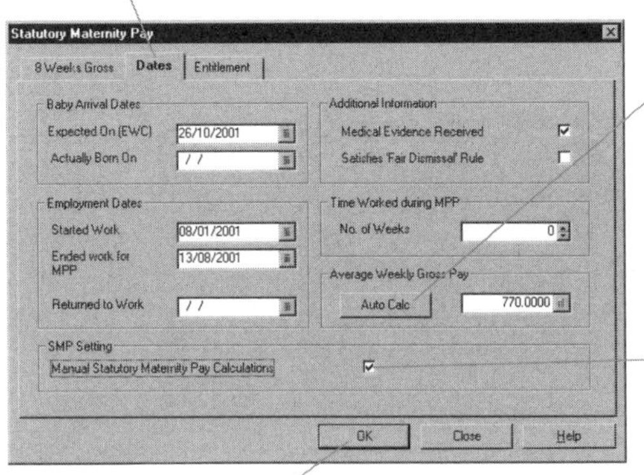

5 Note: Auto Calc will generate calculated average earnings for you.

6 Click here to manually enter your SMP.

7 Click OK to save any changes and return to the Absence tab.

8 Click Save on the Employee Record to return to Payroll desktop.

9 Select the employee and from Payroll stacked toolbar, click Enter Payments.

If, after setting up your Employee record to accept manual SSP payments (page 131) you then wish to process this payment, you must follow the normal processing procedures, i.e., change Process Date to correct date, ensure you have selected your employee BEFORE clicking Enter Payments on the Payroll stacked toolbar.

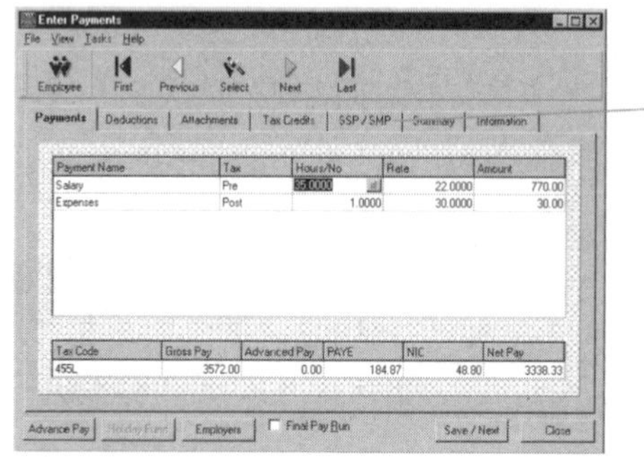

10 Click on the SSP/SMP tab.

11 Select the S.M.P. button.

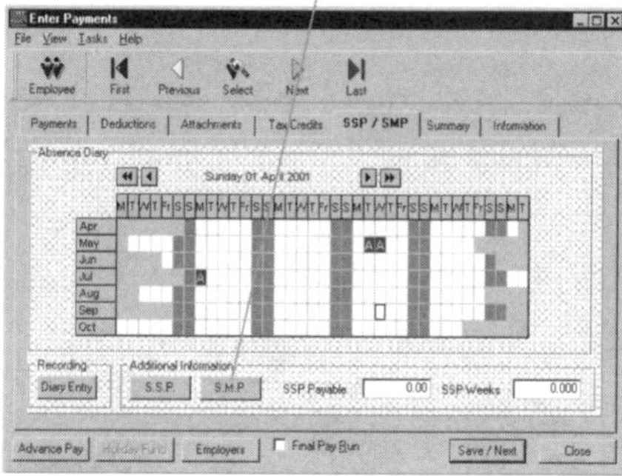

12 Enter your employee's SMP figure here, e.g. £62.20 for this weekly paid employee.

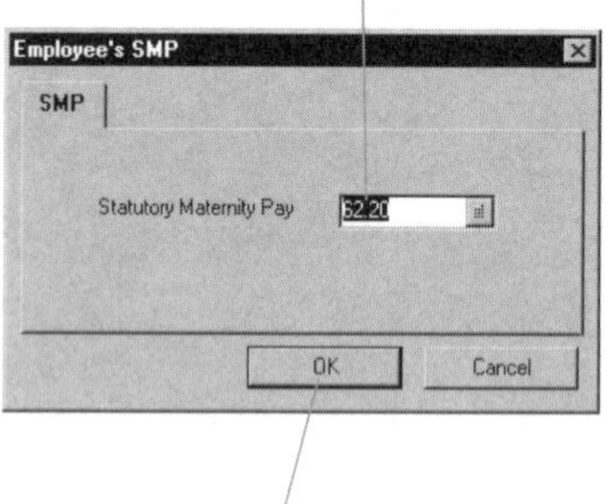

13 Click OK to save changes and return to SSP/SMP tab.

14 Click the Summary tab to view the SMP entry.

15 Click Close.

Click Save/Next before updating a payment.

Use the Information tab to view all payment details, i.e. Income Tax, National Insurance, SSP/SMP and Pension for your employee.

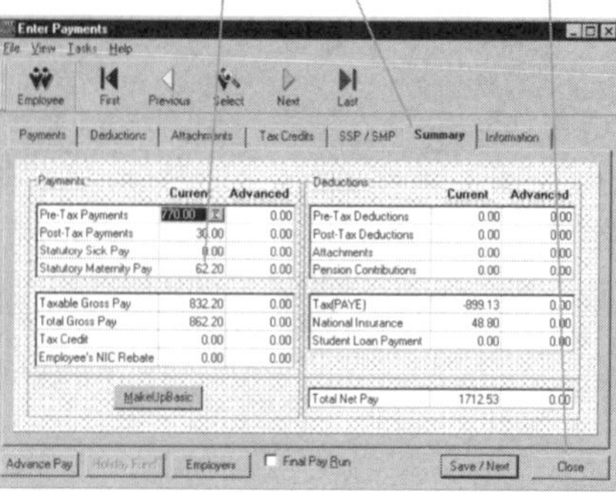

This SMP is now stored with the employee's pay record.

SMP Recovery and SMP Messages

To record any SMP funding you receive from the Inland Revenue, use the SSP/SMP Funding tab from Company Settings.

Working out your SMP Recovery

It is possible for most employers to reclaim 92% of the SMP they have paid out to their employees. If you qualify for Small Employer Relief you can reclaim 100%, plus a percentage of the total gross SMP as compensation for the NICs paid on the SMP. Follow the steps below to quickly check the SMP Rates.

To view SMP Rates

Use the SMP Rates tab to view SMP Rates, Maximum Weeks SMP Payable, Standard Employer Reclaim and Small Employer Reclaim settings.

1 From the Company stacked toolbar select the Government Legislation option.

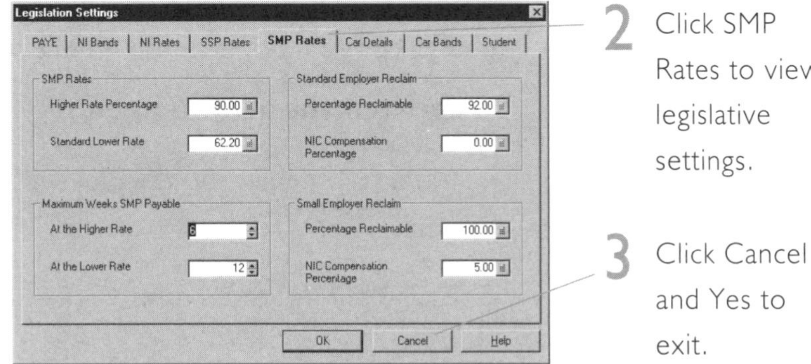

2 Click SMP Rates to view legislative settings.

3 Click Cancel and Yes to exit.

SMP is calculated one week in arrears by Sage Payroll. If the current week needs including in your SMP calculation, select the Company Settings option from the Company stacked toolbar and click the Include SMP Calculation in Current Week check box.

SMP warning messages

When there is a problem calculating SMP, Sage Payroll will display a warning message.

Following are five examples. Some display the problem in the warning message, whilst others include advice on how to resolve the problem.

Sage message: Entitlement Received for Dates Entered or No Payment Due

This indicates that no payment is due because there has not been a complete week, i.e., Sunday to Sunday, since the previous payment was made or the employee stopped work.

Employees not eligible for SMP will need a form SMP1 to claim Maternity Allowance from the Benefits Agency.

Sage message: Employee Is Still Working

SMP cannot be paid until your employee has stopped working.

Sage message: Employment Less Than 26 Weeks

An employee must be employed by your company for 26 weeks prior to the qualifying date to be entitled to SMP.

Sage message: Average Earnings Too Low

Your employee's pay must be above the National Insurance lower earnings limit to qualify for SMP.

Sage message: SMP Liability Exceeded

Where an employee has had more than one child, Sage Payroll stores previous SMP weeks paid information. These values need removing as shown below:

To zero out the SMP figures

To quickly view your employee payments, use Reports from the Payroll toolbar, select Employee section, and Payment Summary (Part 3).

1. From your employee's Employee Record, click the Employment tab.
2. Click YTD Values button.
3. Select Other YTD tab.

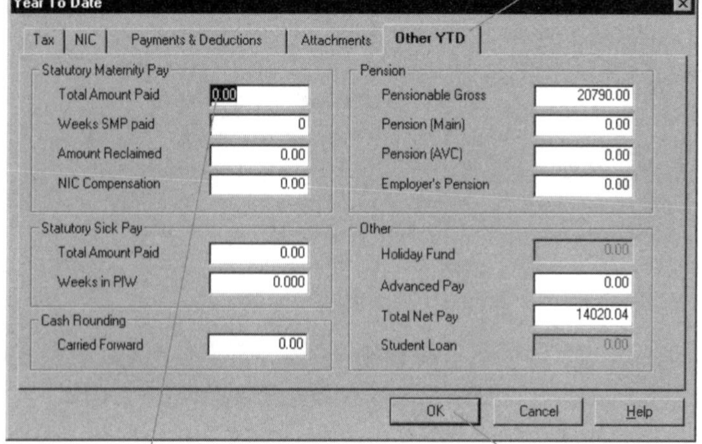

4. Clear SMP values here.
5. Click OK to save and return to Employment tab.

Save time correcting your mistakes by taking regular payroll backups which can then be restored from the File menu.

Company Pension Scheme

This Chapter shows you how to set up company pension scheme details and assign a pension scheme to an employee. The pensions can be either a percentage or fixed amount scheme. Whilst the pension contributions for both employer and employee are calculated for you automatically by the program, you will learn how to view pension details using both information screens and printed reports.

Covers

Chapter Eleven

Company Pension Schemes

The basic state pension and SERPS are the major elements of the State retirement pensions.

When all employed earners reach retirement age, they are entitled to receive the basic state pension. Employees who have paid Class 1 NI contributions are entitled to an additional state pension provided by the State Earnings Related Pension Scheme, better known as SERPS.

Many employers provide their employees with the opportunity to join a company or occupational pension scheme. These schemes provide far better benefits on retirement than the State's basic pension.

You must keep your employees pension contributions up to date. Any changes to the scheme must be recorded, i.e., joiners and leavers, amendments to employees and employer's contributions.

When the employer does not provide their employees with a company or occupational pension scheme, employees can make contributions into their own personal pension scheme to increase pension benefits on retirement.

Sage Payroll V7 allows you to set up an unlimited number of schemes, though you can only assign one scheme to an employee. To view a summary of any pension schemes you may already have set up, do the following:

1 On the Company stacked toolbar, click Pension Schemes.

2 Pension details appear here.

3 Click Close.

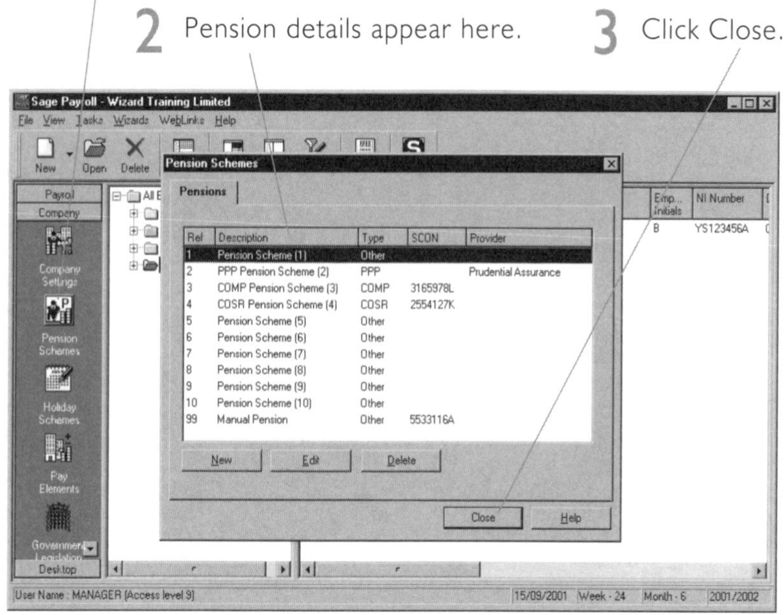

For national insurance purposes, pension contributions and AVCs are not deducted from gross pay prior to calculating NI contributions for the employer and employee.

For contracting out of SERPS the employer must have a contracting out certificate issued by the Occupational Pensions Board. The Scheme Contracted Out Number from this certificate can then be entered in the SCON field when setting up the pension details (page 139).

Contracting in or out

The company or occupational pension schemes can be contracted in or contracted out of SERPS. A contracted in scheme means that the occupational pension is in addition to SERPS, whereas a contracted out scheme means the company pension scheme is in place of SERPS. For a scheme which is contracted out of SERPS, both the employer and employee pay a reduced rate of National Insurance.

Employees contributing to an occupational scheme

Where an employer provides an occupational pension scheme, rules, conditions and benefits must be clearly defined so employees can decide whether or not they wish to become members. Membership is not a compulsory condition of employment.

However, for exempt approved occupational schemes, employees receive tax relief for contributions made through the payroll.

Contributions made from the employee's pay into the pension scheme must be deducted from the employee's gross pay before calculating the tax due on the pay. This is known as a 'net pay arrangement'. Where an employee decides to pay AVCs into the pension scheme, these are treated the same as the pension contributions and are deducted from gross pay before tax is calculated.

Within Sage Payroll V7 you can have an unlimited number of different pension schemes, but only one can be applied to any employee at any one time, i.e., you cannot have a fixed amount and a percentage contribution applied to the same employee.

Employees contracting out of SERPS

Some occupational pension schemes are contracted out of SERPS. For these schemes, both the employees who are members and the employer pay a reduced rate of NICs. The employer must have a contracting out certificate issued by the Occupational Pensions Board. This certificate includes a final salary scheme which provides a guaranteed minimum pension (GMP) increasing in line with inflation and a money purchase scheme that must provide a pension under the protected rights test which gives the employee a similar GMP.

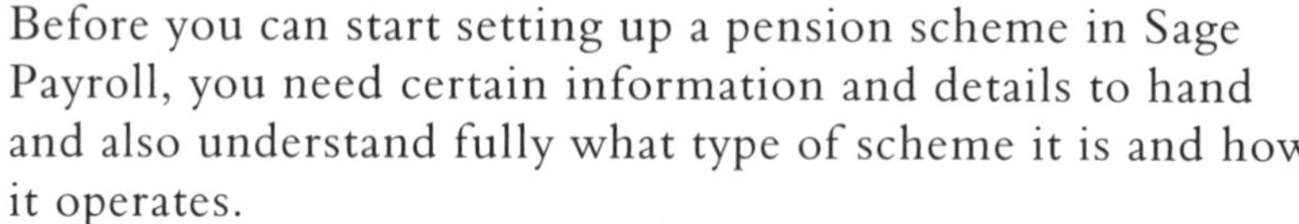

Pension Scheme Checklist

Pensions can be a complicated payroll issue, so make sure you have all the information available and understand pensions fully before setting up your pensions information in Sage Payroll, as correcting mistakes later may prove difficult.

Before you can start setting up a pension scheme in Sage Payroll, you need certain information and details to hand and also understand fully what type of scheme it is and how it operates.

Use the following checklist to determine what type of pension scheme your company has.

Getting started pension checklist

- What is the scheme contribution – a percentage or a fixed amount?
- If the pension contributions are percentage contributions, are they calculated on all elements of gross pay or just certain payments?
- If the pension contributions are a fixed amount, are SSP and SMP payments to be included in the pension calculation?
- If the pension contributions are a percentage, are they to be restricted by the National Insurance limits?
- Are the pension contributions subject to the NIC rebate or Contracted Out Money Purchase Scheme (COMPS)?
- Do you want to have the rebate for COMPS amount added to your fixed or percentage contribution or do you just want the rebate figure only?
- Is your pension amount subject to tax relief?

If you have queries regarding pension contributions, check with your pension adviser BEFORE setting up your pension details.

Your company pensions advisor will be able to answer any questions you may have, if you are still unclear as to the exact details of any pension scheme or schemes your company may offer. It is worthwhile noting that recently introduced government legislation has brought about the Stakeholder pension. This is a simple, inexpensive pension plan aimed at employees with low to middle earnings, i.e., between £10,000 and £20,000.

Refer to page 97 to show you how to enter your manual pension payments.

Setting up Pension Schemes

Sage Payroll V7 provides you with 10 schemes which you can use as templates for your own schemes.

Once you have all the relevant information to hand, you are ready to set up or edit your pension schemes. For example, to edit an existing template and set up a Stakeholder pension, do the following:

1. On the Company stacked toolbar, click Pension Schemes to bring up the templates provided by Sage.

2. Select the existing scheme you wish to change and click Edit.

Pension Schemes

Ref	Description	Type	SCON	Provider
1	Pension Scheme (1)	Other		
2	PPP Pension Scheme (2)	PPP		Prudential Assurance
3	COMP Pension Scheme (3)	COMP	3165978L	
4	COSR Pension Scheme (4)	COSR	2554127K	
5	Pension Scheme (5)	Other		
6	Pension Scheme (6)	Other		
7	Pension Scheme (7)	Other		
8	Pension Scheme (8)	Other		
9	Pension Scheme (9)	Other		
10	Pension Scheme (10)	Other		
99	Manual Pension	Other	5533116A	

Under new Stakeholder pension legislation, employers with five or more employees must offer employees access to a stakeholder scheme by 8 October 2001, unless alternative pension schemes are already being offered. They must be earning over the NI lower earnings limit and minimum contribution must not be set at more than £20 a month. If employees are already members of an occupational scheme, they can also contribute to a stakeholder pension provided that earnings are less than £30,000.

3. Enter a Description and Type here.

4. Enter Pension Provider details in this section.

Once pension schemes and employee records have been set up, the program will automatically calculate the pension value. See Summary tab in Enter Payments option to view pension details.

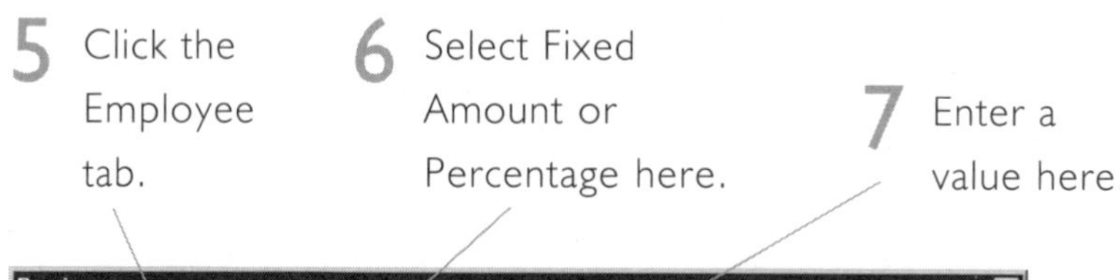

5 Click the Employee tab.

6 Select Fixed Amount or Percentage here.

7 Enter a value here.

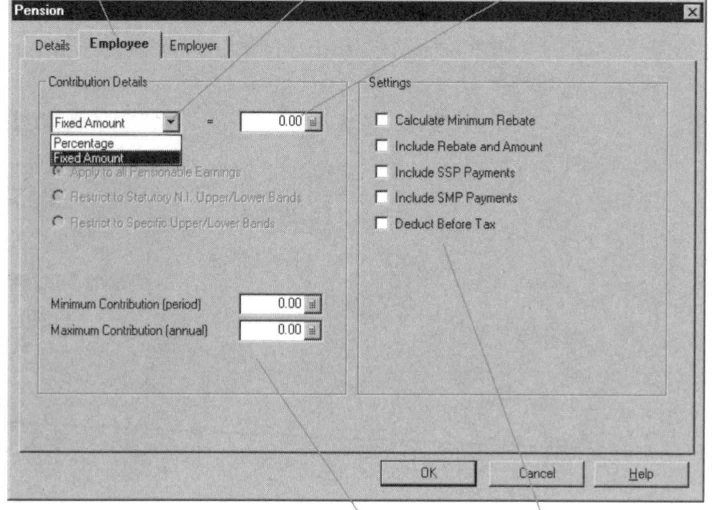

To apply the pension percentage to the NI earnings band only, select Restrict to Statutory N.I. Upper/Lower Bands.

8 Complete the remaining Details and Settings relevant to the type of scheme you have selected.

The Restrict to Specific Upper/ Lower Bands option allows you to set your own defined earnings limit. Once selected, you can enter your own earning limits into the Lower and Upper limits boxes which appear automatically.

9 Click the Employer tab.

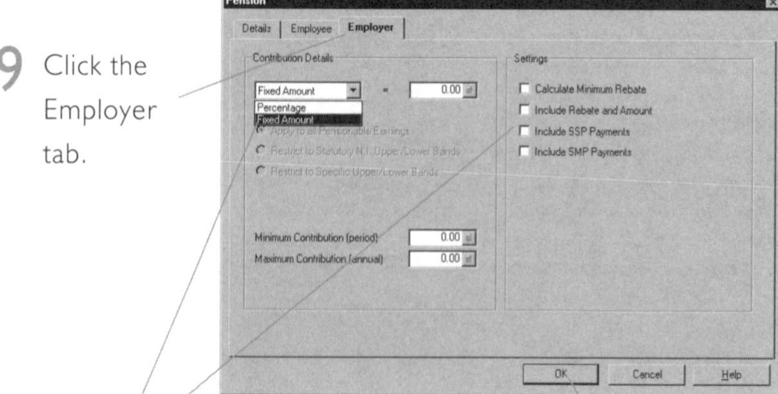

10 Enter the Employer Contribution Details as you did for the employee.

11 Click OK to save details.

Assigning Pension Schemes

Within Sage Payroll V7 you can have an unlimited number of different pension schemes, but only one can be applied to any employee at any one time, i.e., you cannot have a fixed amount and a percentage contribution applied to the same employee.

Once the pension schemes have been set up, you can now assign the appropriate scheme to your employees, either individually or as a group, as follows:

To assign a pension scheme to an individual employee

1 Select and open your employee's record by double clicking the left hand mouse button.

2 Select Employment tab.

3 Click the Pension button.

4 Use Finder button and select appropriate pension scheme.

5 Click OK.

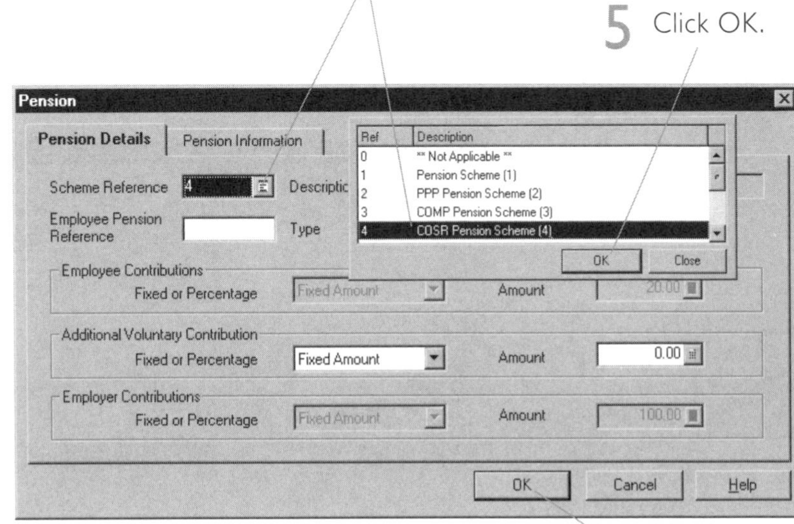

6 Click OK to save details.

To quickly create a new pension scheme simply select and edit one of the ten templates provided.

To assign a pension scheme to a group of employees

Use the AVC button to record details of any additional voluntary contributions.

1 Select relevant employees from employee list then choose Global Changes from the Tasks menu.

2 Choose Pensions, Assign Employee(s) to scheme number.

3 Select pension, click OK then Yes.

Additional Voluntary Contributions

The amount of AVC contributions you can make each year is limited. Refer any enquiries to your pension adviser.

Where an employee is a member of a company pension scheme they can choose to make additional contributions. For example, they may want to pay an additional £50 a month into their pension. Sage Payroll allows you to process any additional voluntary contributions (AVC) your employees choose to make to their company scheme.

To process AVCs, do the following:

If you need to check any details about your employee's pension scheme select the Pension Information tab.

1. Select and open your employee's record by double clicking the left hand mouse button.
2. Select Employment tab.
3. Click the Pension button.
4. Select the type of contribution here.

Use the Employee Details - Pension Cont'ns... report from the Employee section of Reports to view an employee's AVCs to date as well as their main contribution.

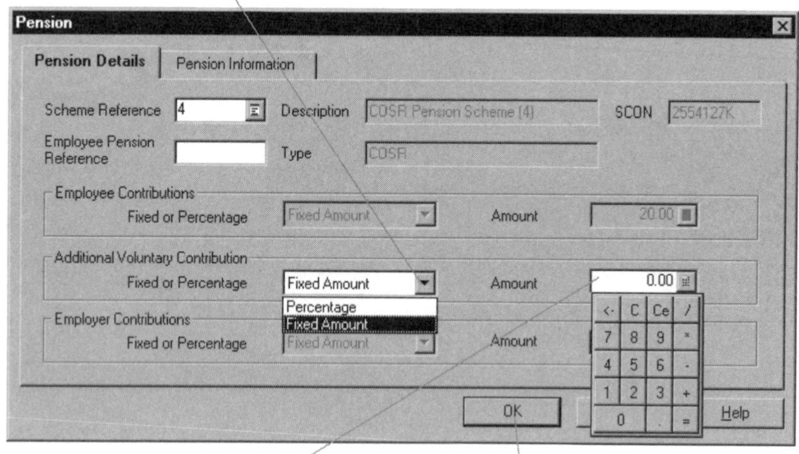

5. Enter the Amount of contribution here, use the calculator if necessary.
6. Click OK to save the AVC details and return to the Employment tab.

The AVC is subject to tax relief.

Deductions and Attachments

Chapter Twelve

This chapter shows you how to set up different types of deductions and attachments of earnings. Once set up you will learn how to allocate these against your employees. This is followed by processing these deductions and attachments of earnings during the payroll run.

Covers

Setting up Deductions

Use Edit or Delete button to amend or delete existing deduction type details.

Within Sage Payroll you are allowed to set up as many deduction types as you require. Once your deductions have been set up, they can be assigned to your employees and automatically deducted from your employees' pay as part of normal payroll processing. To set up your deduction types do as follows:

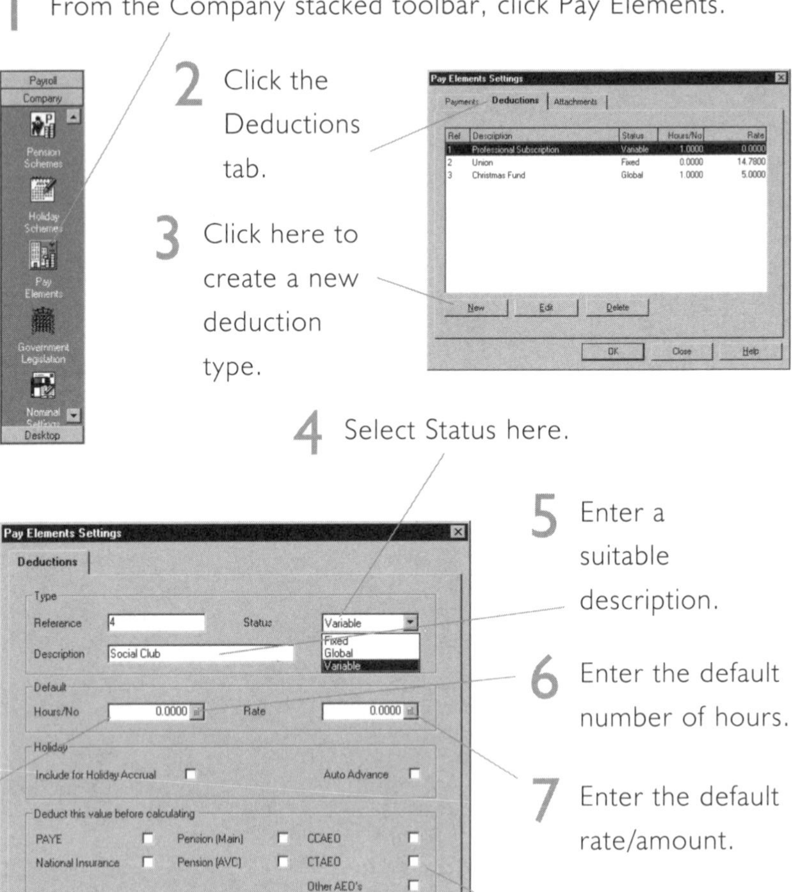

1. From the Company stacked toolbar, click Pay Elements.
2. Click the Deductions tab.
3. Click here to create a new deduction type.
4. Select Status here.
5. Enter a suitable description.
6. Enter the default number of hours.
7. Enter the default rate/amount.
8. Click any appropriate deductions.
9. Click OK to save changes or Close to abandon.

Status can be set to Variable (no restrictions for when rates/hours need changing), or Fixed (rate/amounts are fixed by value entered in each employee record), or Global (any changes made to payments will directly affect all employees who have been assigned to it). To change it use Pay Elements Settings.

It is usually advisable to leave the Default Hours/No and Rate at zero unless all your employees work the same hours.

Allocating Deduction Types

Press function key F1 for further information on the relevant screens.

Once deduction types have been set up you can assign them to your employees following the steps below:

1 Select your employee, and from their Employee Record select the Employment tab.

2 Click Pay Elements button.

Pay Elements...

Use Finder button to select the deduction type you require.

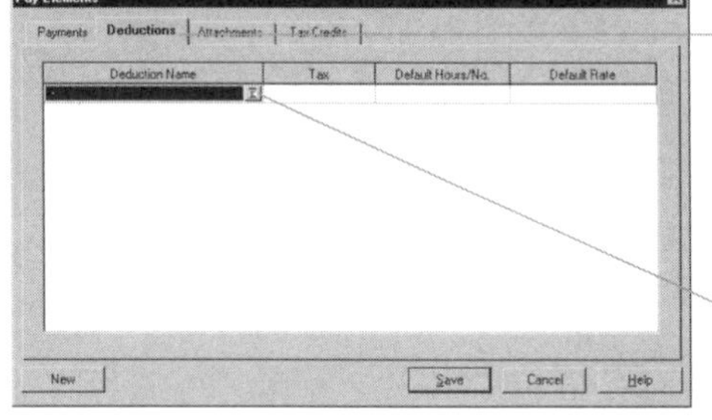

3 From the Pay Elements window click Deductions.

4 Click here for a deduction list.

Use the down cursor arrow key to move down a line.

5 Select desired deduction.

Press TAB key to move right across columns and SHIFT+TAB to move left.

6 Click OK to accept.

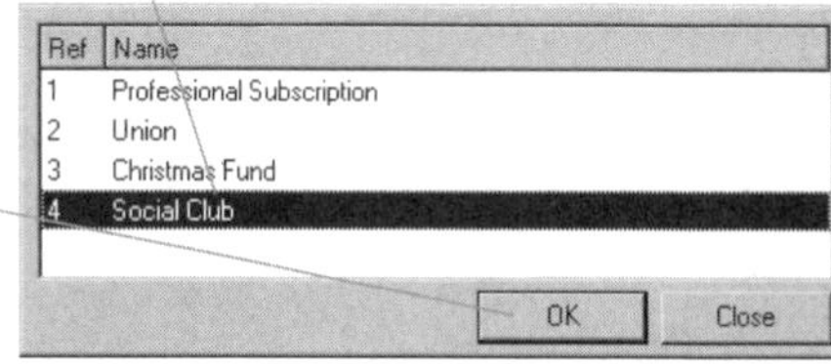

Ref	Name
1	Professional Subscription
2	Union
3	Christmas Fund
4	Social Club

OK Close

7 Enter figures where required.

The Tax field displays Pre or Post to indicate whether the deduction is to be made before or after tax is calculated.

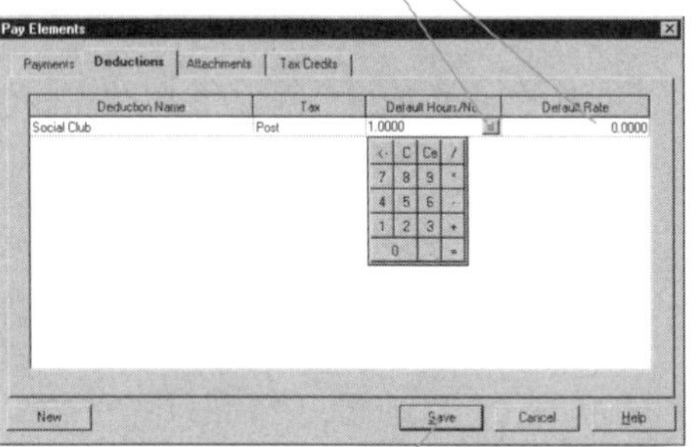

8 Repeat steps 3–7 to add another deduction type.

9 Click Save to close or Cancel to abandon.

Processing Deductions

If a default number has already been set up for the deduction type in the Hours/No field it appears automatically. Likewise for the Rate and Amount field values.

Before processing deductions for your employees, values may need assigning for specific variable deductions using the Deductions tab from the Enter Payments window. Popular deduction types include payments for union fees, recreation activities etc. To enter values and process your deductions do as follows:

1. Select your employee from employee list and click on the Enter Payments button on the Payroll stacked toolbar.
2. From the Enter Payments window click Deductions.
3. Deduction types previously assigned to an employee appear here.
4. Enter number of hours or the number of deduction payments here.
5. Enter the deduction rate for the deduction type here.

Use Reports option from the application toolbar, Employee section to view/print details about your employee's deductions.

6. To add new deductions to this list you need to click the Employee button to return to the Employee Record, then follow steps 2–9 on page 145.
7. Now check that all Deductions have been recorded accurately.
8. Click here to save and move to next record or click Close to return to the Payroll desktop.

You can view total value of deductions paid per employee using the Payments and Deductions tab from the YTD Values window.

Advancing Deductions

Check to see if the employee needs any Tax Credits processing. Refer to chapter 13 if this is the case. To check and advance any Attachment of Earnings Order see page 152 for details.

For occasions where you may need to process an employee's deductions in advance, for example, their holiday period, you can do this following the steps below:

1. Select your employee and click Enter Payments from the Payroll stacked toolbar.

2. Click on the Advance Pay button.

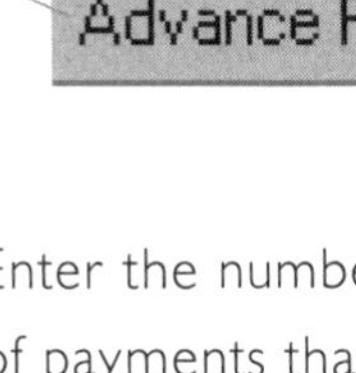

3. Enter the number of payments that you are advancing here, i.e., number of weeks or number of months.

Use the Summary tab to view Pre-tax and Post-tax Deductions for both Current and Advanced pay periods.

4. Click OK.

5. Click the Deductions tab.

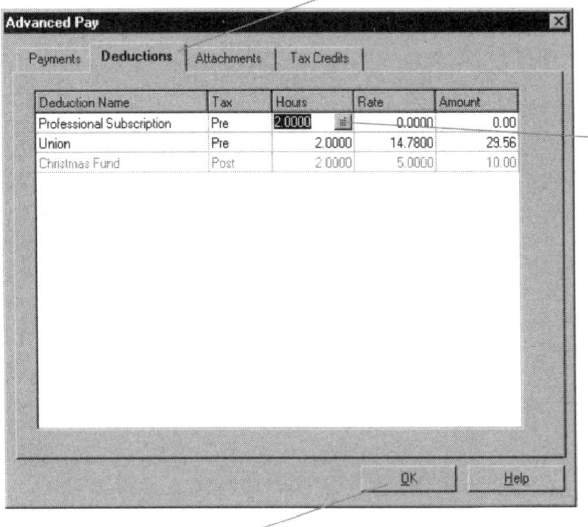

6. Enter the employee's deductions details here.

To print out deduction information use the Reports option, Employee folder, Employee Details – Deductions report.

7. Click OK to accept and return to Enter Payments window.

Attachment of Earnings

Employers are allowed to deduct an admin fee from their employees for administering any attachment of earnings. The rate is £1 per attachment in England, Wales and Northern Ireland and 50 pence per attachment in Scotland.

An Attachment of Earnings Order is an official form issued by a court and legally binding to an employer instructing them to deduct an outstanding debt from an employee's wages. These Attachments are always taken from the employees' net pay, referred to as Attachable Earnings.

The court sets a Protected Earnings Amount to ensure that the employee has sufficient income after deductions have been made. The difference between the protected and attachable earnings is the sum from which the deduction is actually made.

These payments are usually on a weekly or monthly basis. Examples of these orders include the non payment of council tax, fines and child support payments, etc.

Sage automatically provides you with a list of Attachments. A user can add or edit these descriptions where appropriate and later assign them to an employee's details. To view these Attachments do the following:

To deduct an administration fee from an employee's net pay, create a Deductions type within Pay Elements and call it Administration Fee. This Deductions type can then be assigned to the employee.

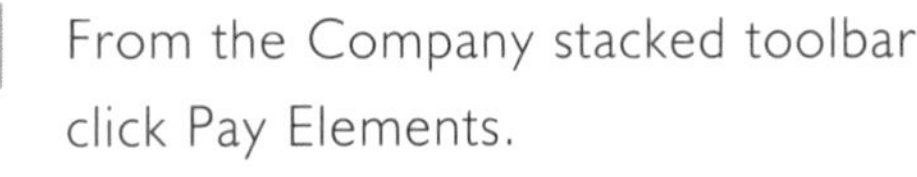

1 From the Company stacked toolbar, click Pay Elements.

2 Click the Attachments tab.

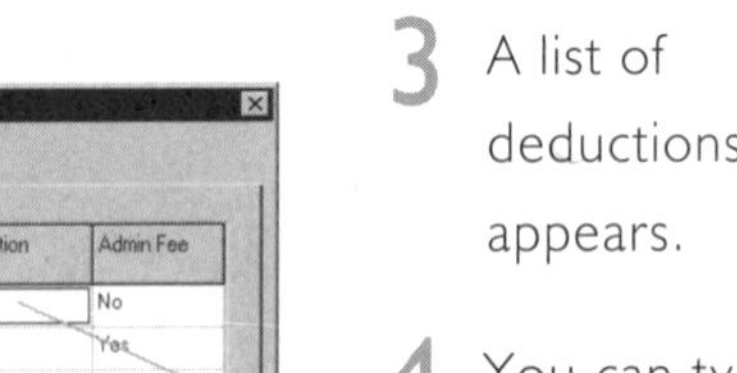

Ref	Standard Description	Replacement Description	Admin Fee
1	1971 Priority		No
2	Child Support	CSA	Yes
3	DEO		No
4	1971 Non-Prty		No
5	Pre 92 CCAEO		No
6	Post 92 CCAEO	Community Charge	No
7	CTAEO		No
8	Earnings Arrest		No
9	CMA		No
10	CAO		No

3 A list of deductions appears.

4 You can type in your own description here. This will appear on reports and payslips.

5 Click OK to save or Close to abandon.

Refer to Sage Help for additional information about attachment of earnings.

Within Sage Payroll you can determine which attachment is to be deducted first, for example, Maintenance Orders and Community Charge Orders have a higher priority than civil debt.

Descriptions for the 10 most commonly used attachments

To help you, here is a list of the more common attachments you are likely to come across whilst processing payroll. Their templates are already pre-defined in Sage Payroll V7:

1971 Priority	This refers to a priority court order, e.g., road traffic fine or non payment of television licence.
Child Support	Deduction to cover child support after parental separation.
DEO	A Scottish child support order.
1971 Non-Prty	This is a non-priority order, e.g., money owing on an unpaid credit card or for work done.
Pre 92 CCAEO	A deduction to recover missing community charge payments from before April 1992 (poll tax).
Post 92 CCAEO	This deduction is to recover missing community charge payments after April 1992 (now council tax).
CTAEO	This is a current council tax order.
Earnings Arrest	This is a Scottish order, an earnings arrestment order, e.g., a fine or civil debt.
CMA	This is a current maintenance arrestment to cover maintenance after a marriage separation/divorce.
CAO	A combined arrestment order, e.g., maintenance, an earnings arrest.

An employee is allocated with a Protected Earnings figure, i.e., a minimum net pay. The attachment cannot deduct all their earnings. If earnings are below the protected level the deduction will not be made. If the order is a protected order any arrears will be carried forward to the next period. Non-protected orders do not carry forward arrears.

Allocating Attachments

Protected Earnings are only applicable on the 1971 Priority Child Support and DEO.

In the Priority Order field, where more than one attachment needs deducting enter 1 for the highest priority, then 2 as next priority, etc.

Where only one attachment is entered you must enter 1 into the Priority Order field. Field entry is mandatory.

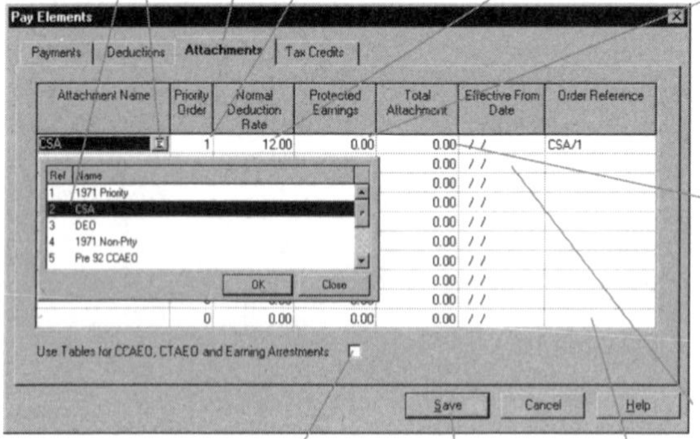

Leave the Total Attachment field as zero for Child Support as this attachment is ongoing.

For employees who are required to pay an Attachment of Earnings Order follow the steps below:

1. Select your employee and from their Employment Record, click Employment tab. 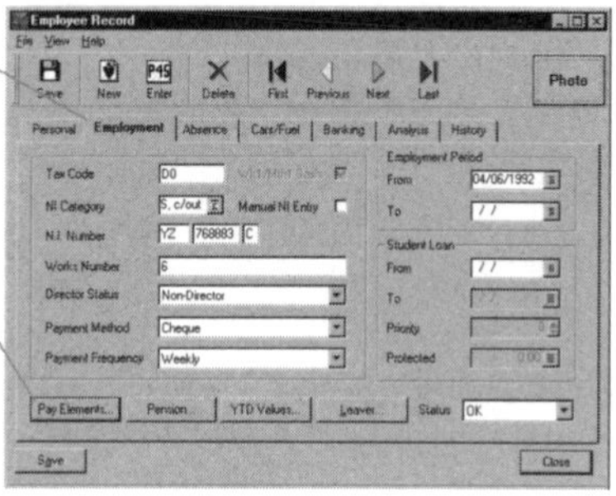
2. Click Pay Elements button .
3. Click the Attachments tab.
4. Click here to select attachment required from list.
5. Enter priority number.
6. Enter normal deduction figure.
7. Enter protected earnings amount.
8. Enter total amount of attachment.
9. Enter date of court order here.
10. Enter a court reference number in this column.
11. Click here to use pre-defined Inland Revenue tables.
12. Click Save.

Processing Attachments

You cannot edit the information in the Name field as this is stored on the Employee Record.

Sage Payroll will process these attachments of earnings automatically for those employees liable for these deductions. To process these attachments follow the steps below:

1 Select the employee and click Enter Payments from the Payroll stacked toolbar.

The Amount/ Percent field shows if the attachment is to be calculated as a percentage of the employee's wages or as a fixed amount.

2 The Attachment tab shows any that have been set up.

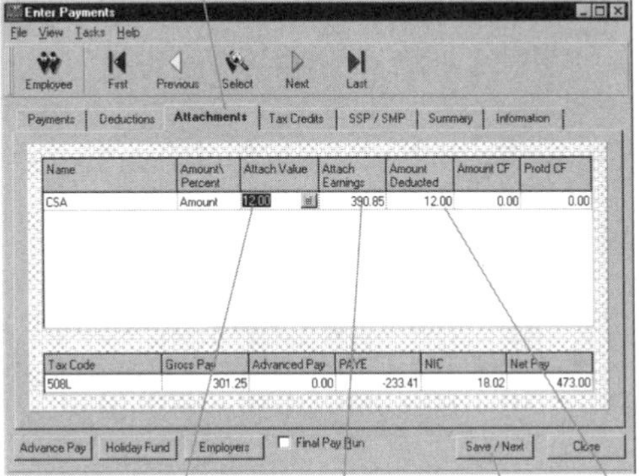

3 To add a new attachment you need to click the Employee button and then follow steps 1–12 on page 150.

For the Attach Value field you need to enter an exact amount for a Child Support attachment, but for a Council Tax attachment, you need to enter a percentage.

4 This shows amount being deducted.

5 This field shows the earnings from which the attachment is deducted.

6 Note actual amount deducted which takes into account any protected earnings.

7 Click Save/Next to save and move to next record or Close to return to the Payroll desktop.

Use horizontal scroll bar to view all attachment details.

Note: If the whole amount is unable to be processed for this period, the Amount CF field shows the value carried forward to the next period. The Protd CF field shows any protected earnings which are also carried forward.

Advancing Attachments

Use the Summary tab to view Current and Advanced Deductions.

There may be an occasion when you need to process an employee's deductions in advance. Sage Payroll allows you to do this as follows:

1. Select your employee and click Enter Payments from the Payroll stacked toolbar.

If you are advancing pay for more than one period, you must enter the total amount of attachments for the whole advance period. For example, if your employee normally pays £20 per pay period in attachments, and you are advancing them two periods of holiday pay, enter £40 in attachments.

2. Click on the Advance Pay button.

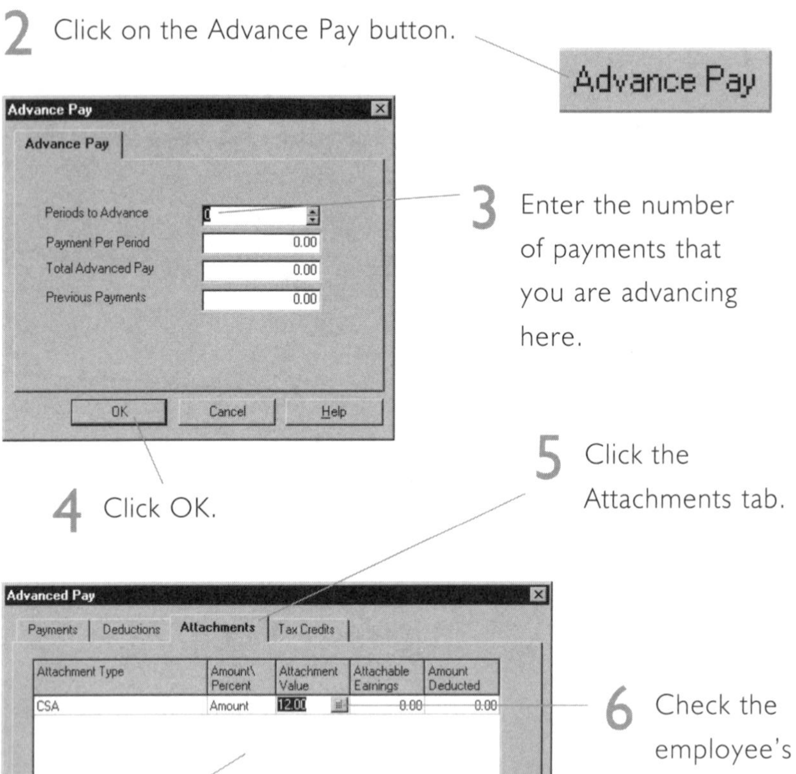

3. Enter the number of payments that you are advancing here.
4. Click OK.
5. Click the Attachments tab.
6. Check the employee's attachment details here and amend if necessary.

If the attachment is deducted as a set amount, you should enter this figure on the Attachment tab on the Enter Payments window.

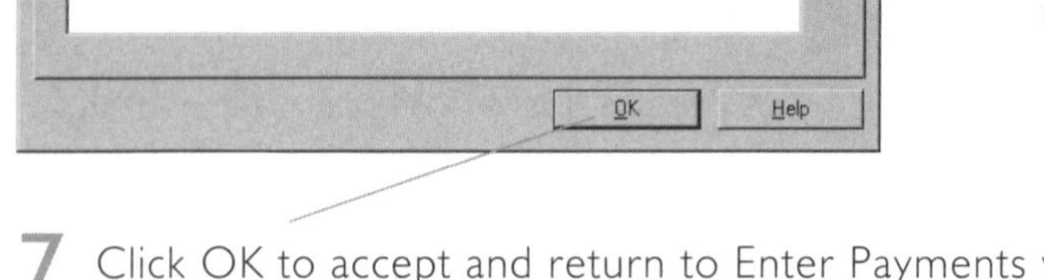

7. Click OK to accept and return to Enter Payments window.

Tax Credits

This chapter shows you how to enter tax credit details for your employees. Once set up, you learn how to process these payments during the payroll run and, when required, how to advance them for a future period.

Covers

Chapter Thirteen

Entering Tax Credits

If an employee who is in receipt of tax credits leaves your company their award stops. The tax credit record is automatically updated with the date and reason, i.e., Leaver.

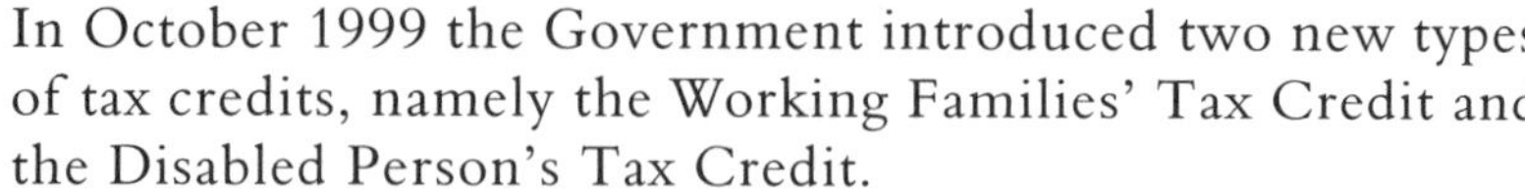

In October 1999 the Government introduced two new types of tax credits, namely the Working Families' Tax Credit and the Disabled Person's Tax Credit.

Since April 2001 this credit is paid to an employee in addition to their net pay through their wages or salary. To enter an employee's tax credit do as follows:

1 From the employee record click the Employment tab, then the Pay Elements button.

2 From the Pay Elements window select the Tax Credits tab.

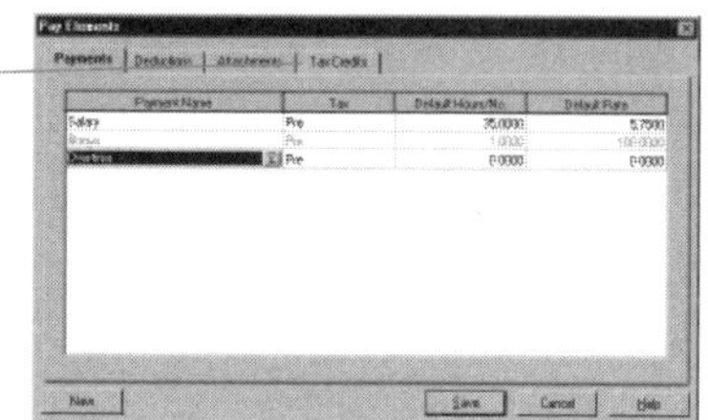

If you have need to remove an employee's leave date you must also manually remove the stop date so their tax credits continue..

3 Enter date tax credits started.

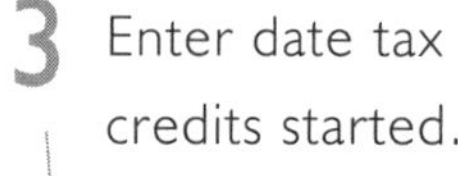

4 Enter date tax credits finish.

5 Enter daily rate of tax credit here.

6 The total amount of tax credit is calculated automatically.

The Leaver Wizard produces a Tax Credit Certificate of Payments for transcription purposes.

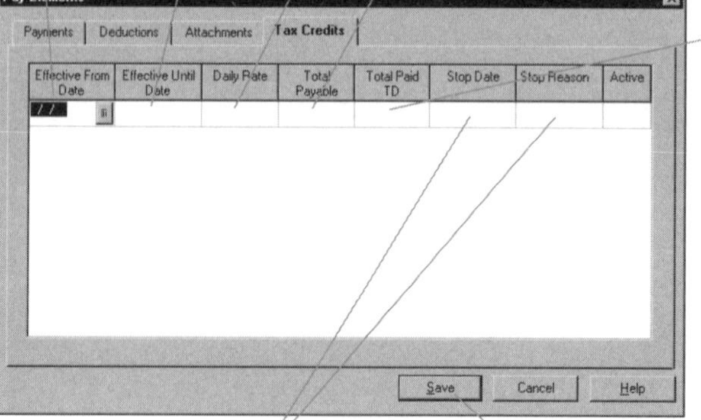

7 Enter total amount of tax credit received to date.

From Stop Reason you can select Leaver, Trade Dispute, No Net Pay or Other.

8 When appropriate, enter a date and reason why tax credit stops.

9 Click Save or Cancel to abandon.

Processing Tax Credits

For more information about tax credits contact your local Inland Revenue.

From April 2000 tax credits are paid direct to employees through their pay. The Inland Revenue furnishes the employer officially with the appropriate documentation. Once the employer receives notification of an employee receiving tax credits, this needs to be set up on the employee record so it can be processed during the payroll run. Once set up, to process these tax credits follow the steps below:

To enter tax credits for your employees, you first need to set them up on their Employee Record. See page 154.

1 Click on the required employee in the desktop list view. From the Pay Elements window click Tax Credits.

2 Click Enter Payments on the Payroll stacked toolbar.

3 Click the Tax Credits tab for details.

4 Enter duration.

5 Number of days between First Day and Last Day is inclusive.

Use Employee button to return to their Employee Record.

6 The Amount shown is number of days times Daily Rate.

7 To view tax credit information for this employee click on the Summary and Information tabs.

8 Click here to save and move to next record or Close.

To record Tax Credit Funding and Tax Refund Received select the Tax Credit tab from Company Settings.

Note: First Day is the first day payments start in the current pay run and Last Day is the last date for these payments. Neither can be before the Effective From Date, or after the Effective Until or Stop Date.

Advancing Tax Credits

Check to see if the employee needs any deductions or attachment of earnings processing in advance. Refer to chapter 12 if this is the case.

For occasions where you may need to process an employee's tax credits in advance, for example, their holiday period, you would do so following the steps below:

1 Select your employee and click Enter Payments from the Payroll stacked toolbar.

2 Click Advance Pay.

Use the Summary tab to view Payments for Tax Credit, both Current and Advanced.

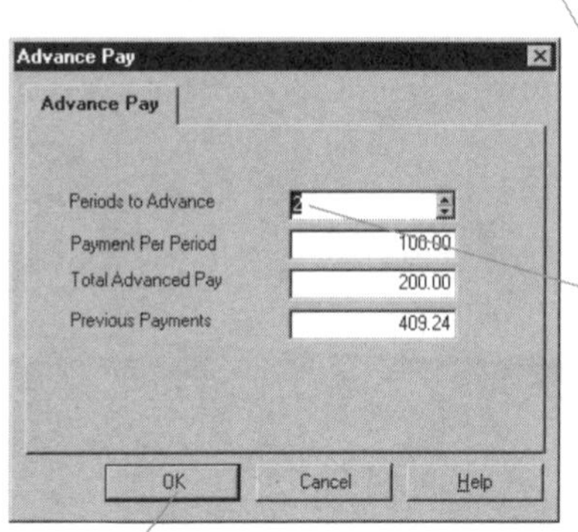

3 Enter the number of payments that you are advancing.

The Information tab, Tax Credits folder produces details about Tax Credit(s) This Period and Tax Credit(s) This Year.

4 Click OK.

5 Click the Tax Credits tab in the Advanced Pay window.

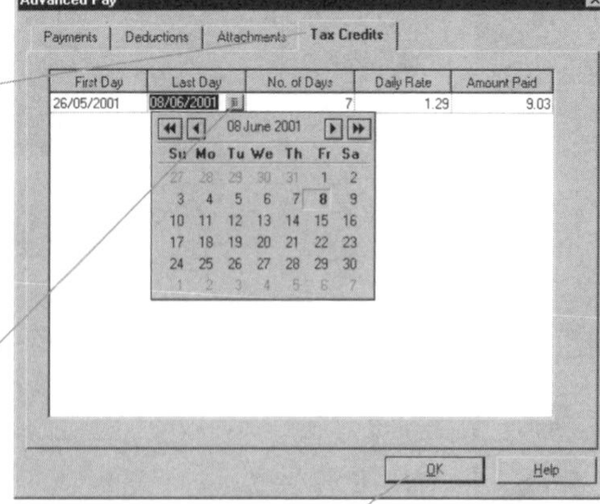

6 Enter tax credit date details here.

To print out tax credit information use your Reports option, Employee folder, Employee Tax Credits report .

7 Click OK to accept and return to Enter Payments window.

The Report Designer

In this chapter you will learn how to create a new report using the Report Wizard, how to prepare a custom report and modify an existing report layout file. The Report Designer is very powerful and provides many features. You will also be shown how to use options for grouping and sorting information, adding calculations such as totals, setting up criteria and filters to search for information as well as designing the layout and format of the report.

Covers

Chapter Fourteen

Introducing the Report Designer

Payroll reports consist of the following sections: Employee, Company, Legislation, Period End, Year End, Absence, Cars & Fuel and User Defined.

When you first install Sage Payroll, you are automatically provided with all of the reports and stationery to suit most business needs. When printing these reports, if you are using stationery supplied by Sage, the data should fit in the pre-printed stationery layouts without adjustment.

There may be occasions though when you need to create a new report or modify an existing one to meet your specific needs. The Report Designer lets you do all of this so you can meet any requirements your business may have. To run Report Designer do as follows:

1. Click the Reports button from the Sage Payroll main toolbar.

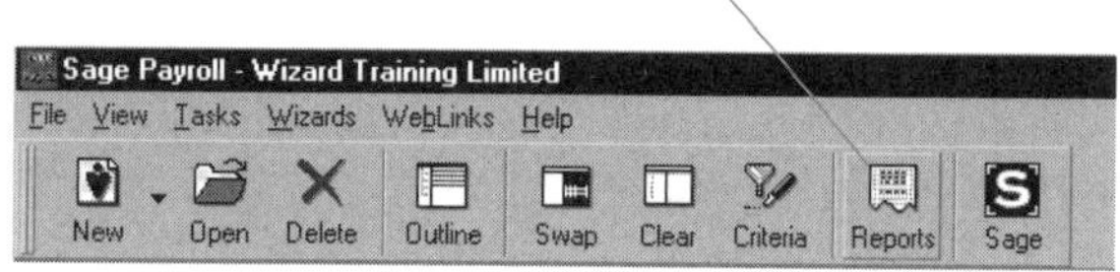

If you only require pre-update reports, select the Pre-update Reports option from the Payroll stacked toolbar.

2. Select the report section you require, e.g., Company.
3. Choose required report from the List View.

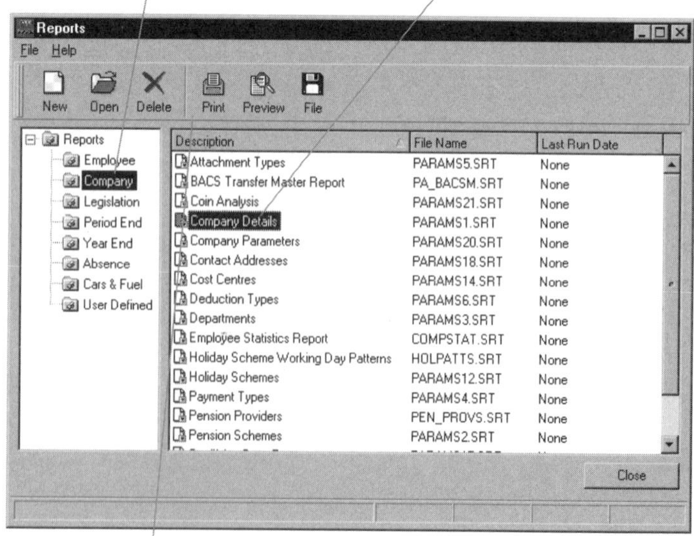

To edit an existing report, select the required layout from the Reports list view, then click the Open button or open the File menu and choose the Edit option.

4. From the Reports toolbar you can now choose whether to create, edit, delete, print, preview or save your report.

Creating a new Report

To print a report, select the required layout and click the Print button.

The following example shows you how to use the Report Wizard to create an Employee report. This will display their name, date of birth, National Insurance number and address details. The report is sorted on the employee's surname and is useful for supplying details to the Contributions Agency. To create this report follow the steps below:

1 Select Reports option from the Sage Payroll main toolbar.

If you wish to preview a report, select the layout you require and click the Preview button.

2 To create an Employee report click here.

3 Click New to create a new report using the Report Wizard.

4 Enter a description here, e.g. NI Employee Report.

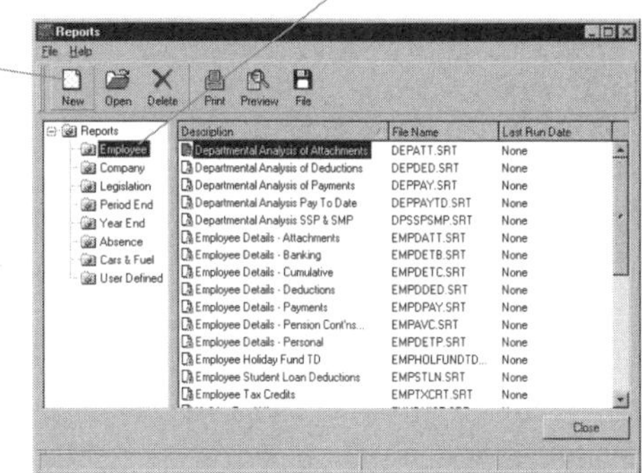

Where you wish to send your report output to a file select the File option.

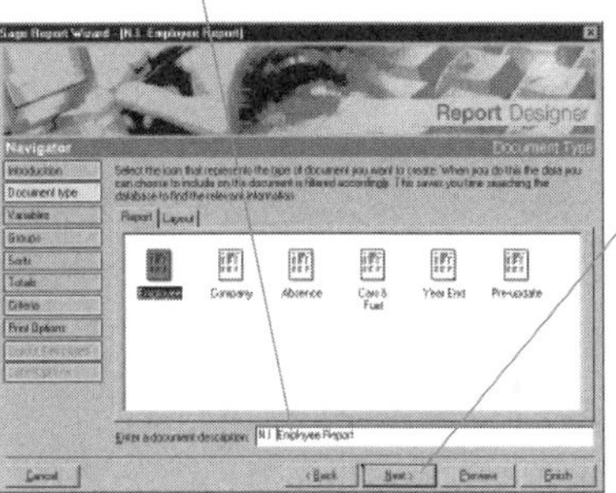

5 Click Next to continue.

6 Note: You can add variables from different tables to your report.

To create a new report select the New option from the Reports toolbar.

7 Click here to select the Sgtbl_EmployeePersonal table.

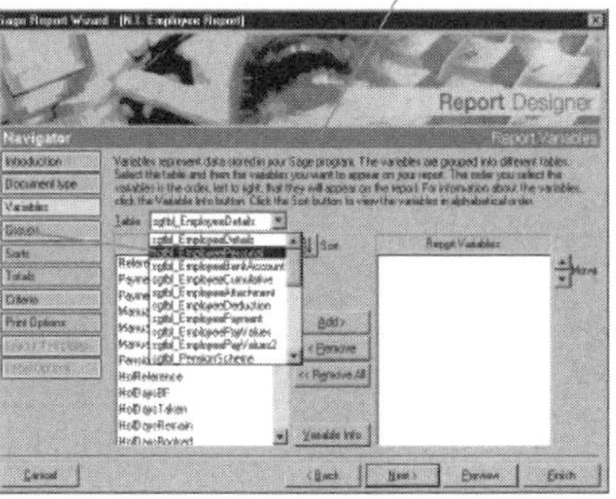

To view variable descriptions in each table select the Variable Info button.

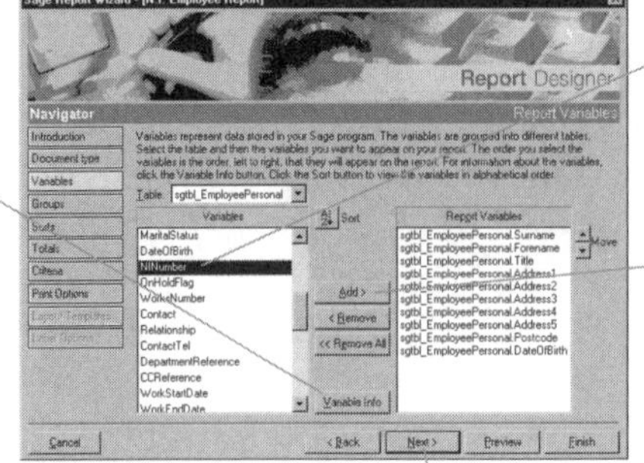

8. Select the variable required from this list.
9. Click the Add > button to copy it to the Report Variables list.

To make a selective choice of variables, hold down the CTRL key whilst clicking on variables required. Click the Add > button to transfer them as a group.

10. Repeat step 9 for all required variables.
11. Click Next.
12. Grouping is not required here, so just click Next.

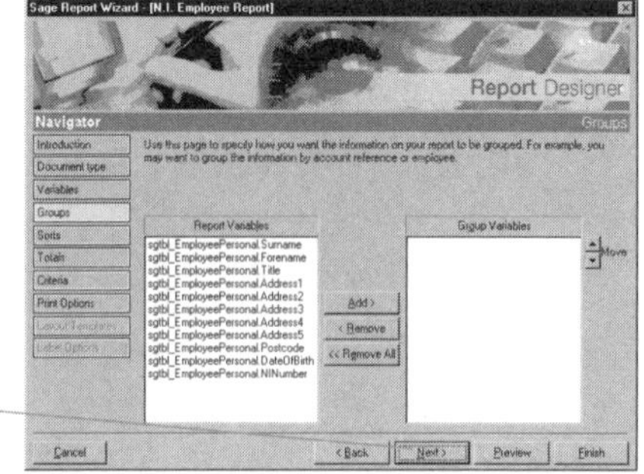

To copy a variable across to the Report Variables list click the Add > button. If you wish to remove any variable from the Report Variables list, use the < Remove button. Where all variables need removing use the << Remove button.

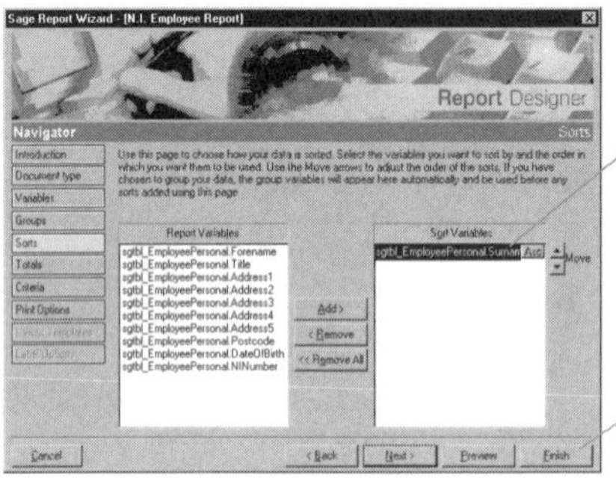

13. Select the surname variable to sort on and add to Report Variables list.
14. Click Finish to generate report layout.

The Report Designer now generates the appropriate report layout for you. You will be able to see how the layout is divided into sections, i.e., Page Header, Details, Page Footer, etc.

If the layout is not as required, you can modify the report later. First you need to check that it provides the information you require by running a report preview.

Maximise your report window to see all your variables and text headings.

To edit an existing report, select the report you require from the Reports window and click File, Edit.

Your report will appear in the Employee Reports folder after saving.

Use drag and drop method to place variables and text headings in correct position, i.e., click on required variable, hold down left mouse button, move mouse pointer to correct position before letting go of the mouse button.

Previewing your Report

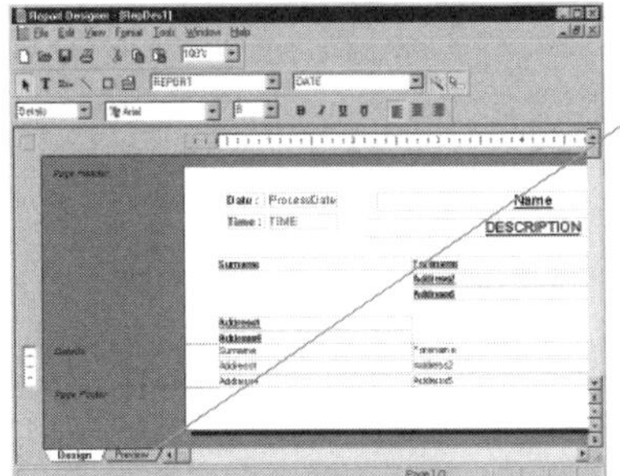

1. Click Preview to run your new report.
2. To Close, click on File menu and Exit.

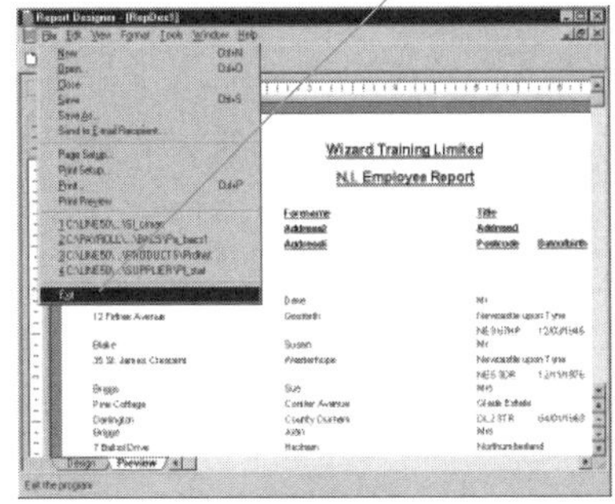

3. To re-arrange the text headings and variables see below and example on page162.

Arranging your variables

The Report Wizard places all text headings and variables in the Report Designer window. These will need re-arranging and positioning in the correct place using the 'drag and drop' method. Any unwanted headings can be removed by selecting and clicking delete.

Variables need to be aligned to produce a neat and tidy appearance. For example, to align the Surname heading in the Page Header with the Surname variable in the Details section, you need to hold down the Shift Key continuously while clicking on the two variables, drag them to the correct position and let go of the mouse button. To align multiple objects use the Select (arrow) on the toolbar, drag a box around the objects you require. From the Format menu, select Alignment, e.g., Left, and click OK to save the new settings.

It is important not to move a variable from one section to another, i.e., from the Detail Section to the Page Header and Footer or vice versa. This will give inaccurate results.

The Page Header normally displays the report's column headings and they print on every page.

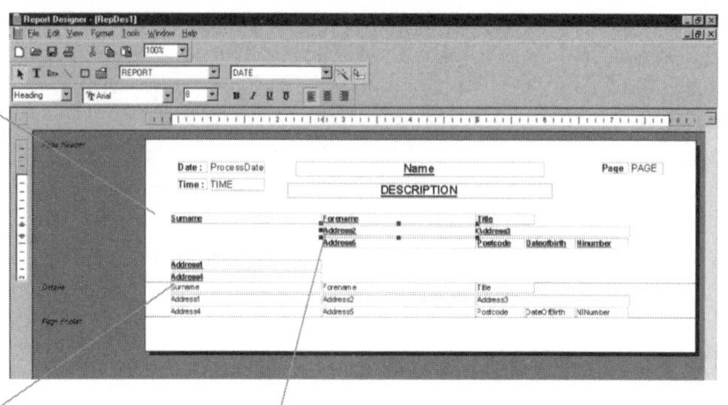

1 Open the report for editing.

The Details section contains the main body of your report.

2 Remove any unnecessary text headers, i.e., Address2 to Address5 and Postcode. To do this, select object first and press delete.

3 Rearrange text headers and variables so your report layout looks like this. Use the 'drag and drop' technique.

The Page Footer section prints at the bottom of every page.

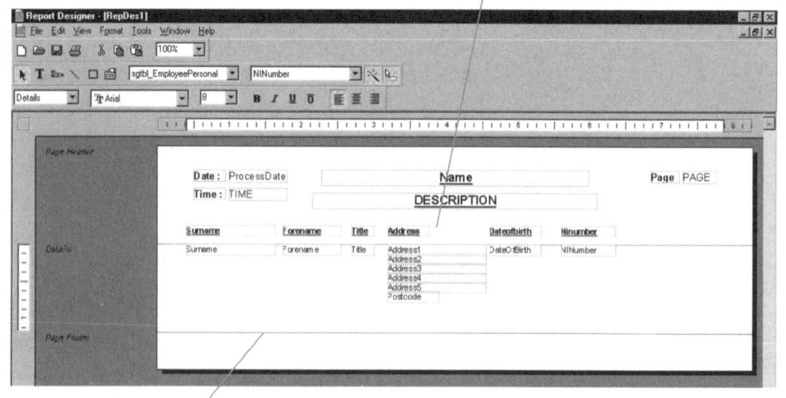

Use the Alignment option from the Format menu to help you position the variables.

4 Click on this line and drag up or down to adjust spacing between employee records.

5 Click Preview tab to check the layout.

6 When satisfied with the result, i.e., headings and variables line up, move to next section on page 163. If you need to make any changes, do so using the Design tab.

During report design, Variables can be added at any time using the Table and Variable drop-down lists on the Report Designer toolbar.

To save and print your new report

1. From the Report Designer toolbar, select File menu.
2. Click on Save As.

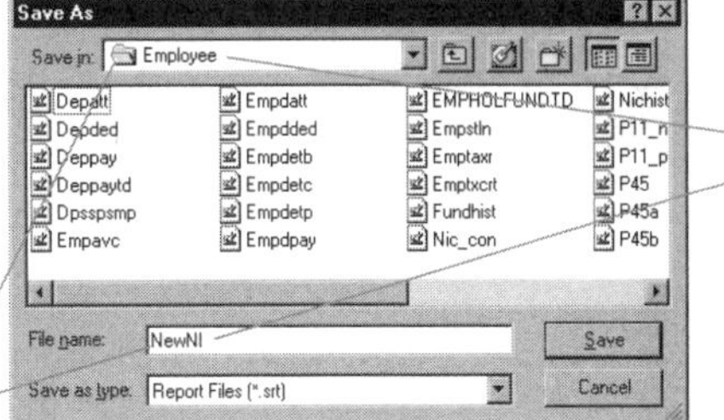

3. Enter the directory and filename you require.

When saving your new report, e.g., NewNI.SRT you could save it to C:\Payroll\Reports\Employee. This will appear in the Employee Reports list on the Reports window.

4. To print your report click Print from the File menu.

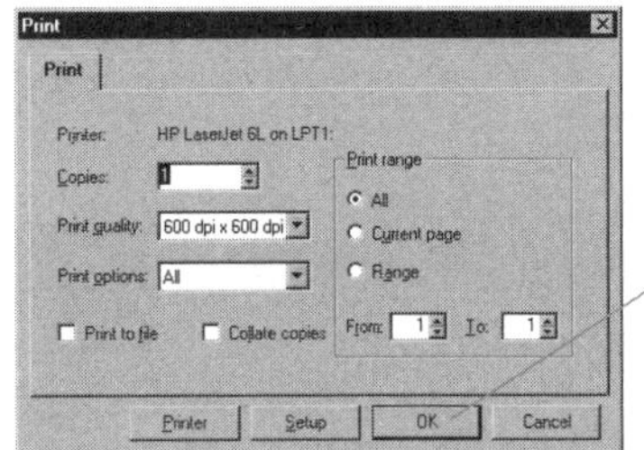

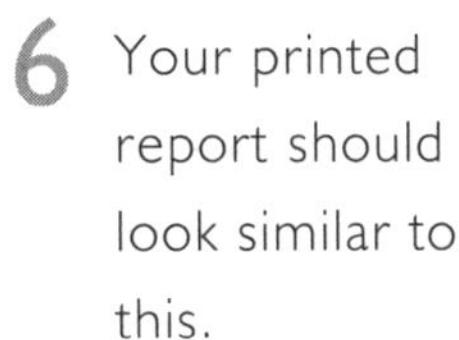

5. Click OK to print.

Be careful not to overwrite any existing reports. They may be useful to you later.

6. Your printed report should look similar to this.

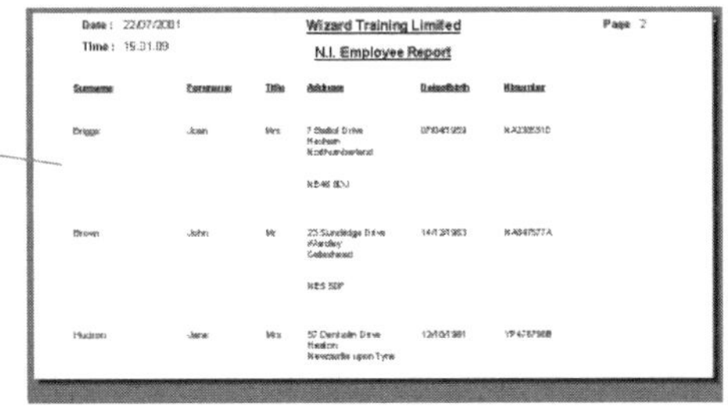

You can use the Print button on the Reports toolbar to quickly print your report.

Note: If your printed report has information missing at the top, bottom, left or right edges of the page, the report needs editing accordingly to increase the amount of space at the top, bottom and sides of your page.

Modifying an existing Report

You will be prompted if there are no employees selected when clicking on the Pre-update Reports option. Select your employees BEFORE modifying your report.

Report Designer lets you modify existing layout files and your program's default reports. However, with some reports, you will be prompted by Sage Payroll to save them with a different filename.

To modify a laser payslip

1 Select an employee and from the Payroll stacked toolbar, click Pre-update Reports.

2 Select the Laser Payslip report layout from the Payslips section.

You can hide details you do not want to display on your payslips, e.g., pension details may not apply to your staff.

3 Click the Open button to make any changes.

4 Click Maximise button to view all your variables.

To delete a variable, select it and click the scissors button.

Adjust position of variables if information is missing from the edges of your report. You may also need to check your margins.

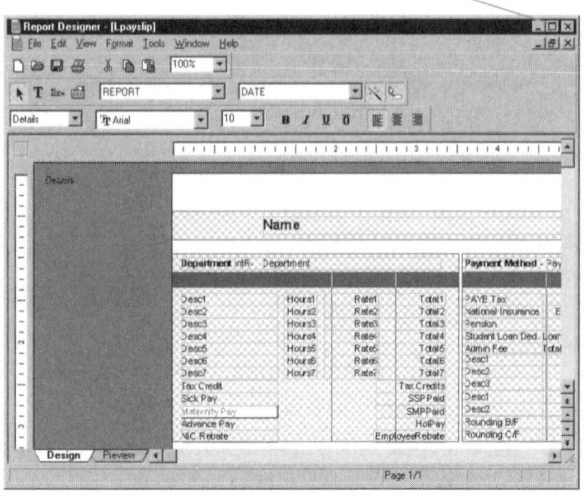

5 Make any changes you require to the report design, using 'drag and drop' technique, deleting unwanted objects etc.

Always preview your reports before printing, for example, check all headings and variables line up correctly etc.

6 For this example, the SMP details are going to be deleted.

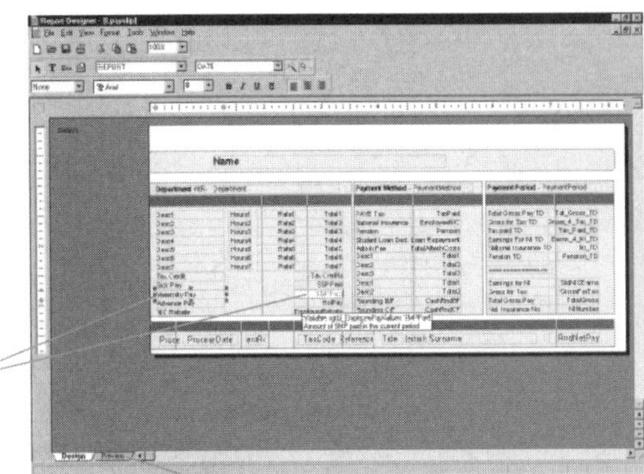

7 Click on field to be removed and press Delete.

Always remember to save any new changes you wish to keep.

8 Click Preview tab to check changes to the layout.

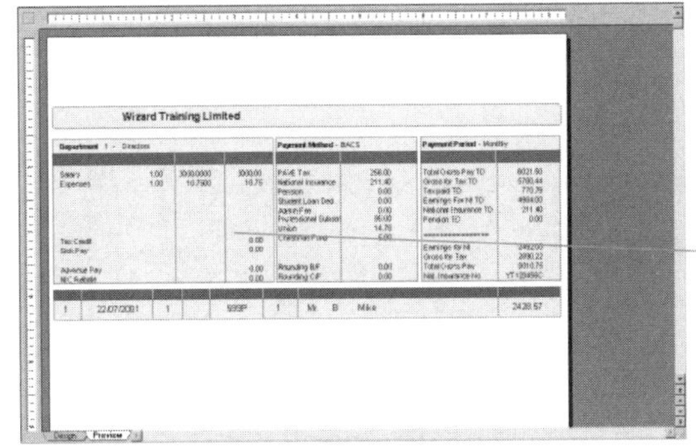

9 Note: SMP details are not displayed.

Custom Reports let you include payment, deduction and attachment information variables in your own reports.

10 To save your changes click Save As from the File menu.

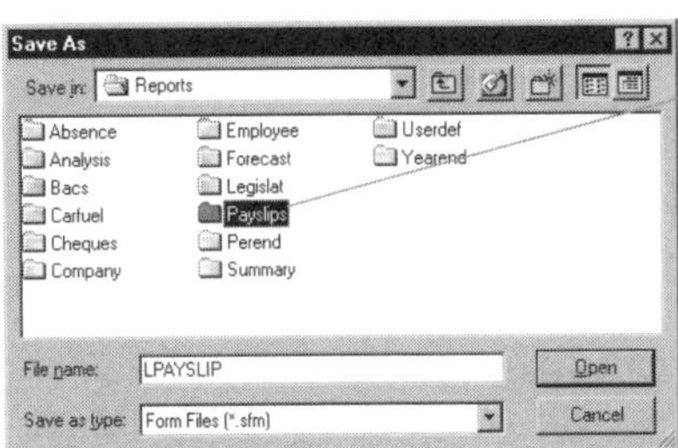

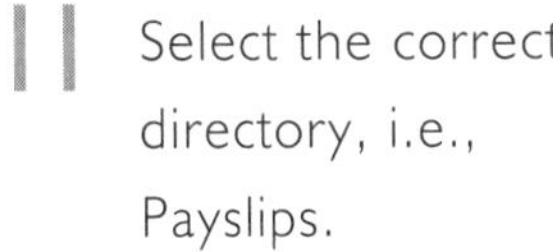

11 Select the correct directory, i.e., Payslips.

12 Enter new filename, e.g., NEWPSLIP.SFM.

Refer to the Sage Payroll Report Designer, Help Topics section for additional information about working with reports.

13 Click Save.

14 To print out the payslips click Print from the Preview window.

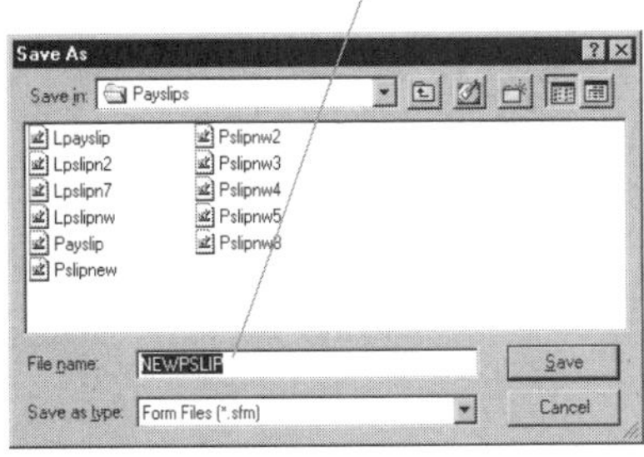

Creating a Custom Report

If you have upgraded from a DOS version of Payroll use this option to recreate any of your reports that included payment, deduction and attachment information.

The Custom Reports option allows you to design your own reports to incorporate payment, deduction and attachment type variables. Below is an example of this type of report, which includes employee payments for salary, overtime and expenses. To set up your variables and create this report do the following:

1 From the Company stacked toolbar click Custom Reports.

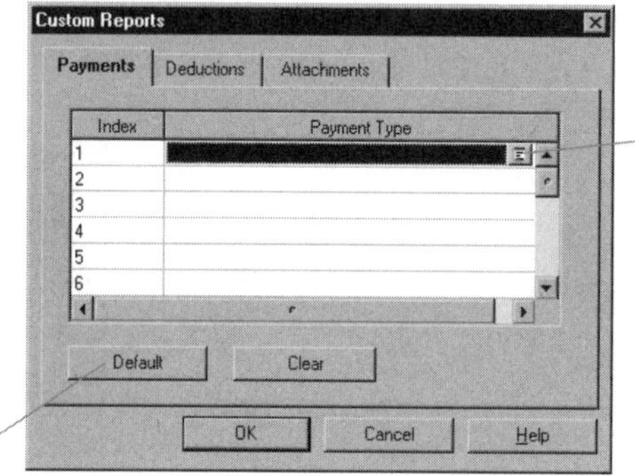

2 Click here to select payment type.

3 From drop-down list select Salary.

If you want to include all payment types as they appear in your Pay Element Settings option click the Default button.

4 Click OK to accept.

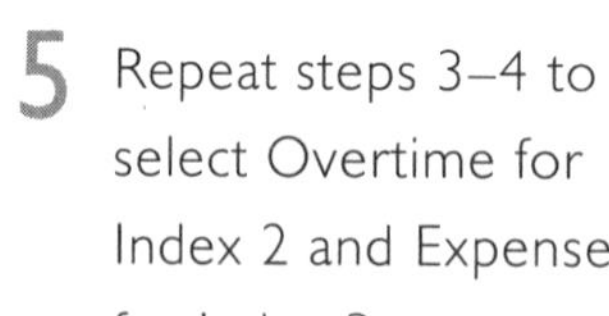

5 Repeat steps 3–4 to select Overtime for Index 2 and Expenses for Index 3.

To remove all payment types from the Payments window click Clear.

6 Click OK to save or Cancel to abandon.

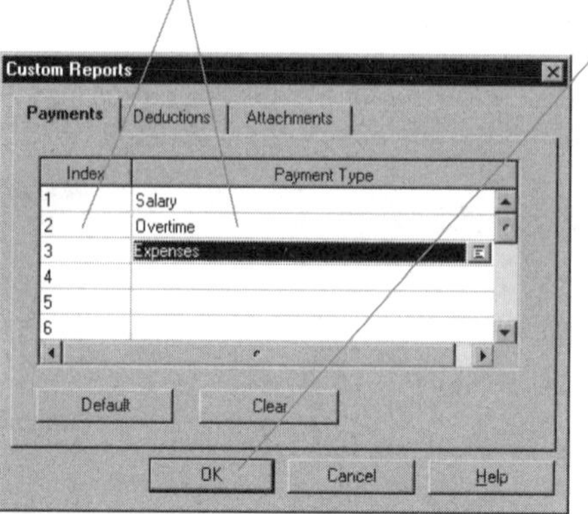

7 You have now entered your custom report variables and are ready to create your report.

You must set up your report variables BEFORE creating a custom report.

You will be prompted if there are no employees selected when clicking on the Pre-update Reports option. Select your employees BEFORE creating your report.

To create the report

1 From the Payroll stacked toolbar, click Pre-update Reports.

2 Click New.

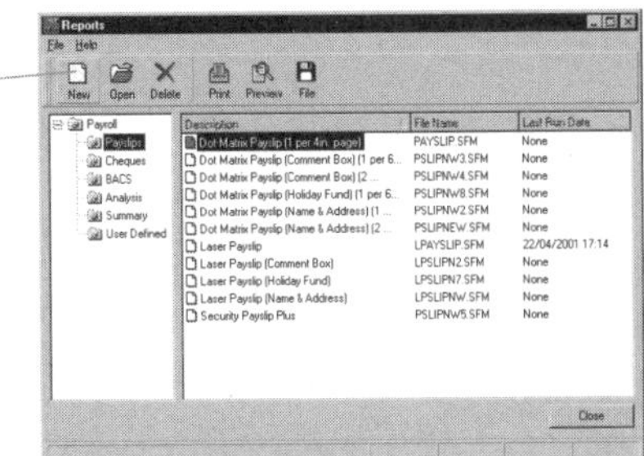

3 Enter a report title here.

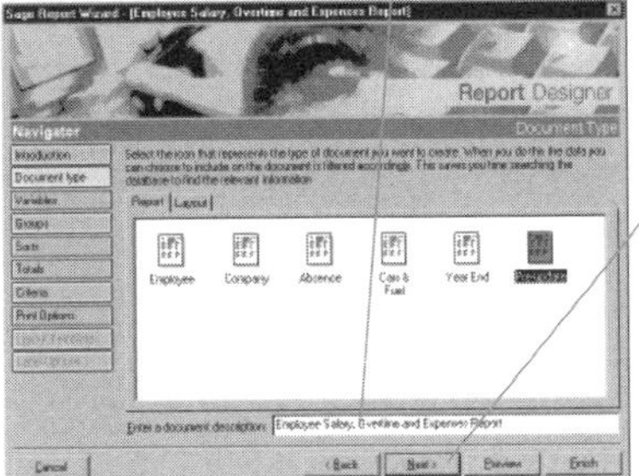

4 Click Next to continue.

Use the <Back and Next> buttons to move between screens.

5 Select table sgtbl_EmployeePersonal from the drop-down list.

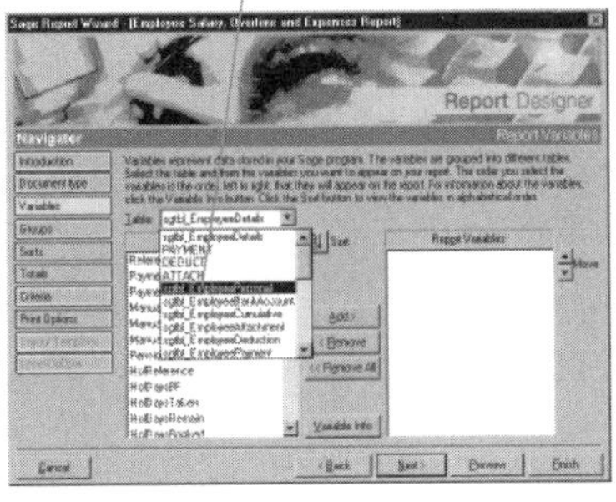

6 Add Surname and Initials to the Report Variables list.

7 Click here to select PAYMENT table.

To copy a variable across to the Report Variables list click the Add > button. If you wish to remove any variable from the Report Variables list, use the < Remove button. Where all variables need removing use the << Remove All button.

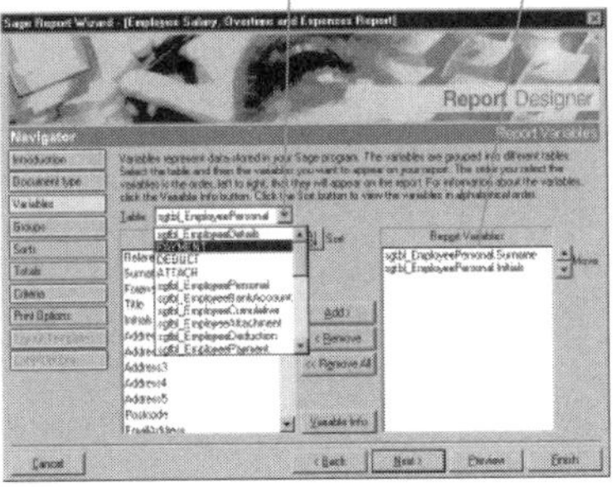

8 You are now going to add variables from the PAYMENT table to the same list as the employee personal details (see step 9).

Refer to page 161 for information about arranging variables.

9 Add these PAYMENT variables to your list.

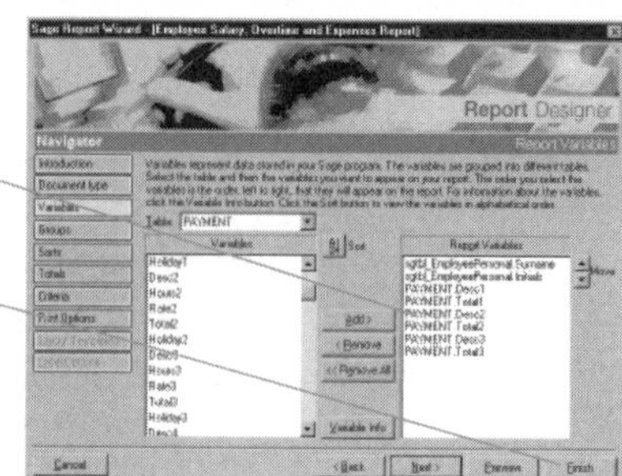

10 Click Finish to view report layout.

11 Click Maximise button to see all your variables.

Press F1 on the Report Designer screens for additional help when creating your payroll reports.

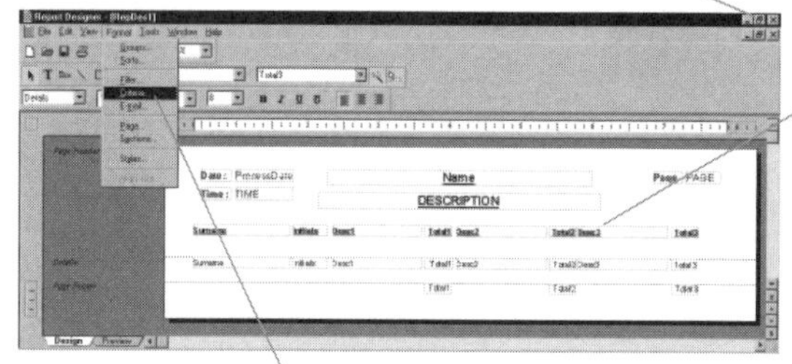

12 Arrange variables using 'drag and drop' technique.

13 From Format menu select Criteria.

To quickly print your report, click the Preview tab from the Report Designer toolbar and then Print.

14 Select Payment Sort and click Preset for Status.

15 Click OK to continue.

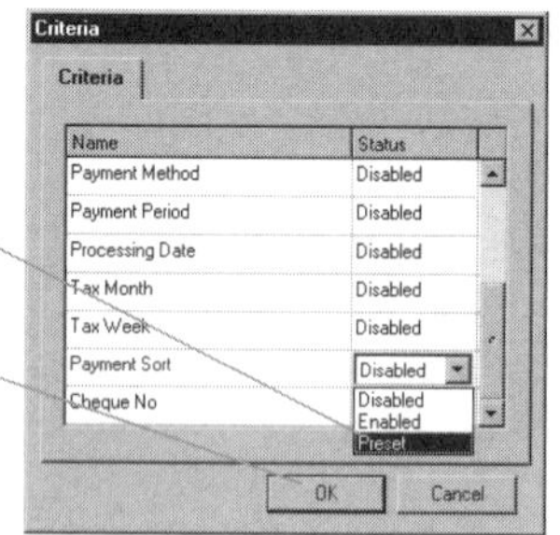

16 Click here, select Custom and then OK.

17 You are now ready to save and print your new report.

You can print your report design by clicking the Design tab, then Print from the Report Designer toolbar.

18 From the Report Designer's window, select File, Save As, select your payslips folder and enter a filename and click OK to save.

19 Click the Preview button and then Print.

Year End Procedure

This chapter shows you how to run your year end procedure using the Tax Year End Wizard. You will learn how to produce your statutory year end forms for submission to the Inland Revenue and Department of Social Security. Advancing absence and holiday years is also covered within this section. Working through, you will learn how to complete all the procedures that finish one tax year and prepare for the next.

Covers

Chapter Fifteen

Year End Checklist

Use the Tax Year End Wizard to guide you through the Year End routine.

Before starting your Year End routine, work through the following list to help you complete the procedure smoothly and successfully.

Year End Checklist

- Run and update your final payroll period for all payment types and process any leavers without company cars.
- Process leavers with company cars.
- Remove leave dates for leavers with company cars.
- Set your process date to the Year End date which is 5 April.
- Take two backups of your data and label them 'Post Update before clearing Year To Date'.
- Print P11 PAYE and P11 NIC Deductions forms.
- Print two copies of your P35 Summary report.
- Check your P35 Summary against the P11.
- Print your P14/P60s.
- Clear your employee's YTD Totals and if required transfer any car mileage records.
- Backup your data and label it 'After Clearing Year To Date Totals'.
- Check your Government parameters against current legislation and update them if necessary.
- Re-enter the leave dates for leavers with company cars so they are not processed again in future payroll runs.
- Enter any tax code changes for your employees.
- Remove any week 1/month 1 tax codes.

If you are linking to your accounts program, quickly post transactions for the last period using the Nominal Link..

Class 1A NIC due on company cars is paid one tax year in arrears. As all leavers are removed from the system during the Year End procedure, the leave date of these employees must be removed to retain the car information and then re-entered after the Year End procedure.

Running the Year End Procedure

Always set your process date to the Year End date, i.e., 5 April and year.

Before running this procedure refer and familiarise yourself with the Year End checklist on page 170. Then, to run your Year End procedure, follow the steps below:

1 From the Tasks menu select Tax Year End.

Check beforehand that you have enough stationery and disks to complete the Year End Procedure.

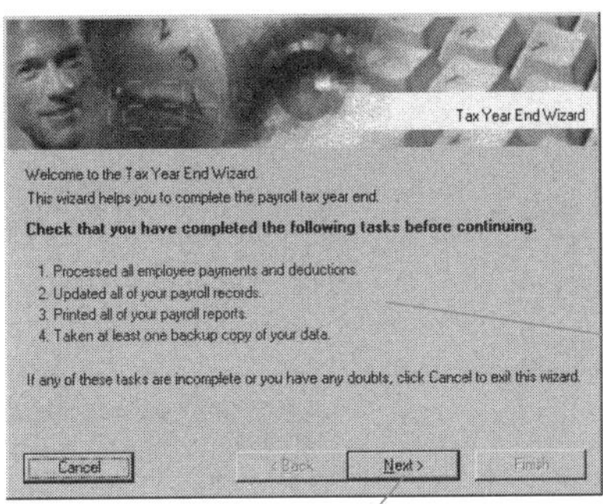

2 Check you have carried out all four tasks before continuing.

Each employer has to submit certain statutory forms at the tax year end. These reports can be printed from the Reports option on the application toolbar, Year End section.

3 Click Next if all four tasks are complete else click Cancel to return to Payroll desktop.

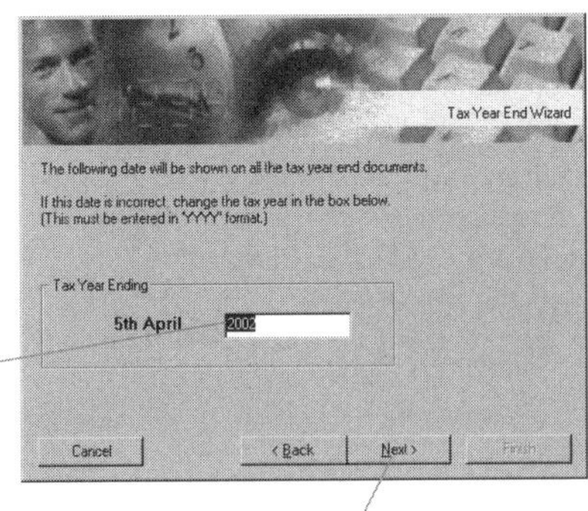

4 Check tax year end date is correct. If incorrect, change it here.

5 Click Next to continue.

Remember to distribute your P60s to your employees and send your year-end returns to the Inland Revenue.

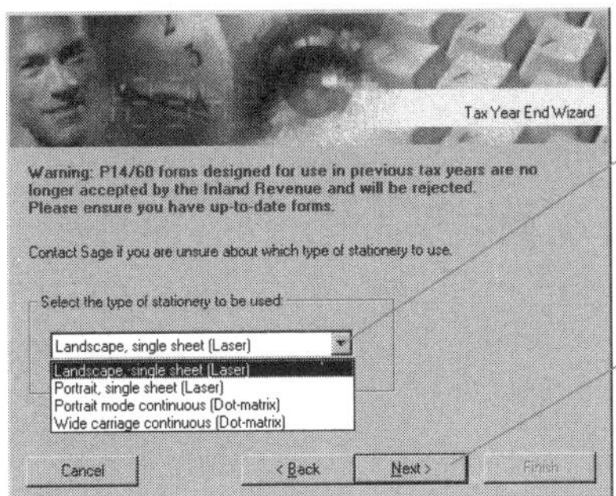

6 Select stationery for your P14/P60 forms.

7 Click Next to go to the Tax Year End tasks window.

If you have already printed your reports from the Reports option just click the Finish button.

Printing your P11 PAYE deduction cards

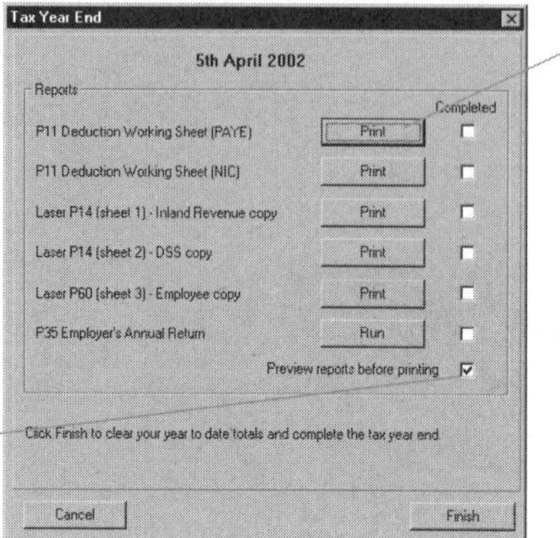

1 Click Print here. If you have chosen to preview your reports before printing them, the P11 PAYE deduction card is previewed.

To preview reports before you print them click the Preview reports before printing check box.

2 Click the P11 window to bring it to the front.

3 Check the report. When satisfied it is correct, click Print.

Read the Wizard screens carefully and if you need to make any changes to the information displayed use the Back button to return and rectify any discrepancies.

4 Click OK.

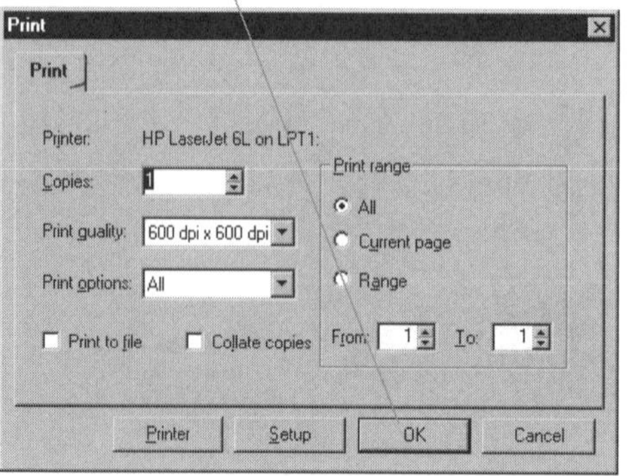

5 Click Close to return to the Tax Year End Wizard.

To submit your Year End information on floppy disk (magnetic media) you need a valid permit number from the DSS and a special disk from Sage.

6 Note: A tick now appears in the P11 Deduction Working Sheet (PAYE) box to show you have printed the P11 PAYE cards.

Printing your P11 NIC deduction cards

Check your P35 Summary against your P11s.

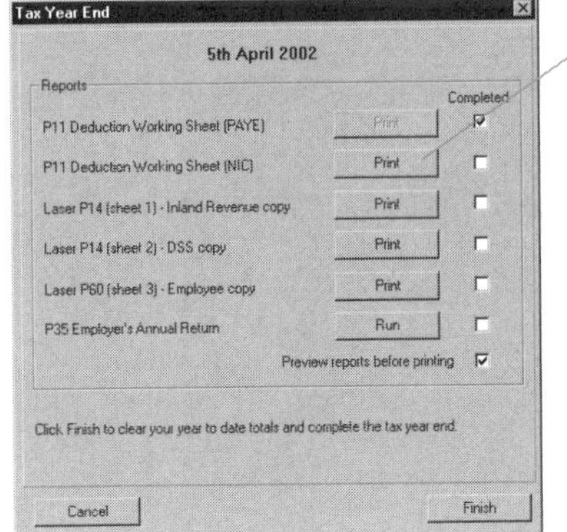

1 Click Print here. The P11 National Insurance Contributions deduction card is now previewed.

A tick will appear in the Completed column when you have printed your P11 deduction cards.

2 Click the P11 window to bring it to the front.

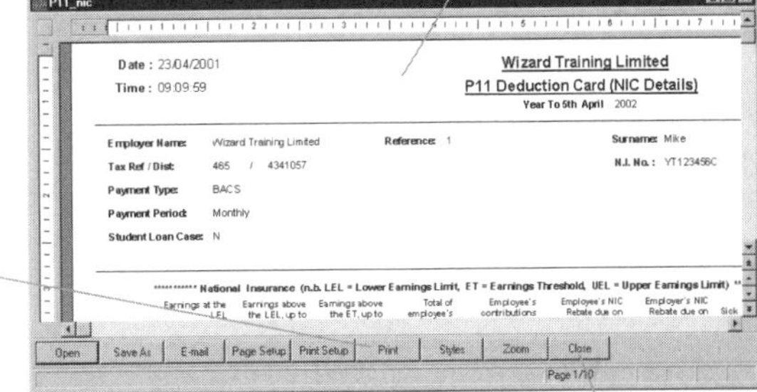

3 Check the report. When satisfied it is correct, click Print.

The Total Tax figure for This Employment on each employee's P11 Deductions Card (PAYE) must be the same as the figure in the Income Tax Column of the P35.

4 Click OK.

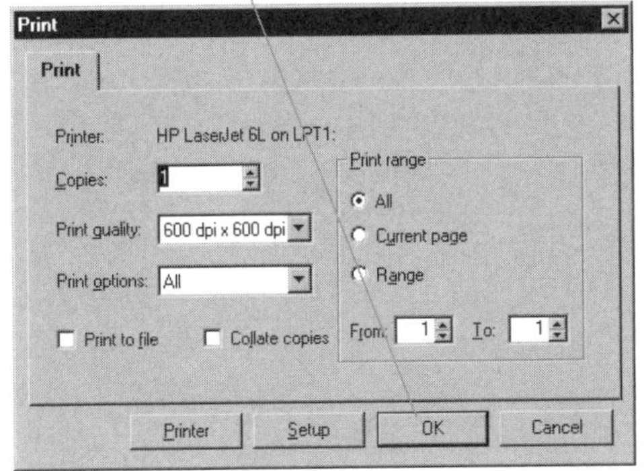

5 Click Close to return to the Tax Year End Wizard.

A B/F value represents cumulative figures entered manually into the payroll system.

6 Note: A tick now appears in the P11 Deduction Working Sheet (NIC) box to show you have printed the P11 National Insurance Contributions deduction cards.

If an employee has a company car the letter Y is displayed in the Nat Ins Category column.

Printing your P35 Summary (two copies)

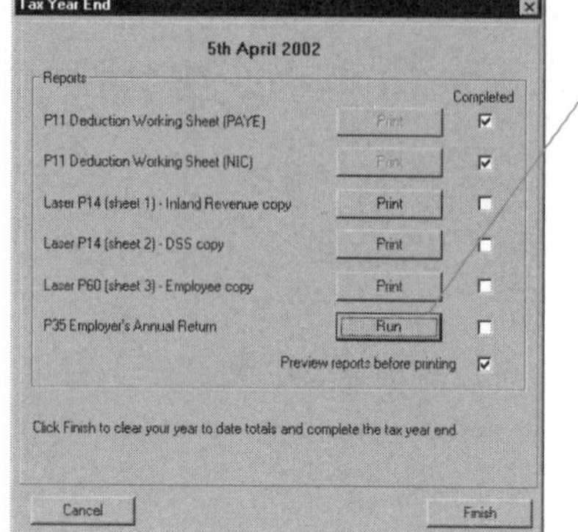

1. Click Run here.

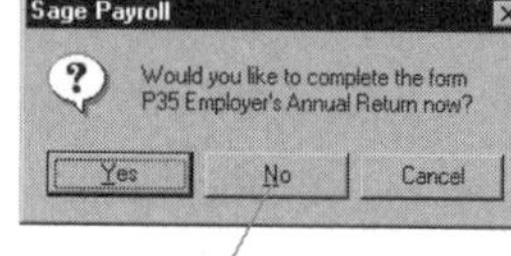

2. Click No for now.

3. Click the P35 window to bring it to the front.

The Total Contributions figure on each employee's P11 Deductions Card (NIC) must be the same as the figure in the NIC column on the P35.

4. Check the report. When satisfied it is correct, click Print.

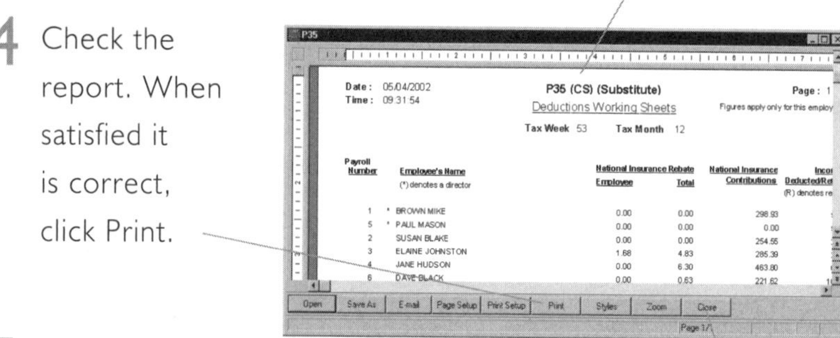

5. Enter 2 here.

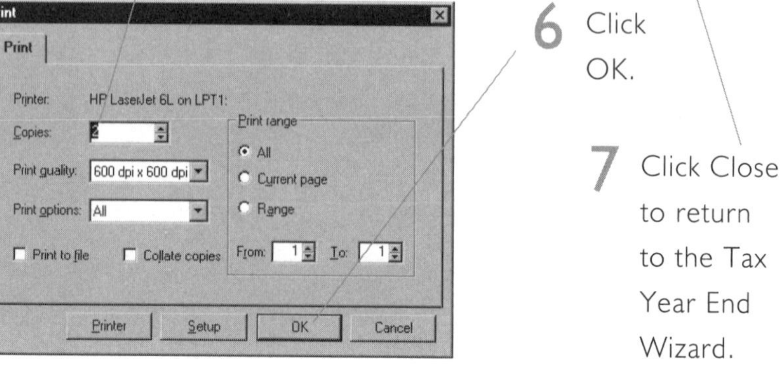

6. Click OK.

7. Click Close to return to the Tax Year End Wizard.

When you are satisfied that your P35 Summary report agrees with your P11 deduction cards you are ready to print your P14/P60s.

8. Now check your P35 Summary against your P11 deduction cards for each employee, ensuring that all the figures correspond accordingly.

Check that your P14s are sorted correctly, i.e., one green Inland Revenue copy, one orange DSS copy and one blue P60 employee copy.

Printing your P14/60 Certificates

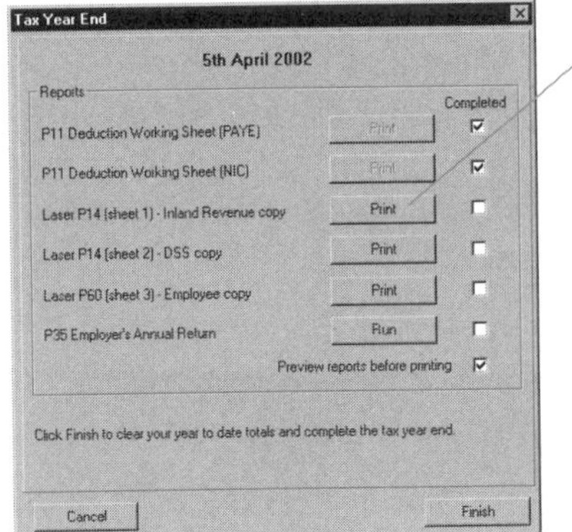

1 Click here to print your P14 Certificate first. Make sure you have the correct stationery ready.

2 Click the P14 window to bring it to the front.

Always test print a couple of P14s to check your pre-printed stationery and printer alignment.

3 Check the report. When satisfied it is correct, click Print.

When alignment is correct, use the Clear button from the desktop window, and then Swap to select all employees before printing your P14/P60s.

4 Click OK.

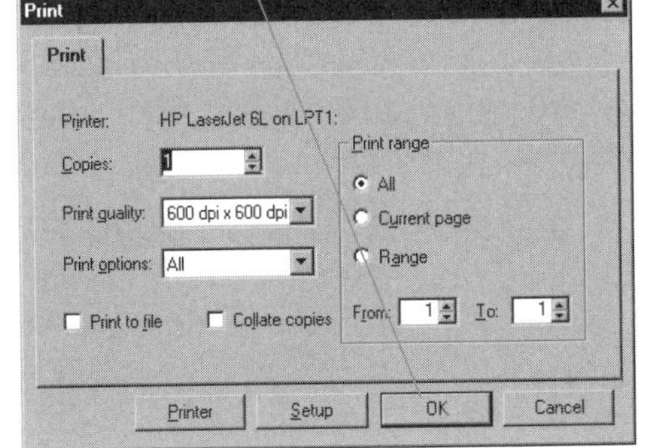

5 Click Close to return to the Tax Year End Wizard.

The P14 displays an x at the bottom right if you have processed the payroll in week 53.

6 Now repeat steps 1–5 to print out your remaining P14/P60 Certificates, clicking on the respective Print buttons for step 1.

The P35 NIC figures include any Class 1A contributions and NIC holiday deductions. They appear as Total Contributions on the employee's P11 Deductions Card (NIC).

Processing leavers with company cars

Class 1A National Insurance Contributions on company cars are paid one tax year in arrears. Therefore, you must keep any leaver who had a company car on the payroll until the following tax year. Do the following:

1. Select the leaver from the list view and open their Employee Record.

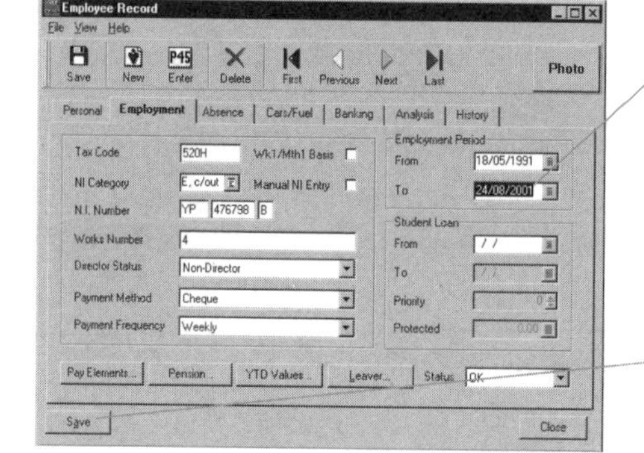

2. Make a note of the leaving date (in the Employment Period To box) then delete it.
3. Click Save and Close.

Income tax deducted or refunded figures appear as Tax Due This Employment on the employee's P11 Deductions Card (PAYE). This applies to current employment only.

4. Once you have completed the Year End, open the leaver's Employee Record and re-enter the leaving date so the Class 1A NIC can be calculated at the next Year End.

Clearing your Year To Date figures

Once you have checked and printed your Year End reports, you are now ready to clear your Year To Date totals. This does the following:

- Removes all payroll cumulative values for the current year, except for the number of SSP/SMP weeks and any NIC holiday cumulatives.
- Deletes the records of all employees who have left.
- Transfers any mileage records for the current year.

The P32 report shows figures updated by the program and ignores cumulative figures entered manually.

Remember, you should now only proceed if you are certain that your reports have all been printed out and their figures are all correct.

Once you have printed your reports click the Clear Tax Year 2001/2002 to zero your employees' YTD values in preparation for the new tax year, except the number of SSP/SMP weeks and any NIC holiday figures.

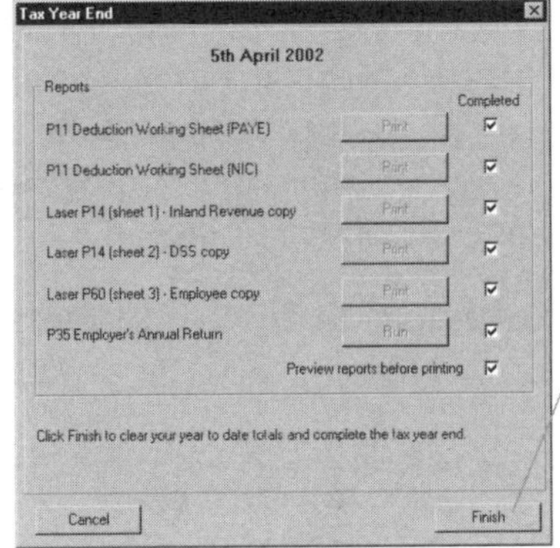

1 Click Finish to delete your YTD totals.

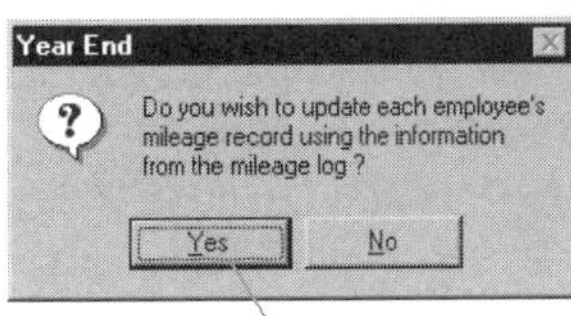

2 Click Yes to process mileage.

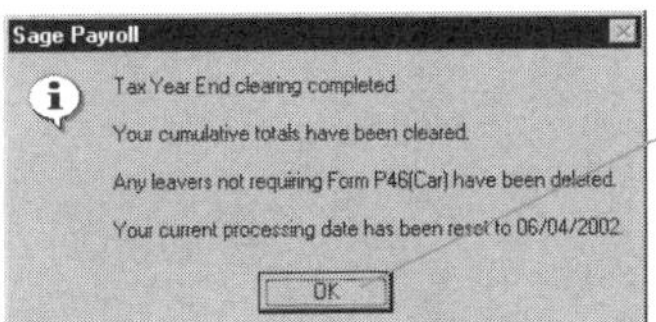

3 You have cleared your Year To Date figures. Click OK to close the Tax Year End Wizard.

The Clear Tax Year option will delete records of employees who have left and transfer mileage records from the previous tax year.

Distribution of Year End Returns

After carrying out your Year End procedure you will need to distribute the documents as follows:

Separate the P14/P60 certificates.

Distribute the P60s to your employees.

Post the P14 End of Year Summary to the Inland Revenue and DSS.

It is important to remember there are deadlines for the submission of statutory forms. Refer to the Sage Help or your Employer's Pack for exact dates. The Inland Revenue may impose fines for late returns:

You will now need to make a backup of your data files and label it Year End after clearing YTD Totals. Include the date and store disks in a safe place.

- Mid-April for payment of PAYE and NIC deductions.
- Mid-May for submission of P35 and P14 Year End Returns.
- Mid-July for submission of the Class 1A National Insurance contributions for the previous tax year for company cars and fuel.

Preparing for the Following Tax Year

By re-entering leave dates for employees with company cars, you remove them from further payroll runs but leave their record on the system so Class 1A NIC can be calculated correctly.

Before you start to process your first payroll for the new tax year, will may need to re-enter leave dates for employees who have left the company but were provided with a company car. Tax codes need updating and any week 1/ month 1 tax codes need removing.

To re-enter leave dates for leavers with company cars

1. Select the leaver and open their Employee Record.

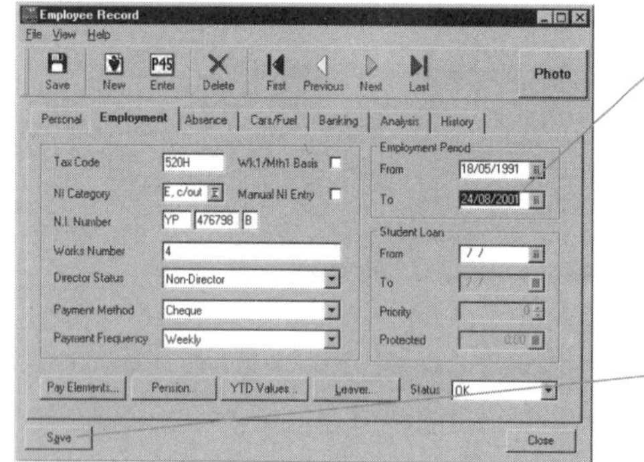

2. Enter their leaving date you noted on page 176, step 2, in the Employment Period To box.

3. Click Save and Close.

To ensure accuracy when transferring your Class 1A NIC figures correctly you should check your car records.

To remove any week 1/month 1 codes

1. Select the Employment tab from the relevant Employee Record.

You will find the Employee Mileage Log by selecting the Employee Record, Cars and Fuel Tab, Enter Mileage button.

2. Click here to deselect this tax code OR use the Global Changes Wizard from the Tasks menu and select the Set or Clear Week 1/Month 1 flags.

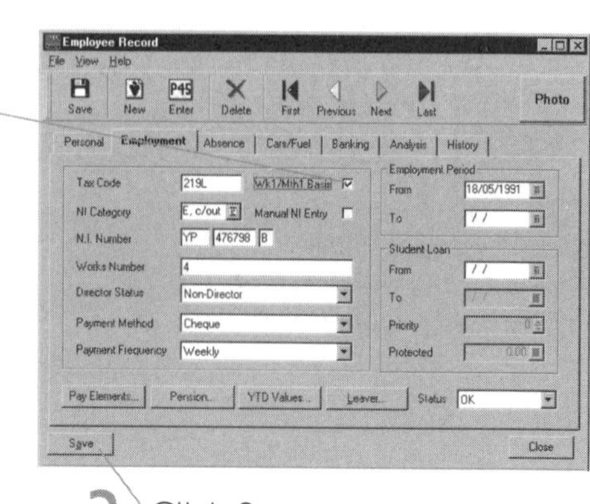

3. Click Save.

Updating Tax Codes

Use the Global Changes Wizard to enter any tax code changes for your employees.

To update your tax codes

When updating your tax codes use the Global Changes Wizard to change information once for a few or all of your records, as follows.

To replace one tax code with another

To help you with any general queries about Tax, National Insurance or VAT registration you can contact the Employers Helpline on 0345 143 143, Monday to Friday, 8.30 am–5.00 pm. For persons hard of hearing or deaf ring 0345 419 402 for text phone.

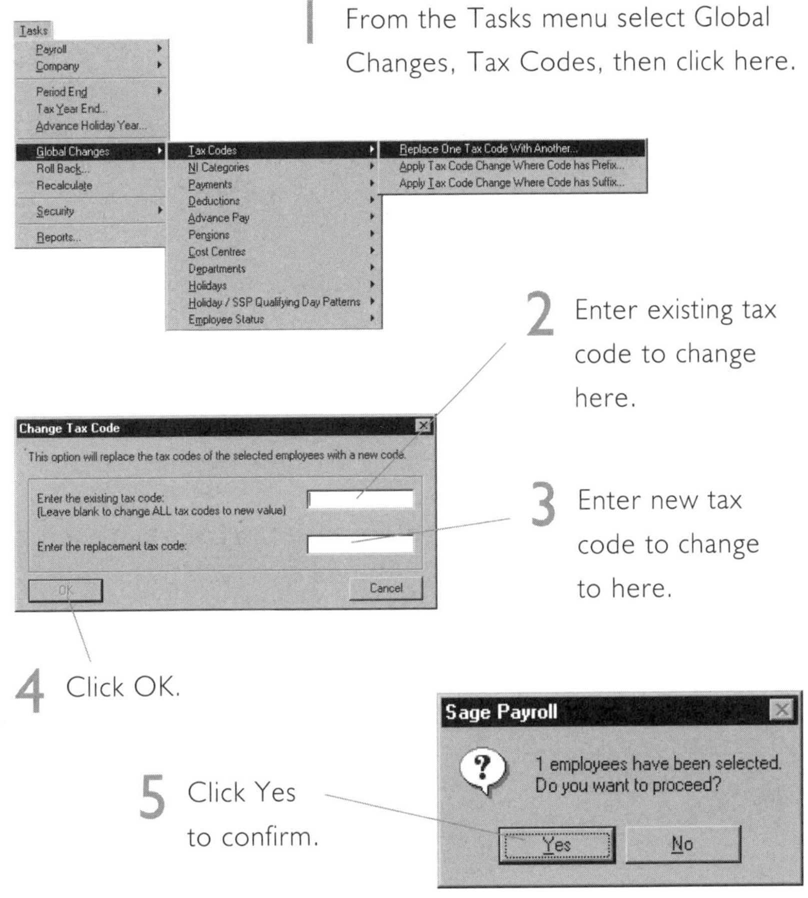

1 From the Tasks menu select Global Changes, Tax Codes, then click here.

2 Enter existing tax code to change here.

3 Enter new tax code to change to here.

4 Click OK.

5 Click Yes to confirm.

Refer to Sage Help for information about Sub-contractors.

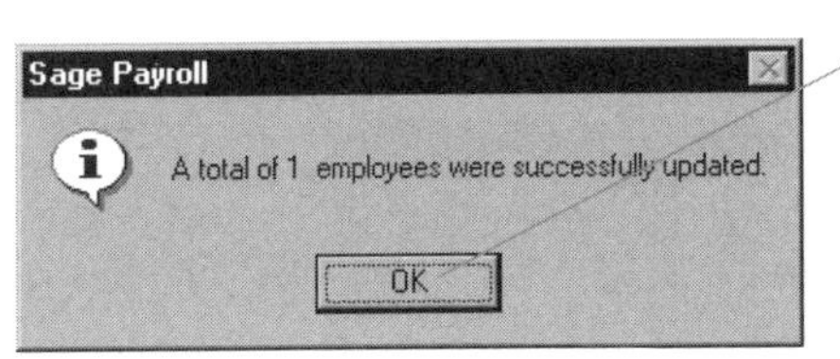

6 Click OK to close the Global Changes Wizard.

The Global Changes Wizard will enable you to make changes quickly and easily to Tax Codes, NI Categories, the Payment Rate, to Remove NIC Holiday entries and Set or Clear Week 1/Month 1 flags.

To replace one tax code with another using Prefix

1. From the Tasks menu select Global Changes, Tax Codes, then click here.
2. Enter Prefix letter, i.e., K.
3. Enter value to change Tax Code by.
4. Click Yes to confirm.
5. Click OK to finish.

Remember to check at the start of the payroll year if there have been any changes to tax codes or the PAYE threshold.

To replace one tax code with another using Suffix

Check your Employer's Pack for changes in Government Legislation.

1. From the Tasks menu select Global Changes, Tax Codes, then click here.
2. Enter Suffix letter, i.e.,L.
3. Enter value to change Tax Code by here.
4. Click Yes to confirm.

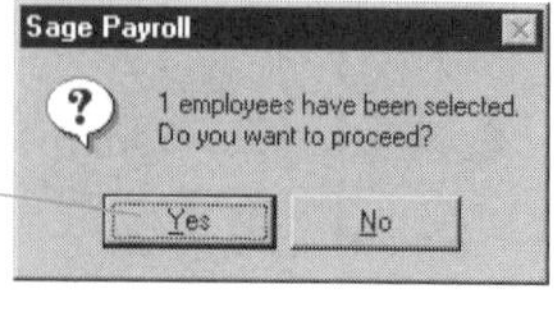

5. Click OK to finish.

You will have to repeat the Global Changes option to amend each suffix code.

Updating Tax Bandwidths

Just ring the Inland Revenue Employer's Orderline for the latest copy of the Employer's Annual Pack.

With periodic changes in Government Legislation you will need to amend your tax bandwidths in order to calculate your payroll correctly. The steps below show you how to make these changes:

To update your tax bandwidths

You can also use the Reports option from the application toolbar to check and print out current legislation settings.

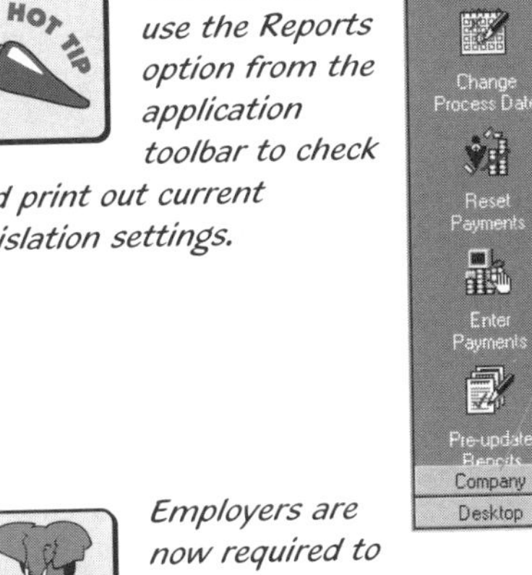

1 Click on Company from the stacked toolbar.

2 Click on the Government Legislation button.

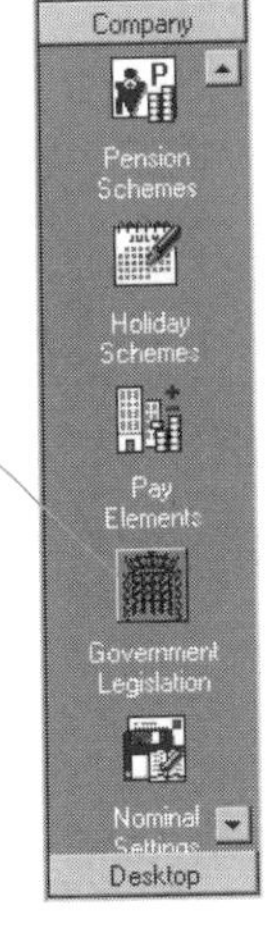

3 Using the PAYE tab, check the Bandwidths and Rates are correct. Amend any figures which have changed due to new Government Legislation.

Employers are now required to deduct student loan repayments from employees who have become liable to repay their loan, if it was taken out after August 1998. However, no deduction will be made if the salary is below the government set threshold. Check with the Inland Revenue for the latest figure.

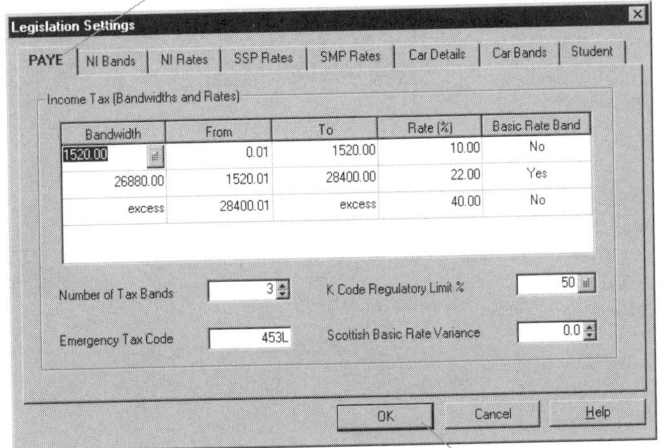

4 After updating all Bandwidth information click OK to save.

Advancing Absence & Holiday Year

You should only use this option at the Year End if your absence/ holiday year runs from 6 April.

After completing your Year End procedure you can advance your current holiday and absence year to the new tax year. This option will automatically carry over any unused days holiday, but only if your holiday scheme is set up for this.

To advance your absence and holiday year

The Wizard allows you to advance your absence and/or holiday year(s) by one year.

1 From the Tasks menu select Advance Holiday Year.

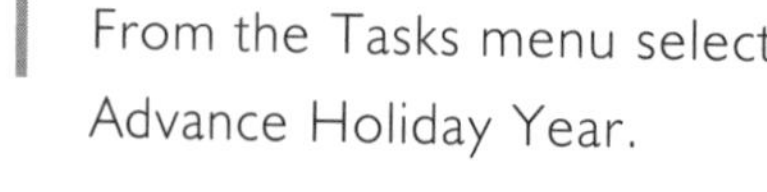

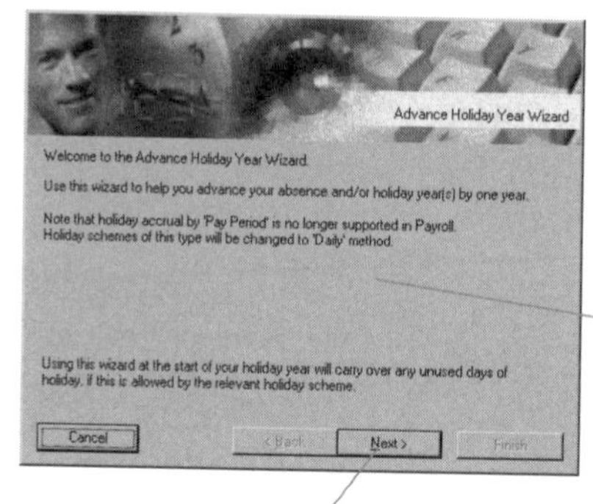

2 Note the information detailed here before continuing.

Holiday Schemes are set up using the Company stacked toolbar, Company Settings option and the Absence tab.

3 Click Next to proceed with the advance, else click Cancel to return to Payroll desktop.

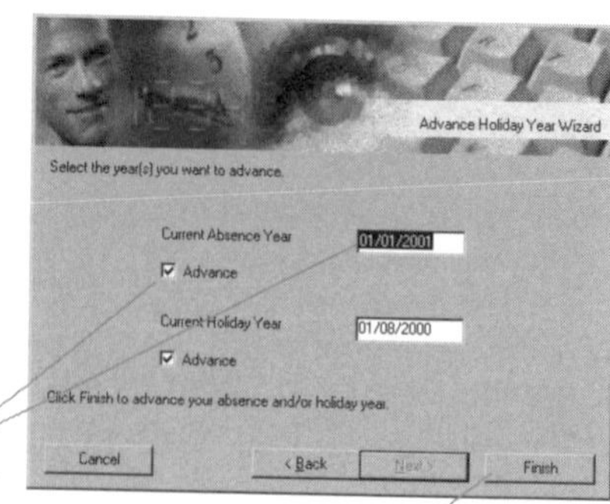

Deselect the check box if you do not wish to advance the Absence or Holiday Year.

4 Note the dates listed and remove tick if you do not wish to advance an item.

5 Click Finish to complete the advance procedure and return to the Payroll desktop.

File Maintenance

This chapter shows and explains the importance of creating regular backups of your data files as part of your payroll routine. You will learn how backing up data files minimises data loss and how to restore from a previous backup using the Sage Restore option.

Covers

Chapter Sixteen

Backing Up and Restoring Data

It is advisable to keep at least one backup copy of each payroll year.

It is very important to keep regular backup copies of your payroll data files. Data can become corrupted, causing a great deal of disruption to the business, for example, loss of payroll information to produce staff wages, time spent re-keying payroll information, fines imposed by Inland Revenue for late returns of statutory forms, etc.

Sage Payroll, therefore, provides you with the facility to create backups and then restore data files as required.

You may also find it useful to keep a backup copy for each payroll period in case data needs restoring.

It is important that you organise and set up a routine for backing up. All disks must be clearly labelled and kept in a secure place. A minimum of two backup copies need keeping as disks can sometimes become faulty. Backup procedures vary. Some businesses use five disks for Monday to Friday and repeat their usage the following week. The important thing is to backup your data at least once a day when using your payroll program!

Although mainly reliable, disks can develop faults through wear and tear, so replace your disks regularly to avoid loss of data, for example, every 3–4 months.

Below is a list of times you MUST create backups:

Backup times

AFTER each payroll run but BEFORE updating your records.

AFTER updating your records with each payroll run.

BEFORE making global updates.

BEFORE running your Year End routine.

AFTER running your Year End.

Restoring data

Use the Backup and Restore Wizard to help you create backups and restore data quickly and easily.

This facility allows you to replace existing data by erasing it and use data from your backup disks, for example if you have made an error whilst processing your payroll or if data has become corrupted, etc.

The Restore facility should only be used, however, if there is a problem. It replaces the data at the time of backup so if any data has been entered since this backup, it will need entering again.

Backing Up Data

You can create a backup copy from the File menu or when exiting from the Sage Payroll program.

Before running this procedure refer to, and familiarise yourself with, the Year End checklist on page 170.

To backup your data

1 From the File menu select Backup.

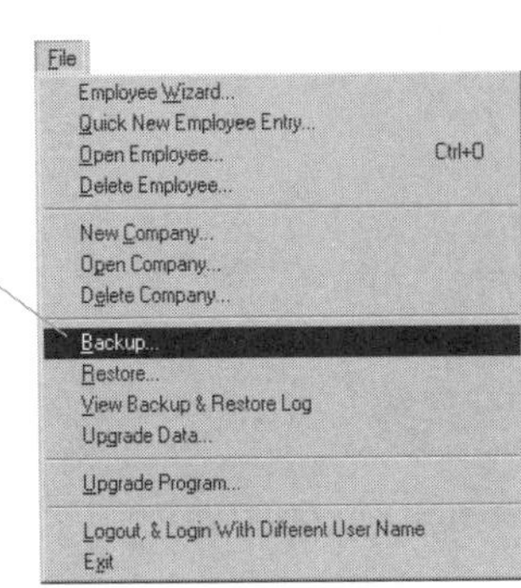

2 Note Backup Wizard details and click Next to continue.

To set up a new destination for your backup data files select Desktop stacked toolbar, Options and Backup tab.

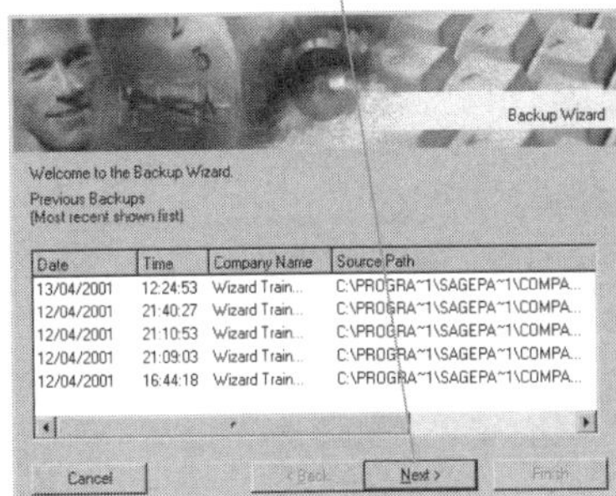

3 Select the files you require.

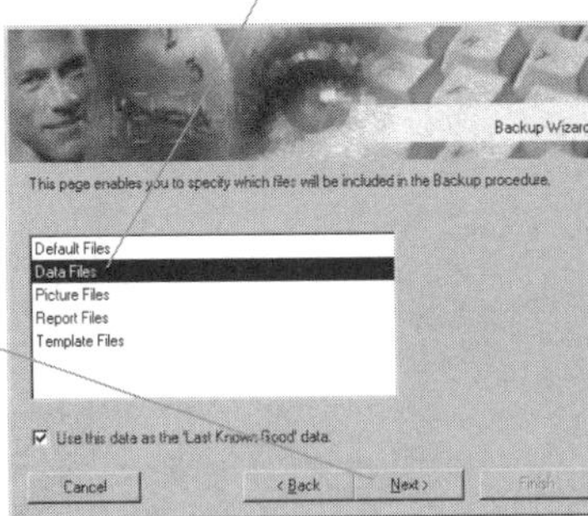

Data Files are automatically selected when creating a backup copy.

4 Click Next to continue.

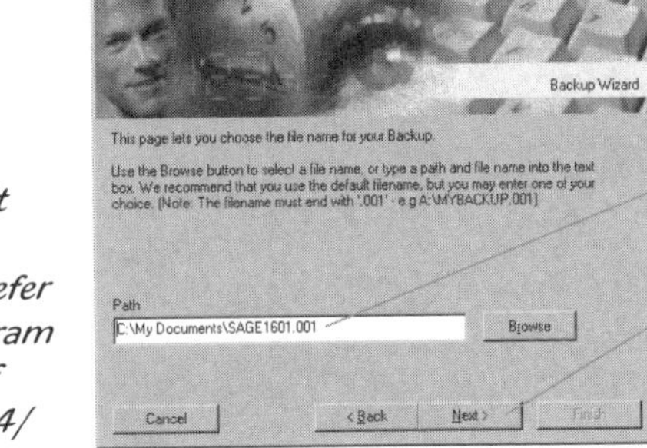

5 Enter a path and filename.

6 Click Next to continue.

Sage default backup filenames refer to the program date, e.g., if payroll date set to 06/04/2001, filename SAGE0101.001 refers to tax week 1 of year 2001.

7 Click Finish to complete the Backup procedure. If backing up to floppy disk ensure you have sufficient formatted disks to hand.

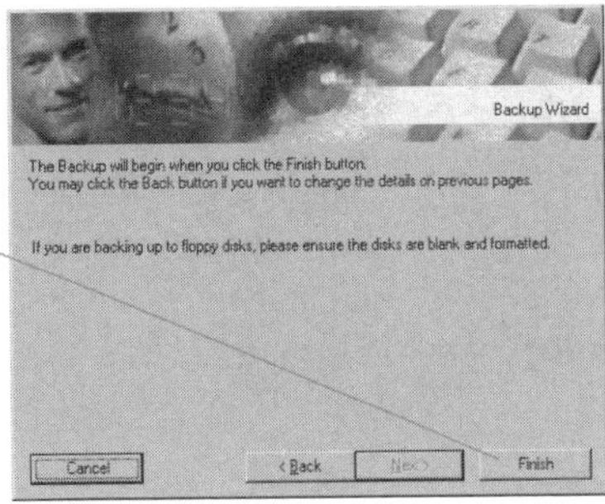

Restoring Data

Restoring data will erase all the current Payroll data.

Hopefully you will not need to restore your data but in case your data is corrupted or contains errors, etc., you can use the Restore Wizard by following these steps:

1 From the File menu select Restore.

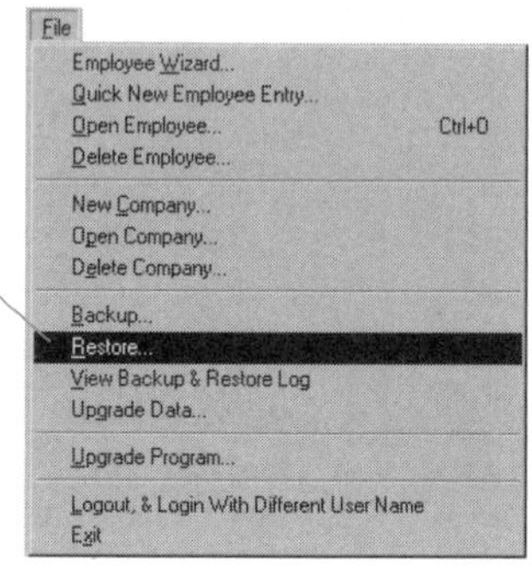

If you need to restore your data you can use the backup filename to identify the tax week.

2 You can select a backup here then click Next.

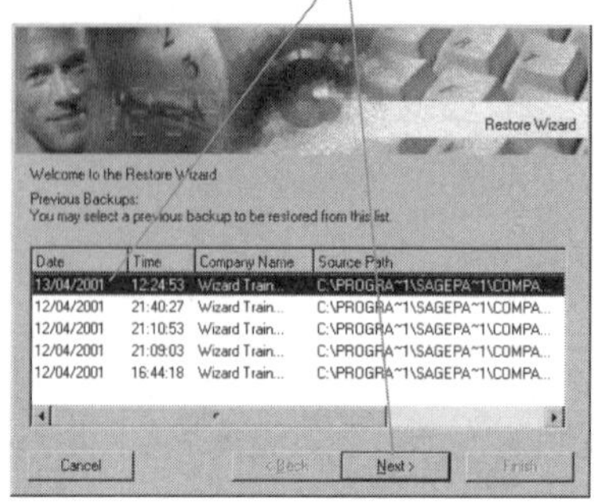

3 Select the files you require.

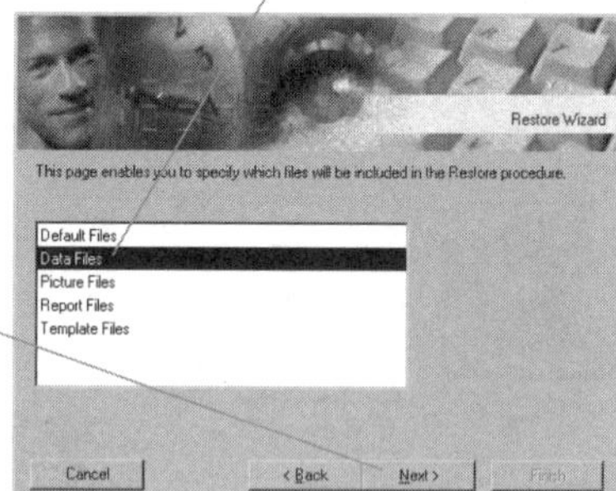

Use the Browse button on the Wizard screen to select the drive letter or directory required.

4 Click Next to continue.

If you are restoring a backup from a floppy disk ensure the path reads A:\.

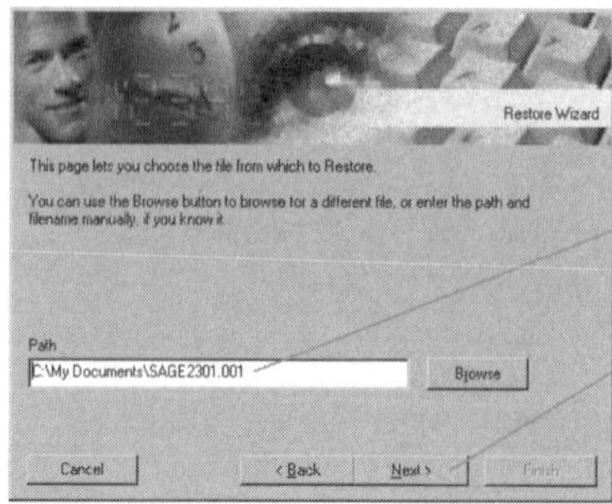

5 Enter a path and filename.

6 Click Next to continue.

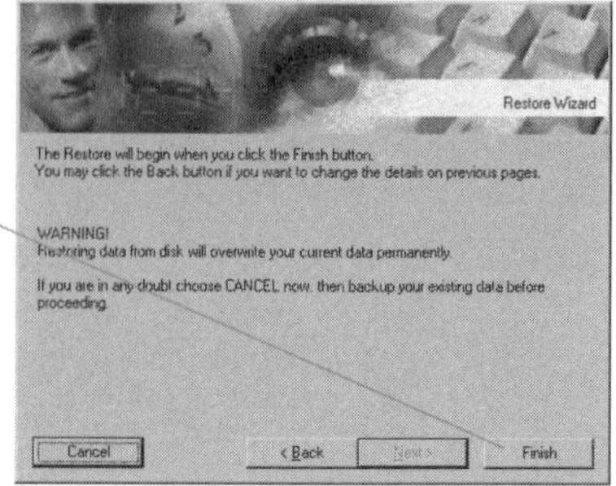

Depending upon the backup date selected, you may have to re-enter some data.

7 Click Finish to begin the Restore procedure, or click Back to make a change on a previous screen.

Index

A

B

C

D

E

F

G

H

I

K

L

P

Q

R

S

T

U

Z